FRANKLIN W. HOUN, the author of this book, was born and educated in China, and served in the Chinese government from 1946 to 1948. Presently a Professor of Political Science at the University of Massachusetts, Mr. Houn has taught Chinese politics and comparative government courses at Michigan State University, the University of Nebraska, and has served as Research Associate at the Hoover Institute at Stanford University. He is the author of *Central Government of China, 1912–1928, To Change a Nation: Propaganda and Indoctrination in Communist China,* and *Chinese Political Traditions,* as well as more than forty articles that have appeared in both English and Chinese journals concerned with political science and Chinese affairs.

COMPLETELY UPDATED

A Short History of CHINESE COMMUNISM

中國共產運動簡史

FRANKLIN W. HOUN

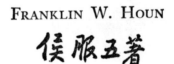

侯服五著

A SPECTRUM BOOK

Prentice-Hall, Inc. Englewood Cliffs, New Jersey

Library of Congress Cataloging in Publication Data

Hou, Fu-wu.

A short history of Chinese communism, completely updated.

(A Spectrum Book)

Includes bibliographical references.

1. Communism—China. 2. China (People's Republic of China, 1949–)
—History. I. Title.

DS777.55.H575 1973 915.1'03'5 73-9532
ISBN 0-13-809426-8
ISBN 0-13-809418-7 (pbk)

A Spectrum Book

PRINTED IN THE UNITED STATES OF AMERICA

10 9 8 7 6 5 4 3 2 1

Prentice-Hall International, Inc. (*London*)
Prentice-Hall of Australia Pty. Ltd. (*Sydney*)
Prentice-Hall of Canada, Ltd. (*Toronto*)
Prentice-Hall of India Private Limited (*New Delhi*)
Prentice-Hall of Japan, Inc. (*Tokyo*)

Preface

I have been greatly heartened by the favorable reception accorded the first English edition of this modest volume and its expanded German and Swedish editions. Equally gratifying has been the fact that some of the long overlooked or misunderstood aspects of the new China, such as the public health program, the improved status of women, and the efficacy of the Maoist approach to nation-building—to which the first edition of this work devoted considerable space—have since been attracting increasing attention from an ever-widening circle of people.

One of the new features of this enlarged edition is the inclusion of a separate chapter on the genesis, meaning, and development of the Great Proletarian Cultural Revolution, with special emphasis on the policy differences between Mao Tse-tung and his faithful supporters on the one hand and Liu Shao-ch'i and the latter's "revisionist" followers on the other. Since that complex and often tumultuous campaign was launched in part to clear the way for Mao to reconstruct the Chinese Communist Party and Chinese society in his image and to develop agriculture and industry in a genuinely innovative manner best suited to China's conditions, all the chapters on these subjects have been thoroughly revised and updated to reflect the new orientation.

A major internal development in the wake of the Great Proletarian Cultural Revolution was the demise of Lin Piao, who had been Mao's designated heir since Liu Shao-ch'i's disgrace in 1966. Although official indictment against Lin has been mostly allegorical and presumably incomplete, nevertheless it is possible to make at least a preliminary assessment of his case and its possible impact on Chinese politics, especially the problem of succession.

The chapter on foreign policy has also been extensively rewritten to take into account the significant developments on the diplomatic front in recent years, including the detente with Washington and Tokyo. In treating these events, I have not refrained from giving my own somewhat unorthodox interpretations.

I wish to take this opportunity to express my sense of gratitude to Miss Sharon Cassidy and Mrs. Vera Smith for their typing of the manuscript of this new edition and to Mrs. Marjorie Streeter of Prentice-Hall, Inc., for her help with the editorial production of the book.

Preface to the First Edition

This volume is intended primarily as an introduction for those who are interested in the Chinese Communist movement and its domestic and international implications. Although the work is based mainly on information drawn from the Chinese Communist press and other publications, Communist and non-Communist, the author owes a substantial intellectual debt to many colleagues in the Chinese field who have contributed to our understanding of various facets of the Communist revolution. In tracing the history of the movement, I have always attempted to keep modern China's overall socio-political scene in view. In the preface to an earlier volume of mine on Communist China, I stated that my task should be neither that of critic nor of apologist, but simply that of dispassionate reporter and analyst—neither to attack nor defend Communist policy, but simply to describe and interpret it as accurately as possible. I only hope that I have successfully adhered to this position in the present work.

In examining the economic, cultural, and social policies of the Peking regime since 1949, I have made extensive use of officially released statistics. It is my belief that except for the grossly exaggerated reports on achievements of the brief period of the Great Leap Forward, which the regime itself shortly felt necessary to correct, the official statistics have been substantially reliable.

To distinguish publications in the Chinese language from those in English, asterisks are added to the former's titles when they appear in footnotes. With reference to transliteration of Chinese words, I have used the commonly accepted Wade-Giles system except for the omission of certain diacritical marks. Some personal and place names, however, are cited in the form widely used in the West.

The elegant Chinese characters for the title of this work and my own name were written by my esteemed old friend, Professor Tse-tsung Chow of the University of Wisconsin. I wish to thank him for his kindness.

I undertook this project at the urging of Dr. Peter C. Grenquist and Mr. James J. Murray III, of Prentice-Hall, Inc.; without their encouragement and cooperation I might not have been able to complete this work on schedule. Mr. Timothy Yohn of the same firm has also been extremely helpful to me. His excellent editorial assistance is much appreciated. My hearty thanks are also due to Mrs. Sophia Zalegowski at the Office of Research Services in the University of Massachusetts for her typing of the manuscript. Mrs. Andrea Bassignani also rendered considerable assistance from time to time. Sincere gratitude is also due to Miss Lynn Horner, who cheerfully assisted me in my regular work during the academic year of 1966–67 and thereby made it possible for me to devote more of my time to the preparation of this work.

Last but not least, I must express my deepest affection to my children, Fred, Florence, and Flora, who sustained me during many long hours of research and writing.

For all errors of omission and commission, however, I am solely responsible.

Contents

I

Historical Background and the Emergence of the Chinese Communist Movement

中國共產運動簡史

The Chinese Communist Party (CCP) was founded in 1921 by a small group of intellectuals in search of a quick and effective solution to modern China's problems of poverty, internal political disorder, and foreign encroachments. By the end of the nineteenth century and the first decades of the twentieth century, population pressure, the administrative deterioration of the Manchu Dynasty (1644-1911), and a lack of industrialization had created in China an environment conducive to the emergence of a thoroughgoing revolutionary movement. Attempts to reform the Manchu Dynasty from within failed, and the dynasty collapsed in 1911; attempts to establish a viable form of republican government after 1911 were futile and served merely to aggravate existing problems. Against this background of continuing misfortune, three circumstances—the so-called "new cultural movement" in China itself, Chinese disillusionment with the Western democracies at the end of World War I, and the success of the October Revolution in Russia—were to bring about the birth of the Chinese Communist Party.

Unprecedented Population Pressure

An unprecedented population growth, beginning in the period between 1750 and 1774, contributed to increasing poverty and the civil disturbances that erupted in the middle of the nineteenth century and progressively weakened the foundation of the hitherto resilient socio-political fabric of Imperial China. Except for periodic famines resulting from drought, flood, war, and other calamities, prior to 1750 overpopulation in China had not been a serious demographical problem; on the contrary, China was occasionally beset by a lack of sufficient manpower. The *Confucian Classics* show that the question of how to increase population was uppermost in the minds of rulers and political philosophers in the pre-Ch'in period (i.e., before 211 B.C.).[1] The Chinese population remained relatively small in subsequent periods, for the approximate size was only 59 million in A.D. 2, 53 million in 755, 44 million in 1102, 60 million in 1290, and 61 million in 1578.

Due to advances in medical science in the sixteenth century, the introduction into China of drought-resistant crops such as peanuts, corn, and sweet potatoes, and a prolonged period of peace and prosperity beginning in the latter part of the seventeenth century, the Chinese population increased from approximately 150 million around 1700 to perhaps 313 million in 1794, more than doubling in one century.[2] According to Professor Ping-ti Ho, the optimum condition (the point at which a population produces maximum economic welfare) for the technical level of the time was reached between 1750 and 1775.[3] From that time on any further growth brought about a formidable socio-economic problem. In the absence of major technological inventions and scientific discoveries in agricultural and industrial production, this continual increase could only result in a progressive lowering of the standard of living, with the rich becoming poor and the poor hungry. Indicative of this general impoverishment was the fact that the amount of land available for cultivation was about 3.86 *mou* (6.6 *mou* equal one acre) per capita in the mid-eighteenth century; in 1812 it was 2.19 *mou;* and in 1833, 1.86 *mou.*[4]

This pressure of population on the means of subsistence posed a difficult problem for the Manchu government and was made all the more serious by the rising prices of land and food.[5] Under these circumstances the traditional order became unusually vulnerable, so vulnerable that from 1795 to the 1820's a series of bloody rebellions occurred, which, of course, further aggravated the economic plight of the country.

[1] See James Legge, trans., *The Chinese Classics* (Hong Kong: Hong Kong University Press, 1960).

[2] Ping-ti Ho, *Studies on Population of China* (Cambridge, Mass.: Harvard University Press, 1959), p. 298.

[3] *Ibid.*, p. 270.

[4] Kung-chuan Hsiao, *Rural China* (Seattle, Wash.: University of Washington Press, 1960), p. 380.

[5] *Ibid.*, pp. 381-382.

Administrative Deterioration of the Manchu Government

The traditional polity was noted for its ability to ensure fairly long periods of national unity and political tranquility, an ability owing in part to a delicate system of checks and balances between various agencies and individual officials.[6] But the Manchu rulers, being suspicious of the Han Chinese subordinates in the government, extended this system so far that there was an absence of coordination and individual responsibility within the government as a whole and in many individual agencies as well.

At the national level, neither the Grand Secretariat (*Nei-ko*) nor the Grand Council (*Chun-chi Ch'u*) was really in a position to act under the emperor as a supreme coordinator and supervisor of the work of the various executive departments or boards. Lacking a specially designated head in either the secretariat or the council, the grand secretaries and the grand councilors acted individually. This practice often led to personal rivalry within the two agencies, thus weakening their position in relation to the emperor on the one hand and to the various executive departments on the other. Furthermore, the two agencies lacked the power to issue directives in their own name to the executive departments of the central government and to the viceroys and governors in the provinces.

The various executive departments too found themselves poorly organized and inadequately empowered. Each of these departments was headed by two ministers, four vice-ministers (positions shared equally by Manchu and Han Chinese), and occasionally, a specially appointed "supervising minister," but none of these officials had any supreme authority in the department. Whenever ministers and vice-ministers of a department could not agree with each other, their only recourse was to present their views individually to the emperor for a final decision.

These as well as many other similar arrangements made unusually heavy demands on the energy, ability, and wisdom of the monarch. Hence, as long as able and energetic emperors like K'ang-hsi (reigned 1662-1722) and Ch'ien-lung (reigned 1736-1795) were in power, the Manchu court functioned quite well, despite its cumbersome structure, and these emperors gave the Chinese one of their golden eras. But once the throne was occupied by men of inferior caliber, such as Chia-ch'ing (reigned 1796-1820) and his successors,

[6] Franklin W. Houn, *Chinese Political Traditions* (Washington, D. C.: Public Affairs Press, 1965), pp. 30-31.

confusion and incompetence marked the top leadership of the imperial administration. Meanwhile, the corruption of the civil service system and the prostitution of the civil service examinations debased and undermined the entire bureaucratic machinery. In dealing with Western powers Chinese officials at the time were also handicapped by their ignorance of Western culture in general and Western diplomacy in particular.

At the provincial level, although no autonomy was legally recognized, the deterioration of the imperial leadership gradually encouraged the resurgence of centrifugal tendencies, which further aggravated the situation.

Finally, the mismanagement of finance and the demoralization of the banner garrisons enfeebled the Manchu Dynasty economically and militarily.

Lack of an Industrial Revolution

Despite the unprecedented population pressure and the administrative deterioration, China might have effected a self-rejuvenation in the nineteenth century and made herself invincible to the aggressive powers from the West, if she had had an industrial revolution. Prior to the industrialization of the West, China's material culture was by no means inferior to that of any other country. On the contrary, as the recently published voluminous works of Dr. Joseph Needham of Cambridge University have indicated, between the third and thirteenth centuries China maintained a level of scientific knowledge unapproached in the West.[7] Beginning in the seventeenth century, however, China gradually fell behind the West in scientific and technological advancement, and in the nineteenth century, when certain countries in Western Europe and North America had industrialized themselves, China suddenly found herself in a position of scientific backwardness. It was mainly this scientific backwardness that made it possible for the industrialized countries of the West to invade and humiliate her from the mid-nineteenth century on. The Chinese musketeers, mounted archers, and banner-decked war junks simply could not resist Western gunboats, which proved decisive during the Opium War (1839-1842) as well as in the wars which followed it.

One of the causes of China's technological backwardness in modern times appears to have been her conservatism—a strain in

[7] Joseph Needham, *Science and Civilization in China,* 4 vols. (London: Cambridge University Press, 1954-1962).

Chinese thinking and habit that became more pronounced in the latter part of the imperial era. Conservatism inclined the Chinese to look back to their ancestry for norms and to carry on their ancestral traditions and customs in daily living. It therefore inhibited innovations in all fields, especially science, technology, and business management. Consequently, Chinese farmers and artisans in the nineteenth century used almost the same kinds of tools that were in use several centuries before. Another contributing factor to China's technological backwardness was the Chinese intellectual's continued preoccupation with humanistic studies after the sixteenth century, while the educated man in post-Renaissance Europe was experiencing a great surge of interest in scientific inquiry. In the absence of modern scientists and engineers, industrialization naturally could not occur in China.

Additional reasons for the lack of an industrial revolution include the absence of substantial investment capital and the lack of powerful stimulation to technological innovations. It was largely due to her possession of these prerequisites that England became the first industrial country in the world.[8] She accumulated investment capital from the seventeenth century on through lucrative foreign trade, maritime shipping, and colonial exploitation. Powerful stimuli to major technological innovations were provided by a combination of circumstances. First, the ever-increasing demand from overseas possessions for goods presented England with virtually boundless opportunities for profit-making if she could only produce the needed goods and transport them to the distant markets. But acute scarcity of labor limited her capacity of production, which, in turn, hindered her pursuit of fabulous profit. To overcome this handicap, every effort was made to economize the use of labor. Hence, the discovery and development of the steam power and the use of machinery set in motion a chain reaction of economic activity that resulted in a thoroughgoing industrial and commercial revolution. Unlike England, China had neither substantial foreign trade nor profitable colonial possessions to enable her to accumulate capital for industrial development. Furthermore, the domestic demand for manufactured goods did not increase enough to call for an unprecedented expansion of production; handicraftsmen were still capable of producing enough goods to meet the limited needs of their fellow countrymen. To be sure, the population of the coun-

[8] I. C. A. Knowles, *The Industrial and Commercial Revolutions in Great Britain During the Nineteenth Century* (London: Routledge & Kegan Paul, 1932), pp. 12-16.

try was increasing by leaps and bounds, but not its purchasing power. As noted above, the rapid increase in population had the effect of impoverishing the nation as a whole, thus making the accumulation of capital all the more difficult. In addition, the availability of cheap labor deprived China of a great stimulus to adopt machinery and other labor-saving devices.

Foreign Encroachments

Imperial China was impoverished by a teeming population, paralyzed by a deteriorating administration, and retarded by the lack of an industrial revolution. For several millenniums she had held the position of primacy in East Asia and regarded herself as the center of civilization, but in the nineteenth century she became the object of Western aggrandizement, first in the economic then in the political, military, and cultural fields. Her early attempts to minimize contact with the West not only prevented her from adopting positive measures to meet the menace in time, but also greatly irritated the Westerners.[9]

Thus, after the Chinese government's dramatic confiscation and destruction, in 1838, of large quantities of opium owned by British merchants in Canton as a measure to enforce interdictions against the drug, England decided to retaliate with force. The British victory in the resulting war opened the gates of China to foreigners and caused her to enter into conflicts with Western powers as well as with modernized Japan. The outcome of these conflicts was a series of defeats for China, and she was forced to sign one "unequal treaty" after another, by which the victorious powers stripped her of all her dependencies and snatched pieces of her own soil—territories totaling over 4 million square kilometers. The victors further extorted concessions and privileges such as the following:

1. The opening of over 60 "treaty ports" for foreigners and foreign trade.
2. The creation of "concessions" within certain Chinese cities such as Shanghai, Hankow, and Tientsin.
3. The designation of some Chinese places such as Kowlow, Tsingtao, Kwangchowwan as "leased territories."
4. The granting of "the most favored nation" treatment to foreign countries, i.e., whenever one country obtained a new privilege from

[9] See Ssu-yu Teng and John K. Fairbank, *China's Response to the West: 1839-1923* (Cambridge, Mass.: Harvard University Press, 1954).

its treaty with China, all the other countries would enjoy the same benefits.

5. The deprivation of China's rights to adjust her tariff rates, to administer her customs, and to appropriate her customs revenues.
6. The right of coastal trade and the right of inland navigations.
7. The right to send missionaries anywhere in China.
8. The right to station foreign troops in the legation areas of the Chinese capital and along the railroad from Peking via Tientsin to Shanhaikwan, as well as in a number of other places.
9. The employment of foreign postal employees and the establishment of foreign postal offices.
10. The right to establish factories in the treaty ports and the right to secure reduced taxes or complete tax immunity for the articles manufactured by such factories.
11. The right to clear the channels of inland water ways and the privileges of employing foreign pilots and erecting buoys, navigating marks, lighthouses, and watchtowers.
12. The right to build railroads, to exploit mineral resources, and to issue currency.
13. The denial to the Chinese of the right to fortify certain strategic seaports.
14. The payment of large sums of indemnity.
15. The establishment of foreign consular jurisdiction (extraterritoriality) in China.

The adverse effects of these concessions and privileges on the socio-political life of the Chinese were numerous and far-reaching. Politically, the extraterritorial rights undermined the judicial power of China and impaired the sovereignty of the nation, while providing protection for foreign subjects carrying on activities injurious to the Chinese. The various "concessions," "leased territories," "treaty ports," and "legation areas" constituted states within a state, from which in time of enmity, the foreign powers could conveniently conduct military operations against China. Even in time of peace, they often served as havens for criminals and political conspirators. The presence of these sanctuaries made it impossible for the Chinese government to cope effectively with elements detrimental to the security and morale of the society. Indeed, many subversive organizations, including the Communist movement, originated in and operated from some of the foreign concessions.

The stationing of troops and police on Chinese soil and the

denial to the Chinese of the right to fortify certain strategic seaports further endangered the Chinese nation. She became an open house in which the imperialists could do as they pleased. Taking advantage of China's defenselessness and their own entrenched position, they more than once extorted substantial privileges from her merely by delivering a strongly worded note to the Chinese authorities. On other occasions, they amplified their previously acquired privileges by a unilateral reinterpretation of the existing treaties. On still other occasions, they effected their encroachments simply by presenting a *fait accompli* to the Chinese.

Foreigners could carry on unrestricted commercial and industrial activities because of their control of tariffs and their special rights to trade along the coast, navigate on inland waters, establish factories in treaty ports, build railroads, open mines, and issue currency. The restricted tariff provided for very low rates on foreign imports and deprived Chinese industry and agriculture of much needed tariff protection. Consequently Chinese markets were flooded with foreign merchandise, and native products lost their outlets. This, in turn, caused a decline of the traditional handicraft industries and doomed the belated Chinese attempt at industrialization. Inasmuch as a considerable portion of the traditional handicraft industries consisted of sideline production on the part of the huge farming population, the bankruptcy of the handicraft industries inevitably led to a reduction of the income of the farmer, thus aggravating the problems already caused by population pressure.

The economic deterioration was further intensified by the ruinous sums demanded as indemnities by the victorious powers after the various wars. These indemnities drained the governmental treasury and increased the burden on the taxpayer. As a result, more people were forced to turn toward insurrection. Notable rebellions in the second half of the nineteenth century included the following:

1. the Taiping Rebellion, 1850-64;
2. the Nein Rebellion, 1848-68;
3. the Miaotze Rebellion, 1855-72;
4. the Mohammedan Rebellion in Yunnan, 1855-73;
5. the Mohammedan Rebellion in the northwestern provinces, 1861-78.

In the Republican period (1912-1949), continued agricultural plight displaced numerous persons from the rural districts. Able-bodied men among the destitute people naturally found a convenient refuge in the armies of the warlords and Communist military organizations. The forces of disturbance were thus sustained, and the task of national reunification and reconstruction was further complicated.

Unsuccessful Attempts at Reform under the Manchu Court

In response to the deteriorating internal condition and the deepening foreign impact in the latter part of the nineteenth century, a first attempt at reform was initiated during the period 1862-1894 by several patriotic, high-ranking officials, including Ts'eng Kuo-fan. Tso Ts'ung-t'ang, and Li Hung-chang. This reform, however, was limited to technical fields and was highlighted by the establishment of modern shipyards and arsenals; the opening of machine shops, cotton mills, and mechanized coal mines; the founding of Western-style naval and military academies; the dispatching of students to the United States for the pursuit of "Western learning"; and the organization of a modern fleet. As the patriotic reformers saw it, what China needed was not an overhauling of the traditional Chinese socio-political institutions, which they still preferred to those in the West, but the adoption of the superior Western technology, to which they attributed the Western powers' victory over their own country.[10]

Due to a combination of reasons, including the extremely limited scope of the technological reform itself, foreign hindrances, the continued administrative deterioration, and the lack of support from the imperial court and the bulk of the imperial bureaucracy, China on the eve of the First Sino-Japanese War (1894-95) remained technologically backward, economically impoverished, and militarily weak. China's defeat by Japan, who derived her military superiority from certain newly adopted modernization programs, caused several scholars, including K'ang Yu-wei and Liang Ch'i-ch'ao, and a few officials, among them Yang Shen-hsiu and Hsu Chih-ching, to feel that if their country were to remain independent, some changes had to be made in administration, education, industry, agriculture, and the armed forces. Even though this movement was sanctioned by the open-minded Emperor Kuang-hsu, it was quickly nullified by reactionary elements in the Manchu court, under the direction of the Empress Dowager Tz'u-hsi.[11]

[10] See Mary C. Wright, *The Last Stand of Chinese Conservatism: The T'ung-chih Restoration* (Stanford, Calif.: Stanford University Press, 1957).

[11] See Meribeth E. Cameron, *The Reform Movement in China, 1898-1912* (Stanford, Calif.: Stanford University Press, 1931).

Although the disastrous national crisis caused by the Boxer movement in 1900 did seem to promote a deeper realization of the need for reform in the hearts of the powerful Empress and royal members of the court, the reform measures in the subsequent years were either too little or too late to cure the principal ills of the Manchu government and the nation as a whole. Meanwhile, there emerged a revolutionary movement seeking to overthrow the Manchu Dynasty and to establish a republican form of government. The revolutionaries were led by Sun Yat-sen and were organized in 1905 in Tokyo under the name *T'ung-meng-hui* (The Alliance Society). Because of the hopeless putridity of the Manchu Dynasty itself, an uprising staged locally by the revolutionaries in Wuchang on October 10, 1911 promptly inspired anti-Manchu revolts in several other cities in the Yangtze River valley and elsewhere. These uprisings, together with a betrayal by Premier Yuan Shih-k'ai, who was hastily called out from his enforced retirement to suppress the rebels, soon caused the infant emperor, Hsuan-t'ung, to abdicate the throne. His abdication ended the Manchu Dynasty as well as the age-old monarchical form of government in the country.

The Phantom Republic

Instead of paving the way for national rejuvenation and modernization, the demise of the Manchu Dynasty and the establishment of a republican form of government in 1912 initiated another period of storm and strain. The nation's crises during this period were progressively intensified by increasing political disorder and more internal military strife. Inasmuch as the establishment of a Western-style democratic government was regarded as the key to national wealth and power, the failure to attain that form of government beyond paper provisions and its disastrous consequences caused more and more Chinese to lose faith in the idea of a constitutional government. They began to look for other models that would yield better and quicker results. The founders of the CCP were people in this state of mind.

In addition to the crushing economic, population, and diplomatic problems which the Republic inherited from the Manchu Dynasty, the nation's tragedy in the early years of the Republic stemmed in large measure from the weakness of the revolutionaries. Lacking broad popular support, handicapped by internal dissension, and confined mainly to the major cities in the central and southern provinces, the revolutionaries succeeded in overthrowing the Manchu Dynasty only with the help of the powerful Premier Yuan

Shih-k'ai. Instead of fulfilling his mission of saving the dynasty by crushing the revolution, he deliberately created a military stalemate at the front, which enabled him to convince the Manchu court that abdication under terms of favorable treatment was the only course open to the dynasty if the country was to be saved from disruption and the imperial family was to retain financial and ceremonial privileges. At the same time he made the revolutionaries recognize his pivotal position and come to terms with him after the abdication of the Manchu court. The price paid by the revolutionaries for Yuan's assistance was his election to the Provisional Presidency of the Republic in February 1912.

Under Yuan the government of the Republic in Peking was in many respects a continuation of the previous regime. It relied mainly upon the support of the former imperial army, which Yuan had trained and commanded; it derived the bulk of its executive and administrative personnel from the conservative and corrupt bureaucracy of the fallen dynasty; and it eschewed the ideals and personalities of the revolutionary party, which now called itself the Kuomintang. These factors attested to the superficiality of the Revolution of October 10, 1911, and clouded the future path of the Republic. The situation was aggravated by the Kuomintang's attempt to use constitutional devices and the legislature (in which it had a majority of seats) to check President Yuan, who as a man of ambition and influence was not only unwilling to accept excessive legislative restrictions but sought total power for himself. The constant friction between the President and the Kuomintang-dominated legislature culminated in the President's illegal dissolution of the parliament and of the Kuomintang in November 1913.

Yuan soon inspired a monarchical movement with himself as the intended emperor. A series of revolts in south and central China erupted protesting the proposed change, and the movement ended with Yuan's death in June 1916. However, his disappearance from the political scene was not an unmixed blessing. As the only magnate of loyalty for the *Pei-yang* ["North Sea"] military faction and the *Pei-yang* officialdom, which had been the pillars of the central government in Peking from 1912 on, Yuan had been the sole stabilizing force in the country from the day the Manchu Dynasty abdicated, and his death plunged the country into unprecedented disunity and disorder. The country witnessed almost uninterrupted political and military struggles not only between the ineffectual Kuomintang in the south and the *Pei-yang* faction in the north, but also among the various cliques of the *Pei-yang* faction itself. No fixed principles and no enduring loyalties marked the multitude of factions. An ally of yesterday could be an enemy of today, and an enemy of today could become a comrade of tomorrow. The presidents, the cabinets, and the legislatures which appeared in Peking in rapid succession during this period of "warlordism" were nothing but tools of whatever militarist happened to be in power. Meanwhile, foreign exploitation and threat, especially the Japanese threat, kept mounting. Throughout these years the nation's fate hung by a thread.[12]

The "New Cultural Movement"

The "New Cultural Movement" began in September 1915 with the appearance of the magazine, *New Youth* (*Hsin-ch'ing-nien*), under the editorship of Ch'en Tu-hsiu (1879-1943), the future founder of the CCP.[13] Since he was convinced that the failure of the previous attempts at strengthening China was due to the superficiality of the programs and popular apathy, Ch'en Tu-hsiu founded the new magazine with the avowed purpose of bringing about a basic change in the Chinese society and civilization through an ideological awakening of the Chinese people in general and the Chinese youth in particular. Believing that socio-political stagnation in modern China stemmed from what he called the decadent traditional ethics, institutions, and ideologies (including Confucianism), Ch'en launched an all-out attack on them in his magazine; he called for the adoption of the modern Western culture, which he regarded as dynamic, progressive, utilitarian, and scientific. Expressed in a passionate and incisive style, Ch'en's radical views immediately struck a responsive chord not only among the youth in the universities and secondary schools throughout the nation but also among a growing number of university professors, particularly in the National Peking University, which, under the leadership of the newly appointed chancellor, Ts'ai Yuan-p'ei, had just abandoned its conservatism in favor of a policy of actively promoting the exposition of divergent points of view, academic as well as political.

In 1917, Chancellor Ts'ai invited Ch'en Tu-hsiu to join the

[12] Franklin W. Houn, *Central Government of China, 1912-1928* (Madison, Wis.: University of Wisconsin Press, 1957); and George T. Yu, *Party Politics in Republican China* (Berkeley, Calif.: University of California Press, 1966).

[13] For the most comprehensive treatment of the new cultural movement, see Chow Tse-tsung, *The May Fourth Movement: Intellectual Revolution in Modern China* (Cambridge, Mass.: Harvard University Press, 1960), p. 232.

faculty of the University as dean of the College of Letters. Many others with new ideas were soon brought into the school. Among them were Hu Shih, who was a disciple of John Dewey; Li Ta-chao, who subsequently collaborated with Ch'en Tu-hsiu in founding the CCP; Ch'ien Hsuan-t'ung, who called himself "the antiquity doubter"; and Wu Yü, who was the most frenzied anti-Confucian scholar. Virtually all these scholars contributed articles to the *New Youth,* and some of them also took part in its editing.

Although these professors expounded vastly different philosophical and literary views, they united in the period of 1917-1918 to introduce Western thought and institutions and to re-evaluate and criticize the Chinese tradition. Through the pages of the *New Youth* and their lectures in the classroom, these men attacked the old pattern of thought and customs as well as the traditional ethics, embodied in loyalty to officials, filial duty to parents, the double standard of chastity for men and women, and the arranged marriage. They opposed superstitions, old religions, and the extended family system (parents and married children living together). They were against the classical literary style and advocated a vernacular literature. Above all, they declared a war on Confucianism. The vehemence in which Confucianism was attacked can be seen from such slogans as "Down with Confucius and Sons" (*Ta-tao K'ung-chia-tien*), "Let Us Deposit the Confucian Classics in the Privy for Thirty Years," and "The So-Called National Quintessence is Nothing but National Refuse." The diverse Western ideas introduced by these new intellectuals ranged from democracy to socialism, from liberalism to anarchism, from utilitarianism to humanitarianism, from realism to romanticism, and from idealism to pragmatism.

These attacks on Chinese tradition were often unjustified and excessive, and the expositions of the Western thought and institutions were frequently superficial and unbalanced. Nonetheless, the bold and fresh ideas of the professors of the new cultural movement aroused the enthusiastic support of the students at the National Peking University and elsewhere. The students regarded the *New Youth* as "the youth's polestar" or "a clap of thunder which awakened them in the midst of a restless dream." Intoxicated by the new thoughts and their iconoclastic attitude toward Chinese heritage, they began publishing their own magazines in support of the new thought and literature movements, the most influential of which was the *New Tide* (*Hsin-ch'ao*) edited by a group of able students at the National Peking University. Reflecting the awakened students' need of organized activity, many organizations of young people were formed with the objective of studying new ideas and promoting social reforms. Mao Tse-tung, who in 1918 was an assistant librarian at the National Peking University with a salary of eight *yuan* a month, joined the Society of Philosophy and the Society of Journalism. Through these organizations he came into contact with some of the brilliant and ambitious young men who later played prominent roles in the Kuomintang, the CCP, and academic and literary circles.

The May Fourth Mass Demonstrations against the Versailles Treaty

The new intellectuals studied and propagated a bewildering variety of Western ideas, yet Marxism received only casual attention in the early stage of the intellectual revolution. The tenets which aroused the greatest enthusiasm at the time were what Ch'en Tu-hsiu called "Mr. Democracy" and "Mr. Science." It was thought that democracy and science were the basic secrets of Western strength and that China's only way to salvation lay in adopting them. Chinese faith in the democratic spirit and institutions of the West was further heightened by the proclamation of Woodrow Wilson's "Fourteen Points" and by the Allied Powers' fine-sounding declarations on "war aims." When the war in Europe ended in November 1918, the Chinese public was jubilant, and the new Chinese intellectuals were particularly optimistic, believing that the Allied victory was one of right over might, of democracy over militarism, and of peace-loving forces over imperialism. Not only did they think that the war had destroyed the ideas and practices of secret diplomacy and the exploitation of one nation by another, they also assumed that China, as one of the Allied Powers, could look forward to Allied support at the ensuing peace conference for the restoration of the territory and interests lost to Germany from 1898 onward and then seized by the Japanese from the Germans during the war.

These high hopes suddenly gave way to profound disillusionment late in April 1919 with the news that the leading powers at the Paris Peace Conference would legitimize Japan's seizure of the former German interests in the Chinese province of Shantung. Greatly shocked, the student organizations in Peking resolved to hold a mass demonstration to protest the Paris Peace Conference's decision on the Shantung question and to denounce some pro-Japanese officials in the Peking regime. The students presented memoranda to foreign legations, set the residence of the pro-Japanese foreign minister on fire, and physically assaulted the Chinese minister to Japan who was then in Peking. In addition they issued a ringing declaration calling upon all agricultural, industrial, commercial, and other groups of the nation to rise and strive for national salvation. The response to this call was fervent and widespread: from May 5 to June 4, students in all major cities of the country demonstrated, circulated leaflets, made street speeches, went on strikes, and organized boycotts against Japanese goods. The students' burning patriotism, the government's repressive measures against them, and the mounting conflict of interests between Chinese and Western economic forces (resulting from the renewed influx of Western goods into the Chinese market after the war) soon stirred other segments of society. Merchants, industrialists, and urban workers joined the students in protesting against the Versailles Treaty by staging strikes, boycotts, and street rallies. Modern China was experiencing the first major mass political action by such social elements.

The immediate result of this nationwide popular outburst, which has since been called the "May Fourth Movement," was the refusal of the Chinese delegation at Paris to sign the treaty. More significant was its impact on some of the new intellectuals who had expected the Western powers to come to China's aid in the postwar years and who had advocated Western democratic thought and institutions as a remedy for the socio-political ills of modern China. Utterly disappointed with the policies of the Western powers at the Paris Peace Conference and impressed with the efficacy of direct mass action taken by the Chinese public (especially the students and urban workers) during the May Fourth Movement, several leading intellectuals, including Ch'en Tu-hsiu and Li Ta-chao, and some young men, among them Mao Tse-tung and Chou En-lai, became increasingly interested in the revolutionary experience of the Bolsheviks in Russia.

In May 1919, during the student demonstration, the *New Youth* dedicated a special number to Marxism, edited by Li Ta-chao. In June 1919, Ch'en Tu-hsiu revealed his growing materialistic views when he stated: "What is politics after all; Everybody must eat—that is important." [14]

In the fall of 1919 socialist study groups were being organized in large numbers among intellectuals. In December 1919, a Society for the Study of Socialism made its appearance on the campus of the National Peking University with Ch'en Tu-hsiu, Li Ta-chao, Ch'ü Ch'iu-pai, Chang Kuo-t'ao, Mao Tse-tung and some 100 other professors and students as its members. By the end of 1919, these

[14] Cited in *Ibid.*, p. 232.

socialist study groups were still fervently debating the relative merits of various kinds of socialism with considerable open-mindedness toward all, and none of these socialistically inclined intellectuals had embraced Marxism or completely rejected the principles of Western democracy. For example, in an article published in the December 1919 issue of the *New Youth,* Ch'en Tu-hsiu still advocated a synthesis of constitutional democracy and "social and economic democracy," though emphasizing that the latter was more important than the former.

Impact of Soviet Overtures

What finally led Ch'en Tu-hsiu and his associates to accept Marxism and organize the CCP were friendly overtures from Soviet Russia. In sharp contrast to the Western powers' continued adherence to the traditional policy of exploitation, the Soviet government, in a declaration issued in Moscow on July 25, 1919 by Leo P. Karakhan, Acting Commissar for Foreign Affairs, announced its readiness to return to the Chinese people, without asking any kind of compensation, the Chinese Eastern Railroad and all other privileges and concessions that had been seized from them by the Tsarist regime. The Soviet government also promised support to the Chinese people in their struggle to regain complete freedom. Due to a long delay in transmission, the telegram containing the Karakhan Declaration did not reach Peking until late in March 1920, but it immediately evoked an enthusiastic response from Chinese who had already been impressed by the success of the Russian Revolution. By early April, more than 30 important organizations had expressed their gratitude directly to the Soviet government.

Amid this pro-Soviet sentiment, the Society for the Study of Marxist Theory was initiated at the National Peking University. In April 1920, the full text of the Communist Manifesto was published for the first time in the Chinese language. The Marxist philosophy now became so fascinating that even some Kuomintang leaders began to use historical materialism in their interpretation of Chinese history.

Birth of the Party

Meanwhile, the Comintern dispatched Gregory Voitinsky, secretary of the Comintern's Far Eastern Bureau, to China. Arriving in Peking in the spring of 1920 with his wife and a Chinese interpreter, Yang Ming-chai, Voitinsky quickly set out to contact intellectuals for the purpose of establishing a Chinese Communist party. He first came into touch with Li Ta-chao, who referred him to Ch'en Tu-hsiu, then residing in Shanghai. After Voitinsky's arrival in Shanghai, Ch'en introduced him to a group of revolutionaries that included socialists, anarchists, Marxists, and some members of the Kuomintang. In May 1920, these heterogeneous elements decided at a secret meeting to form a Chinese Communist party.

Although the party was not formally organized until July 1921 at the First National Congress, Ch'en Tu-hsiu and Voitinsky lost no time in launching a vigorous organizational and propaganda campaign for the new political adventure. They first established a Sino-Russian News Agency and a Foreign Language School in Shanghai. The news agency was designed to be a propaganda medium, and the language school was a disguised center for training Communist cadres, including those who were to be sent to Soviet Russia for further schooling in communism and Bolshevik techniques. In addition, a Socialist Youth Corps was organized, and two party publications—*Labor Circles* (*Lao-tung-chieh*) and *The Communist* (*Kung-ch'an-tang*)—were launched. Fully realizing the importance of forging close links with the emerging working class, Ch'en Tu-hsiu also devoted considerable attention to the labor movement. The first trade union to be organized in Shanghai was the mechanics' union, followed by the printers' union and the textile workers' union.

The emergence of this embryonic party in Shanghai had a profound influence on developments in other major cities. In September 1920, Li Ta-chao organized branches of the party and the Socialist Youth Corps at Peking, and Mao Tse-tung, now teaching at the elementary school of the Hunan First Provincial Normal School, started a Communist group in Changsha. At about the same time, Tung Pi-wu formed a similar organization in Wuhan under the guidance of Voitinsky's assistants. Toward the end of 1920, while serving as provincial commissioner of Kwangtung under a southern warlord governor, Ch'en Tu-hsiu himself organized a cell in Canton. Other Communist nuclei appeared in Hangchow, Tsinan, and Tientsin, as well as among some Chinese students studying in Japan and France. The group in Japan was headed by Chou Fu-hai, who subsequently joined the Kuomintang and then played a prominent role under Wang Ching-wei in the puppet regime of the Japanese in Nanking during World War II. The group in France grew out of the "work-and-study" students, who had been taken by some Chinese educators to Paris after World War I for advanced education while seeking part-time employment. Many members of this group later attained high positions in the Communist regime, among them Chou En-lai, Ch'en I, and Li Fu-ch'un.

Now the stage was set for the formal inauguration of the party. On July 1, 1921, the First National Congress of the party took place in a girls' school in the French concession at Shanghai, beyond the reach of Chinese law. Ch'en Tu-hsiu, who was then busy in Canton, did not attend; however, the 12 delegates to the Congress represented about 50 party members. To guide the Congress, the Comintern dispatched two representatives—one of them Maring, a Dutch Communist whose real name was Hendricus Sneevliet. On the fourth day of the Congress, the proceedings at the school were cut short because the delegates feared surveillance by the concession police. In order to continue deliberations in safety, the delegates proceeded to South Lake (Nan-hu) in Chekiang Province, about 50 miles south of Shanghai, "where they hired a boat, bought food and wine, and carried through the work of the Congress under the pretense of having a quiet and respectful outing." [15]

At the very beginning of the Congress, the delegates, who were men of divergent ideas and political outlooks reflecting the heterogeneous character of the previously organized local groups, found themselves in serious disagreement concerning the organization and tasks of the proposed party. Despite the discord, the delegates finally resolved that the party should build itself in accordance with the Bolshevik principles and that the principles of Marxism-Leninism should guide the party in its work. A decision was made that all those who had non-Communist tendencies would *eo ipso* be barred from the ranks of the party. This "closed-door policy" soon resulted in a *bona-fide* Communist party.

Because of the small membership of the party at that time, the Congress decided not to organize a regular central committee, but to form a provisional central bureau to maintain contact with the local Communist nuclei. The absent Ch'en Tu-hsiu was chosen as general secretary of the party.

Upon his election as general secretary, Ch'en Tu-hsiu left Canton for Shanghai. Under his direction the newly founded party intensified its work in the labor movement by establishing the Chinese Labor Union Secretariat, led by Chang Kuo-t'ao, who concurrently headed the party's Organization Department. To foment agitation, the party organized evening classes for workers and founded a publishing office, which soon turned out such translated

[15] Robert C. North, *Moscow and Chinese Communists* (Stanford, Calif.: Stanford University Press, 1953, 1963), p. 57. Also see Chou Fu-hai's reminiscence in *Ch'un-ch'iu,** No. 208 (March 1, 1966), pp. 3-5; and No. 209 (March 16, 1966), pp. 6-8.

books as *The Program of the Russian Communist Party, Wage, Labor, and Capital,* and *The Soviet System of Power.* Party organizers also met workers at teahouses, cafes, and other places where they relaxed. Despite obstacles and mistakes, the Communists soon succeeded, in the ensuing year, in organizing various labor unions in the major industrial centers and among seamen and railroad workers.

In May 1922 the Communists convened the First All-China Labor Congress in Canton. According to an official party history, the Communist-led labor movement developed so successfully that from January 1922 to February 1923, more than 300,000 workers took part in over 100 strikes throughout the country.[16] On February 7, 1923, however, the movement suffered its first major setback when Wu P'ei-fu, the warlord who controlled the provinces of Hopei, Honan, and Hupeh, ordered his troops to fire on the striking railroad workers at Hankow and Changhsintien. Since about 40 workers were killed and several others were injured, the Communists have since called this incident the "February Seventh Massacre."

Another important step taken by the party shortly after its First National Congress was the reorganization of the Chinese Socialist Youth Corps (renamed the Chinese Communist Youth Corps sometime before February 1925) as an effective instrument for recruiting young men and women into the revolutionary movement. At its First National Congress on May 1, 1922, the Youth Corps resolved to affiliate with the Communist Youth International. The Corps was particularly important to the party at the time since until the "May Thirtieth Movement" in 1925, its membership was consistently two or three times as large as the party's. Some of the promising youths recruited into the Corps and the party were sent to Soviet Russia, where they attended various schools including the University of the Peoples of the East, the Lenin Institute, and, subsequently, the Sun Yat-sen University for Chinese Toilers (founded in January 1926). In these institutions they were trained in Bolshevik doctrine, strategy, and tactics. Some also studied military science and gained experience as officers in the Red Army. Viewing these young men and women as potential leaders of the Asian Communist movement, the highest Soviet dignitaries, including Stalin and Trotsky, found time to talk to them in person. Upon their return to China these well-trained professional revolutionaries greatly strengthened the Bolshevik orientation of the CCP.

[16] Hu Chiao-mu, *Thirty Years of the Communist Party in China* (Peking: Foreign Languages Press, 1954), p. 8.

II

The First United Front with the Kuomintang: 1923-1927

Nature and Objectives of the Policy of Collaboration

Although the Comintern engineered the formal organization of the CCP, it did not envisage an immediate proletarian revolution in China. China, in its opinion, had not yet developed a full-fledged capitalist system but rather was in a stage of development half-feudal and half-colonial. According to the "Theses on the National and Colonial Question," adopted by the Second Congress of the Comintern in the summer of 1920, a Communist party in such a country, instead of staging a socialist revolution at the outset, must first give "active support" to a national revolutionary movement against foreign imperialism and domestic feudal elements, especially in the landowning class. Such support would entail temporary cooperation between the Communists and other revolutionary groups in the national liberation movement, including the bourgeois democrats. At the same time, however, the Communists were to develop an independent proletarian movement and to prepare the working class for the future struggle against the bourgeoisie.

When these theses were adopted by the Comintern, they had no immediate effect on China since a Communist party had yet to be organized. In fact, the theses did not immediately become the official policy of the CCP at the time of its inauguration in 1921, although the delegates to the First National Congress of the party are said to have discussed the question of policy toward Sun Yat-sen. However, at the First Congress of the Toilers of the Far East, held in Moscow and Petrograd in January and February 1922, the strategy embodied in the theses was amplified for

中國共產運動簡史

execution by the CCP. Specifically, the Congress stated that the principal task of the CCP was to wage a joint struggle with other democratic revolutionaries against imperialists and Chinese warlords. Repeating the warning of the Second Comintern Congress against Communist amalgamation with national revolutionary groups, a spokesman of the First Congress of the Toilers of the Far East declared, "The Chinese workers must tread their own path, must not connect themselves with any democratic party or any bourgeois elements," and further stated, "We support any national revolutionary group so long as it is not directed against the proletarian movement." [1]

Following the First Congress of the Toilers of the Far East, the CCP held its Second National Congress in May 1922 in Shanghai. Attended by 12 delegates representing 195 party members, the Congress adopted 11 documents, including the Constitution of the party, a manifesto, and a resolution that the CCP should join the Third International.[2]

In the manifesto, the party analyzed international and domestic conditions and criticized the sundry reformist thoughts of the bourgeoisie of the time.[3] More importantly, the manifesto laid down the "maximum" and "minimum" programs of the party in accordance with the line set by the First Congress of the Toilers of the Far East. Although the "maximum" or long-range aims of the party were to "organize the proletariat to struggle for the establishment of the dictatorship of the workers and peasants, the abolition of private property, and the gradual attainment of a Communist society," the "minimum" or immediate program called for a democratic united front of the proletariat, poor peasantry, and petty bourgeoisie against imperialism and warlordism. In concrete terms, the minimum program meant that in the first stage of the revolution the CCP should work with the Kuomintang, which had long been frustrated in its attempt to bring about a national reunification and rejuvenation.

The proletariat's support for the Kuomintang, the manifesto

[1] *The First Congress of the Toilers of the Far East* (Petrograd: The Communist International, 1922), pp. 165-166.

[2] Ch'un Wen, "Brief Account of the First to the Eighth National Congresses of the Chinese Communist Party," *Selections from China Mainland Magazines* (hereafter cited as *SCMM*), No. 27 (July 24, 1961), p. 39.

[3] An English translation of the Manifesto may be found in Ch'en Kung-po, *The Communist Movement in China*, edited with an introduction by C. Martin Wilbur (New York: East Asia Institute at Columbia University, 1960), pp. 111-123.

emphasized, did not imply surrender to the bourgeoisie. Collaboration was a necessary step for the proletariat to take in order to foster its own strength and shorten the life of feudalism. Upon the conclusion of the national democratic revolution, the proletariat was to struggle against the bourgeoisie and establish a dictatorship of the proletariat in alliance with the poor peasants. The struggle of the second phase could be successfully completed immediately upon the conclusion of the democratic revolution, provided that during the period of the democratic united front the proletariat had carefully retained its political independence, had fought for its own class interests, and had developed its organization (including labor unions) and fighting strength.

On June 10, 1922, the Central Committee of the party issued the "First Manifesto of the CCP on the Current Situation." While criticizing the various defects of the Kuomintang, the CCP called for a joint conference with that party for the purpose of building a united front.[4] The manifesto, however, did not specify the form which the proposed Kuomintang-CCP collaboration should take. Should the Communists work with the Kuomintang as a "bloc without" (i.e., a two-party alliance) or should they help the latter as "a bloc within" (i.e., a system of dual party membership under which individual Communists would enter the Kuomintang while retaining their Communist affiliation)?

Apparently, both the Comintern and the CCP originally preferred the "bloc without" policy. Thus, late in June 1922, Dalin, a delegate of the Communist Youth International, approached Sun Yat-sen in Shanghai with a proposal for an alliance between the Kuomintang and the CCP. Sun rejected the offer but said he might permit members of the CCP and the Youth Corps to join the Kuomintang as individuals. Desperately in need of foreign support for energizing the ineffectual Kuomintang and rebuffed by Western powers in his bid for this aid, Sun was hopeful that by working with individual Communists his party might secure Soviet assistance, and thus enable itself to undertake the arduous tasks of eliminating warlordism and reconstructing the nation.

Partly because of Sun's attitude, and partly due to a realization that the Kuomintang could be conveniently used by the CCP as a Trojan horse for gaining an easier access to the mass movement,

[4] For an English text of the Manifesto, see Conrad Brandt *et al.*, *A Documentary History of Chinese Communism* (Cambridge, Mass.: Harvard University Press, 1952), pp. 54-63.

the Comintern soon decided to adopt the "bloc within" approach. On August 22, 1922, Maring, who had recently returned to China from a trip to Moscow, convened a special plenum of the CCP Central Committee at West Lake, Hangchow. Proceeding from the assumption that the Kuomintang was not a party of the bourgeoisie, but one representing a coalition of classes that could be transformed, under proletarian influence, into a driving force of the national liberation movement, Maring proposed that the Chinese Communists "simply enter the Kuomintang and use its loose organizational structure as a means for developing their own propaganda and contacts among the masses." [5]

There have been conflicting reports on the reaction of the Central Committee members to Maring's proposal. In an interview with Harold Isaacs in 1935, Maring stated that a majority of the Central Committee, including Ch'en Tu-hsiu, immediately accepted his view. Those who opposed his plan, particularly Chang Kuo-tao, "did so on the grounds that they doubted the weight of the Kuomintang as a political force and did not believe it would or could develop into a mass movement." [6] According to Ch'en Tu-hsiu, however, all the Central Committee members attending the plenum initially opposed Maring, contending that the suggested scheme could blur class distinctions and curb the CCP's independent action.[7]

The plenum eventually accepted Maring's proposal, Ch'en asserted, only after the Dutchman had invoked the discipline of the Comintern. Nonetheless, shortly after the adjournment of the Hangchow plenum, individual Communists began to join the Kuomintang, the first one to take the step being Li Ta-chao. The collaboration between the Kuomintang and the CCP was not formalized until the issuance of the Sun-Joffe Declaration of January 26, 1923, in which Sun Yat-sen was assured by Adolph Joffe, a representative of the Soviets, that the proposed cooperation between the Kuomintang and the CCP was for China's national unification and liberation instead of the establishment of a Communist system, which was deemed inapplicable to China. At its Third National Congress held in June 1923, the CCP officially adopted the policy of encouraging its members to enter the Kuomintang. Meanwhile it ostensibly rec-

[5] Harold R. Isaacs, *The Tragedy of the Chinese Revolution* (Stanford, Calif.: Stanford University Press, 1951, 1961), p. 58.

[6] *Ibid.*, p. 59.

[7] Ch'en Tu-hsiu, *A Letter to All Comrades of the Party** (dated December 10, 1929), pp. 2-3.

ognized the Kuomintang as the central force and the leader of the National Revolution and called upon all revolutionary elements to rally around it.

CCP-Kuomintang Collaboration in Canton: 1924-1926

While Sun Yat-sen was negotiating with Joffe, some pro-Sun generals in Kwangtung captured Canton from a local warlord and offered to place that strategic city under his control. On February 21, 1923, Sun arrived in Canton where he addressed himself to the task of establishing a revolutionary base and of revitalizing his party. Under the guidance of Soviet advisors headed by the politically gifted Michael Borodin, who came to Canton in October 1923, the Kuomintang reorganized itself in accordance with Bolshevik party-building principles. The reorganization was accompanied by a systematic formulation of its program embodied mainly in Sun's *Three People's Principles*. To enlist mass support, the Kuomintang stepped up its organizational and propaganda efforts among workers, peasants, student groups, and people in other walks of life. A more important step was the establishment of the Whampoa Military Academy in May 1924. Under the superintendence of the young general Chiang Kai-shek, who had been in Moscow in the summer of 1923 to study the organization of the Red Army, the academy was to provide the nucleus for a Kuomintang army that would fight for national reunification and reconstruction.

The Communists who had entered the Kuomintang now actively participated in the latter's work and their influence grew steadily. From January 1924 to May 1926, they occupied approximately one fifth of the Kuomintang Central Executive Committee seats and one third of the Standing Committee seats. In addition, T'an P'ing-shan, Lin Tsu-han, and Mao Tse-tung headed the Kuomintang Departments of Organization, Peasant Movement, and Propaganda, respectively.

The Communists' growing influence in the Kuomintang was bound to cause enmity between the two parties, but friction was avoided before the death of Sun Yat-sen in March 1925. Soon after Sun's death, some orthodox members of the Kuomintang began to complain about the Communist control of strategic positions in the party. Spearheading the anti-Communist campaign was Tai Chi-t'ao, a veteran Kuomintang leader, who subsequently headed the Examination *Yuan* [Council] of the National Government from 1928 to 1948. In a pamphlet published in July 1925, Tai contended that only the Kuomintang and its doctrines could save China; that the Communists did not really believe in the *Three People's Principles* but merely wanted to used the Kuomintang to expand their own organization; and that therefore the Communists' parasitic existence within the Kuomintang should not be allowed to continue.[8] Although Tai's views greatly worried the Communists, they resolved to remain in the Kuomintang and pursue the policy of "allying with the Kuomintang's Left Wing and of fighting against its Right Wing," of which Tai Chi-t'ao was regarded as a spokesman.

This policy of supporting the Left Wing only served to reinforce the apprehension of the Kuomintang leaders who had been alarmed by the Communist infiltration of their party. On August 20, 1925, Liao Chung-k'ai, an influential Kuomintang leader, ardently in favor of working with Soviet Russia and the CCP, was mysteriously assassinated in Canton. On November 23, fifteen members of the Kuomintang Central Executive and Supervisory Committees convened what they called the "Fourth Central Executive Committee Plenum" before Sun Yat-sen's embalmed body in the Western Hills of Peking. Subsequently known as the Western Hills Group, these prominent Kuomintang leaders adopted resolutions for the expulsion of all Communist elements from the Kuomintang; the dismissal of Michael Borodin as chief Soviet advisor to the party for his connivance with the CCP; and the suspension of Wang Ching-wei's party membership for six months. Wang Ching-wei was then Chairman of the Kuomintang Political Council and of the National Government Council and advocated a close alliance with Soviet Russia and the CCP.

When the Western Hills Group was trying to purge the Kuomintang of its Communist elements, Chiang Kai-shek, by virtue of commanding the newly organized Kuomintang army, had already emerged as one of the two most influential leaders in the Kuomintang party and government in Canton, sharing supreme authority with Wang Ching-wei, an able, ambitious, and unpredictable politician. Distrustful of both Soviet Russia and the CCP from the very beginning of the Kuomintang-CCP entente, Chiang now felt, however, that the time for a split with the CCP was not yet ripe, because the Kuomintang still could not afford to risk losing Soviet assistance to the projected military campaign against the Northern warlords. Given Chiang's conciliatory attitude toward the Communists, Wang Ching-wei responded to the Western Hills

[8] Tai Chi-t'ao, *The National Revolution and the Kuomintang** (Shanghai: published by the author, 1925).

Group's challenge with the convocation of the Second National Congress of the Kuomintang in Canton in January 1926. This Congress resolved to expel the leaders of the Western Hills Group from the party and to continue the alliance with the Communists.

Despite his desire not to jeopardize Soviet aid, Chiang Kai-shek soon felt impelled to curb the Soviet and Chinese Communist influence in the Kuomintang because of the Soviet advisors' collusion with the CCP for controlling the Kuomintang armies; their opposition to the launching of a Northern Expedition against the warlords at an early stage (the Soviet advisors felt that the preparations were incomplete and that an early Kuomintang unification of China might preclude Communist control of the revolution); the appearance of handbills in Canton portraying him as a new warlord; and Captain Li Chih-lung's (a Communist) alleged plot to seize Chiang on the gunboat *Chung-shan*. On March 20, 1926, in his capacity as Canton's Garrison Commander, Chiang declared martial law, ordered the arrest of Li Chih-lung and a number of other Communists, disarmed the Communist-dominated Canton-Hong Kong Strike Committee, and put Soviet advisors under surveillance. He executed this *coup d'état* when the shrewd and influential Borodin was temporarily in Moscow for consultation.

Before Borodin's return to Canton there was a division of opinion among the Chinese Communists as to how their party should respond to the latest development. Some members of the CCP Kwangtung Regional Committee advocated an independent direct struggle to seize leadership of the Kuomintang, whereas Ch'en Tu-hsiu, General Secretary of the party, proposed immediate withdrawal from the Kuomintang. In keeping with the Comintern policy of continuing the Kuomintang-CCP entente, the Soviet consul in Canton adopted a conciliatory attitude toward Chiang, promising to send home the objectionable Soviet advisors. Soon the official attitude of the CCP also fell in line with the Comintern policy. Early in April the party decided to withdraw its representative from the Kuomintang First Army and to disband the League of Military Youth organized by Communist officers and cadets in the Whampoa Military Academy.

Meanwhile, Chiang Kai-shek also let it be known that he wanted to restore unity. After Borodin's return to Canton on April 29, 1926, he and Chiang reached an agreement for conciliation, which comprised the following major points: (1) the Chinese Communists accepted Chiang's demand for restricting their activities within the Kuomintang; (2) Borodin agreed to support the

Northern Expedition against the warlords; and (3) Chiang yielded to Borodin's insistence that steps be taken against the Western Hills Group and other rightist elements in the Kuomintang. Although preventing an open rupture, this agreement failed to check the animosity between the Kuomintang on the one hand and the CCP and the Soviet advisors on the other. In May 1926, the Kuomintang Central Executive Committee adopted a resolution proposed by Chiang Kai-shek, which, among other things, prohibited Communists to serve as departmental heads in the Kuomintang Central Party Headquarters. The Communists responded to this by stepping up their efforts to control the Kuomintang and to check Chiang Kai-shek by giving more support to its Left Wing, headed by Wang Ching-wei. Lacking both military and popular support of its own, and jealous of Chiang's rapid ascendancy, the Kuomintang Left Wing easily fell into the Communist trap. To set the Left Wing against Chiang, the Communists went so far as to help it form mass organizations outside the party, especially among the petty bourgeoisie. Thus suspicion and unrest so much infected the Kuomintang high councils in Canton as well as its branches elsewhere that Wang Ching-wei soon left his post as Chairman of the National Government and went abroad for "reasons of health."

The Final Split

The rivalries within the revolutionary front were progressively intensified in the course of the Northern Expedition, which began in July 1926. In the territories recently taken from the warlords, the Communists endeavored to establish their political leadership with the help of labor unions and peasant associations under their control. In some places they even armed workers and peasants for carrying out radical urban and rural policies. While Chiang was in the front, the Communists and the Soviet advisors availed themselves of the opportunity to strengthen the position of the Kuomintang Left Wing in the National Government Council. In the meantime, Ch'en Kuo-fu, Chiang's deputy in the Kuomintang Organization Department was working assiduously to weed out the dual-party elements from party organs at various levels, a step that did not endear Chiang to the Communists.

The friction between Chiang and the Left Wing leaders came to a head in January 1927 when the National Government controlled by the Left Wing moved the capital from Canton to Wuhan against the wishes of Chiang, who was in favor of Nanchang (the site of his headquarters) where he could assert his influence and check that of the Communists. Instigated by Borodin, the Chinese Communists and the Kuomintang Left Wing leaders in Wuhan stopped funds to Chiang's army in Nanchang and organized strikes at the Canton arsenal to prevent shipment of military supplies to Chiang. Accusing Chiang of practicing "personal dictatorship," the Left Wing leaders launched the "Movement to Restore Party Power" on February 24, 1927. They openly declared that it was necessary to centralize the revolutionary forces by enabling Communists to participate in the high councils of the Kuomintang and in all other political and mass organizations. Resolutions were passed to curtail Chiang's military authority and to urge Wang Ching-wei to cancel his leave of absence and resume his duties at once.

At the Third Plenum of the Kuomintang Central Executive Committee, held on March 10 through March 17, 1927, the Left Wing leaders, with the support of the Communist elements on the Committee, formally reduced Chiang's authority as the Commander-in-Chief, dismissed him as head of the Kuomintang Organization Department, and named Wang Ching-wei his successor in that strategic post. Moreover, the Plenum passed a resolution "On Unification of Revolutionary Forces" calling upon the Communists to participate in the National Government. In effect, this resolution transformed the original policy to admit Communists into a policy of a two-party coalition. As expected, the Communists immediately set out to use the government apparatus to effect land confiscation and tax reduction. On March 24, 1927, following the capture of Nanking, the Communists even attempted to embroil Chiang with foreign powers by inciting some pro-Communist Kuomintang troops in the city to loot and destroy foreign property, including those of consular staff members and missionaries. However, Chiang was able to settle the so-called "Nanking Affair" through negotiations.

Shortly after the entrance of his troops into Shanghai, where he secured the support of the bankers, merchants, secret societies, non-Communist labor leaders, and anti-Communist Kuomintang leaders, including the Western Hills Group, Chiang at long last decided to take open action against the Communists. On April 12, 1927, he broke the Communist stronghold in the Chinese part of the city by disarming the Red labor pickets and executing many Communists—an event that has often been indignantly referred to by the CCP as the "Shanghai Massacre."

The Kuomintang leaders who supported Chiang's anti-Communist stand resolved to expel Communists from the party as a whole.

When the Left Wing of the party, under the leadership of Wang Ching-wei, reaffirmed the policy of collaboration with the CCP and the Soviet Union, Chiang and his supporters set up a rival party headquarters and a rival National Government in Nanking on April 16, 1927, declaring that the Wuhan regime was Communist-controlled and therefore no longer legitimate.

The alliance between the Communists and the Wuhan faction of the Kuomintang did not last long. The Kuomintang leaders in Wuhan, who had advocated collaboration with the Communists largely because of their personal opposition to Chiang Kai-shek, were soon alarmed by the Communist attempts at violent land reform and labor control of industries. When a Comintern agent, the Indian M. N. Roy, committed the indiscretion of showing Wang Ching-wei a telegram from Stalin instructing the CCP to tighten its grip on the Wuhan regime, the Kuomintang leaders in Wuhan also decided to purge the party of the Communists. Meanwhile, they sent Borodin and all the other Soviet advisors back to Russia.

The Comintern and the Chinese Communist Debacle

The CCP's failure to exploit what they have since called the "First United Front" with the Kuomintang was due to a multiplicity of causes, including Chiang Kai-shek's shrewdness and the CCP's own weaknesses and shortcomings. But a substantial share of responsibility must be charged to the Comintern, or to be more exact, to Stalin personally.[9] Lacking intimate knowledge of the Chinese scene and unwilling to effect a reversal of policy as advocated by Trotsky, who was challenging him, Stalin stubbornly insisted at the crucial moment of the Kuomintang-CCP alliance that the CCP must continue to work through the Kuomintang and avoid an open breach at all costs. He instructed the CCP to restrain the rising peasants' and workers' movements even though the party could have exploited these movements to great advantage. In fact, on March 31, 1927, when Chiang Kai-shek was preparing to disarm the Communist-organized labor pickets in Shanghai, the Comintern under Stalin's leadership instructed the Chinese Communists in that city not to launch any "open struggle" but to hide or bury all arms.

[9] See Conrad Brandt, *Stalin's Failure in China: 1921-1927* (Cambridge, Mass.: Harvard University Press, 1958); M. N. Roy, *Revolution and Counterrevolution in China* (Calcutta: Renaissance Publishers, 1946); Leon Trotsky, *The Stalin School of Falsification* (New York: Pioneer Publishers, 1937); *Problems of the Chinese Revolution* (New York: Pioneer Publishers, 1932).

After Chiang's coup in Shanghai on April 12, Stalin, while writing off Chiang as a revolutionary ally, still fought against Trotsky's demand for an immediate Communist withdrawal from the Kuomintang Left and the formation of Soviets of Workers' Deputies. Stalin insisted that the National Government in Wuhan was a better instrument for building Communist strength and for the eventual establishment of Communist hegemony.

Although Stalin insisted on continued cooperation with the Kuomintang Left Wing in Wuhan, he also wanted to convert the latter into an organ of "the revolutionary-democratic dictatorship of the proletariat and the peasantry." In accordance with this policy, the CCP, at its Fifth National Congress held in Wuhan toward the end of April 1927, adopted a policy of land confiscation (lands of "small landlords" were exempted) but stipulated that property belonging to members of the Kuomintang or the officers of the Kuomintang army was not subject to seizure. The preferential treatment for the Kuomintang elements was proposed on the assumption that they would not oppose an agrarian revolution if it did not directly injure their personal interests. The CCP also resolved to organize "village people's councils" and a "people's army." Under Communist agitation the poorest section of the peasantry in Hunan and Hupeh rose in revolt, killing landlords and committing other terrorist acts. The excesses in the peasants' movement soon alarmed the public and the Kuomintang regime in Wuhan, especially its military officers, most of whom came from landlord families. The "Equine Day" Incident occurred in Changsha, capital of Hunan Province, on May 21, 1927, when Colonel Hsu K'o-hsiang, commander of the local garrison, ordered his troops to march into the headquarters of the Hunan Provincial General Labor Union and the offices of other Communist-dominated organizations. Some labor and peasant leaders were executed and others were arrested. Similar anti-Communist episodes took place elsewhere.

At this critical moment Trotsky again advocated a bold policy, calling upon the Chinese workers and peasants to organize themselves into powerful councils that would win the soldiers' allegiance away from the Kuomintang generals. It is problematical whether his policy would have averted the catastrophe which the CCP shortly suffered, but Stalin's policy was certainly doomed to failure. In a telegram which reached Wuhan on June 1, Stalin instructed the CCP to preserve the alliance with the Kuomintang Left Wing and to check the peasants' excesses, while at the same time demanding the immediate liquidation of the unreliable Kuomintang generals, the creation of a new army of workers and peasants, and a drastic transformation of the Kuomintang and its leadership in particular. As noted above, after Roy committed the indiscretion of showing Stalin's telegram to Wang Ching-wei, the latter began immediate preparations for the expulsion of Communists from the Kuomintang in Wuhan.

Forbidden by Stalin from breaking up the alliance with the Kuomintang Left Wing and yet faced with a grave danger, the CCP held an enlarged meeting of its Central Committee on June 1. An 11-point resolution on reconciliation was adopted in which the CCP recognized anew the "leading position" of the Kuomintang in the National Revolution against warlordism and imperialism; warned labor unions and workers' pickets not to assume judicial or administrative functions, arrest people, or patrol the streets without authorization from the Kuomintang; and prohibited the labor unions from insulting employers, making excessive demands, or interfering with management's handling of personnel matters. On July 3, the CCP and Borodin decided to send Roy back to Russia and to cease all agrarian activities. All these gestures availed them nothing, and on July 15, the Kuomintang Political Council in Wuhan formally decided to expel the Communists. The "expulsion" order was carried out by execution squads. Communists who were not caught up in the net fled. Conveniently ignoring his role in the debacle, Stalin now heaped all blame on the CCP leaders. They were criticized for their failure to "develop the agrarian revolution," to anticipate the betrayal of the Kuomintang leaders in Wuhan, and to "prepare the working masses for decisive action." [10]

The Rise of Ch'ü Ch'iu-pai

At the August Seventh Conference (1927) held in the Japanese concession in Hankow under the direction of Heins Neunmann and Besso Lominadse, who had just been sent to China by Stalin as the Comintern's new agents, the Russian-speaking and Russia-trained Ch'ü Ch'iu-pai and more than a score of other party members, acting in the name of the CCP Central Committee, made Ch'en Tu-hsiu the principal scapegoat for the catastrophe. Accused of pursuing "an opportunistic policy of capitulation," Ch'en was deposed from leadership. The Conference also abolished the office of

[10] "Resolution of the ECCI on the Present Situation of the Chinese Revolution," *International Press Correspondence* (July 28, 1927), p. 984.

general secretary and set up an emergency Politburo with Ch'ü Ch'iu-pai as its head. While ostensibly asserting that the Chinese Communists should remain within the Kuomintang in order to continue the bourgeois-democratic revolution in cooperation with its new Left Wing headed by Madame Sun Yat-sen, Teng Yen-ta, and Eugene Ch'en, the Conference actually adopted a policy of military insurrection, thus ushering in a new era for the party.

III

The Second Revolutionary Civil War (1927-1937)

中國共產運動簡史

The period of collaboration with the Kuomintang for launching the Northern Expedition has been designated by the CCP as the era of the "First Revolutionary Civil War." In the ensuing ten years (1927-1937) the Communists pursued a course of armed insurrection, which has officially been called "The Second Revolutionary Civil War." During the period of the Second Revolutionary Civil War, important changes were made in the party's top leadership as well as in its strategy and tactics. Despite its repeated setbacks, the Chinese Communists in this period steeled themselves, created a party army, established soviets, experimented and refined the tactics of guerrilla warfare, and learned the wisdom of using the united front policy. All these valuable achievements and experiences contributed to their final triumph in 1949.

The Policy of Urban Uprising and the Ch'ü Ch'iu-pai Leadership

After the Kuomintang Left Wing in Wuhan had expelled the Communists, Stalin and his allies in the Comintern, to ward off further criticism from the opposition led by Trotsky, felt the need for immediate, impressive victories in the Chinese Communist movement. This policy plunged the CCP into a series of adventures in the cities in the fall of 1927. The first involved an uprising at Nanchang, capital of Kiangsi Province,[1] which, planned by Besso Lominadse,

[1] Ho Lung, "The Nanchang Uprising and the Building-up of Our Army," *People's Daily,** August 1, 1958; see also J. Guillermaz, "The Nanchang Uprising," *The China Quarterly,* No. 11 (July-September, 1962), pp. 161-168.

was led by Ho Lung and Yeh T'ing, two Communist officers in the Kuomintang armies stationed in Nanchang.

On the night of August 1, 1927, Ho and Yeh, with the support of Chou En-lai, T'an P'ing-shan, and Chu Teh, staged a mutiny, which resulted in their more than 30,000 troops disarming some 10,000 loyal Kuomintang soldiers in the city; tribute was exacted from local businessmen, and a large number of Kuomintang members were arrested. At the same time they proclaimed a Revolutionary Committee that included the names of the new Kuomintang Left Wing leaders, Madame Sun Yat-sen, Teng Yen-ta, and Eugene Ch'en, then en route to European exile. When news of the uprising reached Moscow, the Comintern press hailed it saying, "A new revolutionary center had been formed." [2] However, in less than four days Kuomintang forces moved toward the city, and the rebels were forced to flee. The first occasion on which it resorted to armed insurrection, "August First" is now commemorated each year by the CCP as the "Founding Day of the People's Liberation Army."

Upon evacuating Nanchang, the Communists marched straight southward to Swatow and Chaochow in eastern Kwangtung, where they were defeated and dispersed in battles. In the middle of October, one group of the remnants fled to the counties of Haifeng and Lufeng, where they joined P'eng P'ai, who soon formed an abortive soviet.[3] Another group, under the command of Chu Teh (Lin Piao and Ch'en I were in his group), retreated to southern Hunan, where in the spring of 1928 they joined the guerrillas of Mao Tse-tung in Chingkangshan.

At the August Seventh Conference the party resolved to organize "Autumn Harvest Uprisings" in the countryside in preparation for establishing a worker-peasant army and instituting Communist power on local levels. Thus when the forces under Yeh T'ing and Ho Lung were retreating from Nanchang to eastern Kwangtung, Communist-inspired outbreaks of limited magnitude also occurred in several other places in central China. They too met with quick defeat since the masses, instead of making the "tremendous response" which Stalin had predicted, simply refused to cooperate.

One of these unsuccessful "Autumn Harvest Uprisings" was led by Mao Tse-tung in Hunan Province.[4] On September 8, 1927, Mao's

[2] *International Press Correspondence* (August 18, 1927), p. 1069.

[3] S. Eto, "Hai-lu-feng: The First Chinese Soviet Government," *The China Quarterly*, No. 8 (October-December, 1961), pp. 161-183; No. 9 (January-March, 1962), pp. 149-181.

[4] Lo Jung-huan, "The Autumn Harvest Uprising and the Formative Period

over 5000 followers, who were mostly poor peasants belonging to the peasant associations that Mao had organized in the preceding months, raised the banner of revolt in the county of Hsiu-shui with the seizure of the provincial capital of Changsha as their declared objective. Poorly armed and rejected by the bulk of the local population, the rebels were quickly surrounded and forced into a disorderly retreat. Mao himself was captured by Kuomintang forces but soon escaped. Fleeing southward he re-established contact with his remnant forces, which now numbered only about 1000 men. After having suffered further defeats, Mao and his little band finally (in October 1927) sought refuge in a mountain stronghold called Chingkangshan on the Hunan-Kiangsi border, and there he established his first revolutionary base. The immediate consequence of the unsuccessful Autumn Uprising in Hunan was Mao's repudiation by the Central Committee of his party. Accused of failure to seek the Central Committee's approval of the program of the uprising, Mao was dismissed from both the Politburo and the Party Front Committee.

In November 1927, a plenum of the CCP Central Committee, in accordance with Comintern instructions, proclaimed a new course for the party. Discarding the Kuomintang banner completely at long last, the plenum put forward the slogan of soviets. Despite the repeated defeats at Nanchang, Swatow, Hunan, and elsewhere, the plenum declared that "the Chinese revolution not only did not ebb, but rose to a new higher stage." This sanguine estimation of the revolutionary situation led the Communists to stage an abortive uprising in Canton on December 11, 1927.[5] This along with the previous defeats in Nanchang, Hunan, and Swatow caused heavy losses to the CCP. Indeed, in the midst of the Kuomintang's successful take-over of labor organizations, the CCP's very existence in the urban areas was in grave danger. Faced with this precarious situation, the party convened its Sixth National Congress in Moscow from June 18 to July 11, 1928. Under Comintern supervision the Congress placed responsibility for the various unsuccessful uprisings on the Chinese Communist leadership. Condemned for his "ill-prepared, ill-directed putschism" or leftist deviation, Ch'ü Ch'iu-pai was ordered to remain in Moscow. Hsiang Chung-fa, a virtually illiterate former boatman on the Yangtze River, was elected general

of Our Army," *People's Daily,** July 31, 1958. See also John E. Rue, *Mao Tse-tung in Opposition* (Stanford, Calif.: Stanford University Press, 1966), pp. 73-81.

[5] Yeh Chien-ying, "The Failure of the Great Revolution and the Canton Uprising," *People's Daily,** July 30, 1958.

secretary, but real power fell into the hands of Li Li-san, who was officially a member of the Politburo and director of the Propaganda Department. In line with the program sketched at the Sixth World Congress of the Comintern in July 1928, the Sixth National Congress of the CCP stressed the importance of gaining leadership over the peasantry, of establishing soviets, and of linking peasant uprisings with urban insurrections.

The "Li Li-san Line"

In the next two years the Comintern issued to the CCP a series of enigmatic and contradictory instructions concerning the revolutionary situation and the configuration of political forces in China. Confused by these directives from Moscow and encouraged by the impending revolt of Yen Hsi-shan and Feng Yü-hsiang against Chiang Kai-shek, the Politburo declared in January 1930 that a new revolutionary upsurge was emerging. In March and April, Li Li-san, while dutifully reiterating the necessity of linking up the worker and peasant movements, expounded the policy of "the cities leading the villages" and ridiculed "the talk of encircling the cities with the villages." His policy has since been known as the "Li Li-san line."

In July 1930 when Chiang's forces were suppressing the anticipated revolt of the two northern militarists, Li Li-san ordered the poorly equipped Communist armies in Kiangsi, Hunan, and Hupeh to capture Nanchang, Changsha, and Wuhan, capitals of the respective provinces. Attempts to seize Nanchang and Wuhan were unsuccessful, but the Fifth Red Army under the command of P'eng Teh-huai was able to capture Changsha on July 28. Communist leaders both in China and Russia were exultant over the success in Changsha, hailing it as "a great step forward in the Soviet movement." However, the jubilation was quickly followed by disappointment, for by August 3 P'eng's forces were withdrawing from the city as General Ho Chien's Kuomintang troops closed in for a counterattack. During their brief reign of terror in the city, the Communists set fire to numerous buildings and took the lives of over 2000 persons. Unwilling to accept defeat, Li Li-san ordered P'eng Teh-huai to attack Changsha again, but P'eng was unable to carry out the new order.

Ascendancy of the "Returned Students Clique"

Although the Comintern never gave an unequivocal forewarning about the danger of the "Li Li-san Line," once the military adventure in Changsha failed, it quickly made Li Li-san responsible for the blunder.[6] In addition, hostile factions within the CCP itself were eager to take advantage of Li Li-san's discomfiture. At the Third Plenum of the Sixth Central Committee held in September 1930, Li was criticized for his "leftist adventurism," and the plan to organize a nationwide uprising and concentrated attack on the large cities was called off. The Third Plenum found only minor errors in the policies of Li Li-san.

At the Comintern's insistence, the Li Li-san line was more severely condemned at the Fourth Plenum of the Sixth Central Committee held in January 1931 in the international settlement at Shanghai. Controlled by the Soviet-trained "Returned Student Clique" centering around Wang Ming (Ch'en Shao-yü), who had the support of Pavel Mif, former director of the Sun Yat-sen University in Moscow and now Comintern representative to the CCP, the Fourth Plenum extracted abject confessions of error from Li Li-san, Chou En-lai, and others. Li was sent off to Moscow, where he made another self-criticism before the Far Eastern Commission of the Comintern and was then told to attend the Bolshevik school there.[7] However, Chou En-lai succeeded in retaining his seat on the Politburo now dominated by the Returned Student Clique. He did this after he had helped the latter defeat the challenge mounted by Ho Meng-hsiung and other moderate labor leaders who had previously spearheaded the campaign to oust Li-Li-san.

When the Returned Student Clique assumed the reins of the party, the prospect of establishing Communist power in urban areas had become so dim that it could not but abandon, at least temporarily, the ultra-adventurist policy of attacking the big cities in favor of an all-out effort to strengthen the Red Army and establish a central soviet government in one of the existing soviet districts for

[6] There has been a division of opinion among scholars on the genesis of the "Li Li-san Line." According to most writers on the subject, prior to the defeat at Changsha, "Moscow at least acquiesced in Li's policy of seizing the cities, if it did not initiate it through its ambiguous and contradictory directives to the CCP leadership. However, Professor Tso-liang Hsiao of the National Taiwan University recently concluded, on the basis of his investigation of captured Communist documents, that the "Li Li-san Line" was made locally rather than imported. See his *Power Relations Within the Chinese Communist Movement, 1930-1934: A Study of Documents* (Seattle, Wash.: University of Washington Press, 1961), pp. 14-31. See also Benjamin Schwartz's comments on Hsiao's conclusion in *The China Quarterly,* No. 12 (October-December, 1962), pp. 231-234.

[7] Fifteen years were to elapse before Li was sent back to China to work in Manchuria, following the Soviet army's entrance into that region in the last few days of World War II.

future expansion. In conformity with the Comintern instructions contained in its letter of November 16, 1930, this new decision signaled the completion of the shift from urban uprisings to rural insurrections as well as the shift from using the proletariat to using the peasantry as the primary instrument of revolution. Under the new leadership, the party continued its clandestine organizational and agitational activities in the urban centers, but these activities were now a "rear support" for the soviet districts in the mountainous hinterlands.

Mao Tse-tung on Chingkangshan

The creation of rural soviets and Red armies in the hinterlands after the Kuomintang-CCP rupture in the summer of 1927 was not the result of any single individual's strategy or effort. Mao Tse-tung, however, was primarily responsible for the formation of the principal units of the Red Army and for the establishment of the largest soviet district in southern Kiangsi, where the Chinese Communists maintained a Provisional Central Soviet Government from 1931 to 1934. Fleeing in defeat from an unsuccessful attack on Changsha, Mao finally retreated in October 1927 into the mountainous Chingkangshan on the border between Hunan and Kiangsi Provinces. Soon after his arrival in Chingkangshan, Mao's small band was augmented by a local bandit force headed by Wang Tso and Yuan Wen-ts'ai. Mao lost no time in unfolding his policy of exploiting the discontent of the poor for the building up of a revolutionary army and the creation of rural military bases. Specifically, he put into effect, though not without glaring deviations, a land redistribution program in accordance with the principle of relying upon the poor peasants and farm hands, uniting with the middle peasants, restricting the rich peasants, and liquidating the landlords, "local bullies," and "bad gentry."

Mao also laid down the policy that (1) the Red Army must be thoroughly indoctrinated and strictly disciplined; (2) in addition to waging war, the Red Army must actively participate in all local activities of the party, such as organizational and propaganda work; and (3) unless the military situation had reached a basic turning point in favor of the revolution, the Red Army must rely on guerrilla or mobile warfare, marshaling the support of potentially friendly elements among the population, avoiding battles with superior enemy forces, and concentrating superior forces to encircle and annihilate inferior and isolated enemy troops swiftly. To ensure continued supply of daily necessities for his troops in their formative stage, Mao also resorted to the expediency of "protecting small industrialists and businessmen" within his domain—a policy that incurred the displeasure of the ultra-Leftists on the Southern Hunan Special Committee, under which Mao operated. Despite these relatively moderate policies, Mao's Red force was for a long time isolated from the local peasantry, who were either apathetic or hostile to it. Peasant associations set up by the armed Red forces invariably disintegrated and disappeared as soon as the Communist guerrilla bands passed on. Poorly equipped and unable to secure local support, the Red army on Chingkangshan suffered repeated defections and endured dire hardships.

In November 1927, the first Chinese soviet was proclaimed in Tsalin, on the Hunan border. In April 1928, Mao's army was joined by the forces of Chu Teh. The two forces were merged and took the name of the Fourth Red Army, with Chu as its top commander and Mao as the Party representative. In July, this newly amalgamated but still ill-fed and ill-clad army was ordered by the CCP Hunan Provincial Committee, then under the control of Ch'ü Ch'iu-pai's followers, to launch an adventurist expedition to the south of Chingkangshan that almost jeopardized the existence of the base itself. For his opposition to the adventure, Mao was even replaced as the leading party representative in the border area. However, before long Mao was able to regain political control on Chingkangshan as a result of the blunders committed by his replacements.

Founding of Guerrilla Bases in Southern Kiangsi and Elsewhere

Soon after Mao's resumption of power on Chingkangshan, he and Chu decided to abandon their existing stronghold in favor of a better base in the border region between Kiangsi, Fukien, and Kwangtung. In January 1929, they marched down the mountain passes at the head of a starving, freezing, ill-armed, and straggling column of a few thousand men. During the journey the Red Army suffered heavy casualties at the hands of the Kuomintang forces and local peasants. Finally, late in February 1929, the Chu-Mao force reached the remote mountainous districts in southern Kiangsi near the Fukien and Kwangtung borders, where it established a new base. By insisting on the application of his recently developed military, agrarian, and social policies, by strengthening the discipline and internal "democracy" of Red Army units, and by skillfully exploiting contradictions among the Kuomintang commands, Mao and Chu gradually extended their control in the rural areas and expanded the size of their army.

In the process of expansion Mao came into conflict with the political organizers and military officers affiliated with the Li Li-san faction and certain local cliques of the party. To guard against sabotage and ensure the security of the Soviet area. Mao, in November 1930, deemed it necessary to have some 4,400 dissident elements arrested. A major clash in the southern Kiangsi soviet area occurred on December 8, 1930, when Liu Teh, a battalion political commissar of the Twentieth Red Army, rose in revolt at Tungku and led several hundred men in an attack on Fut'ien, a Communist stronghold. The rebels set free a group of Communist leaders of the Kiangsi Provincial Action Committee who had been arrested by Mao's office, the Central Front Committee, on charges of being agents of the Kuomintang's A-B (Anti-Bolshevik) Corps. Bringing forward anti-Mao slogans, they also overthrew the Kiangsi Provincial Soviet Government, forced its chairman to flee, and arrested Liu T'ieh-ch'ao, commander of the Twentieth Red Army, and other pro-Mao elements. Although the revolt, which has been known as the "Fut'ien Incident," was quelled in two months, Mao's foes in the party, oblivious to the role of the A-B Corps, were to blame the tragedy on his "ruthlessness."

While Mao was busy establishing military bases in southern Hunan and southern Kiangsi, other Communist leaders also organized Red guerrilla bands and created soviets in scattered mountainous districts in central China and northern Shensi, always taking advantage of Chiang Kai-shek's embroilment in the incessant revolts of dissident Kuomintang generals and turncoat warlords. Like the partisan band led by Mao and Chu, these Red armies "were not even primarily peasant force"; "they were composed in the main of dispossessed peasants, jobless agricultural laborers, mutinous soldiers, local bandits, all declassed elements, playing no direct role even in agricultural production." [8] Again, like the band under Mao and Chu, these partisan units frequently manifested the psychology of the *lumpenproletariat* by engaging in aimless burning, plundering, and killing in the first few years of their existence. However, as a result of intensive political indoctrination, they were gradually steeled into well-disciplined fighting forces, which, to be sure, did not forsake terrorism completely but were to resort to it only when it would advance the Communist cause.

[8] Isaacs, *The Tragedy of the Chinese Revolution*, p. 328.

The Chinese Soviet Republic

After these Red armies and rural soviets were first formed, the successive central party leaderships regarded them as only a "side current" supporting the urban labor movement. Since the labor movement was receding and the party's influence in the cities was being drastically reduced, the Red armies and their rural bases came to receive increasing recognition as the "determining factor," the "source spring," or the "driving force" of the revolution. Thus, upon their assumption of the reins of the party, the Returned Student Clique, in its underground headquarters in Shanghai, took immediate steps to strengthen its leadership over the various scattered rural bases and to draw them together under a centralized soviet. First, it established the Central Bureau of Soviet Areas on January 15, 1931 to take charge of all party affairs in the soviet areas and Red armies. The Bureau was composed of nine members with Chou En-lai as its chairman and Hsiang Ying as its secretary.

Preparations for the inauguration of a Chinese Soviet Republic were stepped up. On December 7, 1931, the First All-China Soviet Congress met in Juichin, Kiangsi, with 610 delegates from the various soviet districts, the Red armies, the All-China Federation of Trade Unions, the Seamen's Union and the CCP. The Congress proclaimed the establishment of a Chinese Soviet Republic, set up a Central Soviet Government, and adopted a political program, a constitution, a land law, a labor law, and resolutions on the Red Army and economic policies, all proposed by the CCP Central Committee. Based on the principle of "the democratic dictatorship of the proletariat and peasantry" and aimed at, among other things, "the destruction of all relics of feudalism," "the elimination of the influence of the imperialist powers in China," and "the transition to the dictatorship of the proletariat," the Central Soviet Government, with Juichin as its capital, was headed by Mao Tse-tung. Chu Teh was made chairman of the Revolutionary Military Council, which had overall control of the Red armies.

Shortly after the inauguration of the Chinese Soviet Republic, the central organs of the party that were controlled by the Returned Student Clique were moved from Shanghai underground to Juichin. Although this was primarily necessitated by security considerations as Kuomintang pressure in Shanghai was mounting, it greatly facilitated the Returned Student Clique's control over the newly created Central Soviet Government and diminished Mao Tse-tung's authority. According to Chang Kuo-t'ao, who was then a vice-chairman of the Central Soviet Government and a leader of the O-yü-wan Soviet (on the Hupeh, Honan, and Anhwei borders), from the time when the central party organs arrived in Juichin toward the end of 1931 to the convocation of the Tsun-i Conference in January 1935 in the midst of the "Long March," supreme political power in the soviet districts was in the hands of Ch'in Pang-hsien (Po Ku), with Chou En-lai in charge of military affairs.[9] Ch'in Pang-hsien, also a member of the Returned Student Clique, became the General Secretary of the party in the Fall of 1931, replacing Ch'en Shao-yü, who gave up the post to go to Moscow as chief Chinese delegate to the Comintern.

Chiang Kai-shek's Five Campaigns Against the Soviet Districts

When the Red Armies and soviet districts were first organized in the hilly regions of central China, the National Government at Nanking was preoccupied with suppressing a series of revolts staged by dissident Kuomintang generals and former warlords. Since these revolts posed greater immediate threats to his leadership than did the Communist forces, Chiang was unable to direct his attention to the Communist insurrection until after the collapse of the gigantic revolt of Feng Yü-hsiang and Yen Hsi-shan in October 1930. By then the Communists were already entrenched in their mountain strongholds, and from December 1930 to May 1931 the Red forces in Kiangsi successfully foiled two "annihilation campaigns" launched by Chiang's armies with their guerrilla warfare tactics. In July 1931 Chiang Kai-shek started a third drive, but it had to be called off prematurely in October as the Japanese invasion of Manchuria was disrupting the National Government itself.

After the political storm in Nanking was over, Chiang resumed his task of "annihilating" the Communists. In June 1932, he began a fourth campaign against the soviet districts. In November his troops succeeded in dislodging the Communist armies under Chang Kuo-t'ao and Hsu Hsiang-ch'ien from the O-yü-wan Soviet District, forcing them to flee westward into northern Szechwan. The offensive against Ho Lung's forces in western Hupeh also progressed satisfactorily, but the attack on the Central Soviet District on the Kiangsi-Fukien borders was bogged down. Then, in February 1933, the National Government had to abandon the anti-Communist campaign in order to check the Japanese aggression along the Great Wall in northern Hopei.

[9] North, *Moscow and Chinese Communists,* p. 158.

After the battle of the Great Wall, which ended in a temporary truce between China and Japan, Chiang Kai-shek returned to the campaign against the Communists. The fifth campaign, which began in November 1933, was based on a new strategy conceived by Chiang and his German advisors, including General von Seeckt: instead of rushing his troops into the Communist strongholds, Chiang threw a tight blockade around the entire Central Soviet District, depriving the Communists of vital supplies, which they could not find locally. One item denied by the blockade was salt, and the shortage of salt in the diet of the soviet area soon endangered the health of the local population and the Communist personnel. Chiang also built a series of highways, stone fortresses, and pillboxes to hem in the Communists. A further advantage was gained by his maneuvering the Red armies (over 300,000 men) into abandoning their guerrilla tactics for positional warfare.

The "Long March" and the Rise of Mao

The combined pressure of the Kuomintang economic blockade and military attack was so effective that by the summer of 1934 the total size of the Soviet districts in central China was reduced to less than 1600 square miles or 15 per cent of the size in 1932. With mounting casualties in the field, the Communist position in southern Kiangsi and the neighboring provinces became increasingly precarious. Faced with the prospect of being completely annihilated, the CCP leaders, with Comintern approval, made an agonizing decision to evacuate the main surviving Red forces (about 120,000 to 130,000 men) from their hard-won bases in Kiangsi. In October 1934, the Red Army broke out of the Kuomintang encirclement to the west and started on the "Long March" which has been hailed by the Chinese Communists as the most glorious exploit in the history of their party.

Although the Communists were actually in forced retreat, their long trek was indeed "one of the great triumphs of men against odds and man against nature." [10] This journey on foot took the Communists over a distance of more than 6000 miles, touching upon the territory of 12 provinces in West China. The Red Army marched through some of the world's most arduous trails in forbidding forest domains of aborigines, miasmatic jungles, and headwater marshlands, crossing treacherous and swift rivers and passing over 18 high mountains, five of them permanently snow-capped. In some

[10] Edgar Snow, *The Other Side of the River: Red China Today* (New York: Random House, 1961), p. 142. Reprinted by permission.

of these places there was nothing to eat but wild vegetables and herbs; there were no houses or even trees for shelter, and at night the Communists huddled under bushes tied together. The journey lasted 368 days, out of which 235 were spent in day marches and 18 in marches by night. Except for a stay of 56 days in the high grassland of northwestern Szechwan, the Communists took only 44 days of rest. The remainder of the time they marched an average of 24 miles per day, an unquestionably impressive feat in view of the difficulties of the terrain added to the fact that minor skirmishes took place almost daily and 15 full days were devoted to major pitched battles with the enveloping Kuomintang armies and provincial troops. Yet in spite of all this, in the towns and villages they passed through, the Communists took the opportunity to foment class struggle and invite uprisings with a view to recruiting new converts. They held mass meetings with inflammatory speeches, revolutionary songs, and propagandistic plays and set fire to the homes of landlords and merchants encouraging the destitute people to plunder. They took foodstuff, clothing, and other property from the wealthy and distributed them among the poor. To make the poor people's commitment to the revolution irretrievable, the Communists also instigated them to kill some of the local officials and well-to-do inhabitants.

Mao's Emergence as the Top Leader and Chang Kuo-t'ao's Challenge

Despite this tremendous display of valor, tenacity, and cunning, the Communists found themselves in an unprecedented predicament from the very beginning of the march, for they ever ran the risk of falling into the enemy's ensnarement and never knew for sure when they would eat again or where they would lie down exhausted. This critical situation provided Mao Tse-tung with an opportunity to challenge the Returned Student Clique leadership in the party, which had previously reduced Mao's influence in the soviet districts and the Red Army and had often ridiculed him for his "countryside policy" and "banditry doctrine." At an enlarged meeting of the Politburo held in January 1935, at Tsun-i, Kweichow Province, where the main column of the Red Army stopped briefly after leaving Kiangsi, Mao and his supporters opened a fierce attack against Ch'in Pang-hsien and his group, holding them responsible for the loss of the soviet bases in Kiangsi and the disasters in the course of retreat. Among other things, Mao accused the Returned Student Clique of failing to exploit the internal contradictions within the Kuomintang, of refusing to cooperate with the revolt of the Kuomintang general, Li Chi-shen, in Fukien, and of resorting to positional warfare after Chiang Kai-shek unleashed his fifth annihilation campaign. Dubbed as a leftist dogmatist and condemned for his "pure proletarian line," Ch'in Pang-hsien stepped down from the chairmanship of the Politburo in favor of Mao. Mao's leadership over the whole party was thereby formally established. During this power struggle, the ever-adaptable Chou En-lai gave his support to Mao.

As the new leader of the party, Mao assumed supreme responsibility for political as well as military strategy, but his newly acquired authority was soon challenged by Chang Kuo-t'ao in June 1935, when the Red forces from Kiangsi met at Maoerhkai, western Szechwan, with the troops which Chang had earlier brought to the region from the O-yü-wan Soviet District. Viewing Mao as an upstart in the party and controlling a stronger army (about 100,000 men to Mao's approximately 30,000), Chang refused to recognize Mao's leadership and abide by other decisions of the Tsun-i Conference, where he was not represented.[11] Opposing Mao on both political and military issues, Chang questioned the utility of the soviet form of government to the Chinese revolution and insisted that the Red Army should not proceed to northern Shensi as Mao had advocated but should either strive to establish a new base in western Szechwan or withdraw to Sikang, which would be closer to Sinkiang, then under virtual control of Soviet Russia. After nearly two months of disagreement as to the next move, in August, under the pressure of the Kuomintang forces, the factions finally decided to go their own ways. While Chang Kuo-t'ao's forces moved westward toward Sikang, the Kiangsi column continued its northward advance under Mao Tse-tung, accompanied by Chou En-lai, P'eng Teh-huai, Lin Piao, and Ch'in Pang-hsien.

[11] The personal animosity between Chang and Mao might have originated as early as 1918 at the National Peking University when Chang was a prominent student and Mao a poorly paid assistant librarian. Mao told Edgar Snow in 1936 that because of this humble position many of the active and influential students on the campus snubbed him when he attempted to converse with them on socio-political problems about which the students had professed a keen interest. Chang could have been one of those snobbish students referred to by Mao. It is true that Chang and Mao subsequently helped Ch'en Tu-hsiu organize the CCP, but for a decade or so thereafter Chang played a more prominent role in the central headquarters of the party than Mao did. This background could have made it difficult for Chang to reconcile himself to Mao's accession to supreme power in the party in 1935.

After suffering intolerable hardships in the Great Grasslands of the Szechwan-Kansu borders, where they saw no human habitation for ten days, and fighting more critical battles in the Yellow River basin in Kansu, they finally reached northern Shensi on October 25, 1935, where the local Communist leaders, Kao Kang and Liu Tzu-tan, had maintained a soviet district with a small Red force. In October 1936, Chang Kuo-t'ao, after having been blocked in his westward movement toward Sikang, also emerged in northern Shensi with his now decimated troops. The arrival of Chang's troops coincided with that of the Second Front Red Army under Ho Lung, which had been forced to abandon its old base in western Hupeh in June 1936. By now all the surviving Red forces totaled less than 30,000 men.

IV

The Second United Front with the Kuomintang and the War Against Japan

中國共產運動簡史

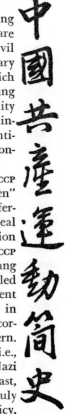

Clamor for an Anti-Japanese United Front

As the Red Army suffered mounting casualties during the Long March, the CCP leaders became increasingly aware of the danger of their eventual extermination if the civil war was not halted soon. To bring about a temporary cessation of the civil war and to create a situation in which a third force would engage and weaken the Kuomintang army while providing the Communists with an opportunity to gather strength for another struggle against the Kuomintang, Mao Tse-tung and his associates decided upon an anti-Japanese National United Front at the Maoerhkai Conference.

On August 1, 1935, while still in Maoerhkai, the CCP issued a proclamation calling upon "all fellow countrymen" to "unite as one man" to fight against Japan, despite differences of political opinions and interests. In a special appeal to Chiang Kai-shek, for whose overthrow and liquidation they had been struggling for more than eight years, the CCP promised to cooperate with the Kuomintang if only Chiang would halt the fight "against his own people," and called also for the organization of a National Defense Government and an anti-Japanese allied army. This abrupt change in the Chinese Communist strategy was in line with a corresponding shift in the international line of the Comintern. With a view to defending "the fatherland of socialism" (i.e., the Soviet Union) against the mounting threat of Nazi Germany in the West and Japanese militarism in the East, the Comintern's Seventh Congress, held in Moscow in July and August 1935, adopted a global united front policy, calling upon Communists, socialists, and other anti-aggression elements throughout the world to fight jointly against Fascist and imperialist war mongers.

Shortly after the issuance of its open appeal on August 1, 1935, the CCP, as alleged by Chiang Kai-shek, dispatched Chou En-lai to Hong Kong, where he indirectly approached a Kuomintang representative to voice the hope that the National Government would designate someone to negotiate with him for a speedy cessation of the internal strife and for a united front against Japan.[1]

The Communists entertained no illusions about Chiang Kai-shek's voluntary acceptance of their overtures for reconciliation at a time when the final triumph of his protracted and arduous anti-Communist campaign seemed in sight at long last. Conscious of the Chinese public's growing dejection and indignation over the increasing Japanese encroachments on China, they did their utmost to bring a strong popular pressure to bear upon Chiang Kai-shek, who had been reluctant to oppose a foreign enemy effectively until he had achieved domestic unity. Through such emotion-charged slogans as "Fight Japan and Not the Communists," "Chinese Must Not Fight Chinese," and "The Kuomintang and the CCP Must Co-operate to Save the Nation," the Communists' call for popular support for their new stand quickly struck a responsive chord among various segments of the Chinese population, especially the intellectuals and student groups.

On September 18, 1935, the Anti-Japanese National Salvation Grand Alliance appeared in Shanghai. Founded by Shen Chün-jui, Shih Liang, and other prominent leaders of Shanghai's cultural and educational circles, this supposedly nonpartisan organization advocated a policy toward Japan completely in agreement with the Communist line. It agitated for the immediate cessation of the war on the Communists and the formation of a national front of salvation in order to resist Japan. Because of the prestige and articulation of its leaders, the group contributed much to the Communist campaign to arouse popular impatience with the Kuomintang policy of "effecting internal pacification before resisting external aggression." Meanwhile, Communist underground agents led by Liu Shao-ch'i succeeded in instigating the formation of similar organizations in all major cities under Kuomintang control. North China alone had no fewer than 30 such organizations, all clamoring for a "national salvation united front." Their most effective weapons

[1] Chiang Kai-shek, *Soviet Russia in China* (New York: Farrar, Straus & Cudahy, 1957), pp. 77-78.

were student strikes and demonstrations, and the most dramatic of these was the "December Ninth Movement" in 1935 in which students in Peking clashed in the streets with the local garrison force. The resultant bloodshed gave rise to a tremendous upsurge of popular sympathy and support for the "national salvation" movement.[2] These demonstrations and petitions caused considerable embarrassment and anxiety to Chiang Kai-shek, but they failed to make him call off his anti-Communist campaign and start a premature war against Japan. After the Red Army's new setback in Shansi Province, the CCP presented the Kuomintang with two proposals, in May and August 1936, for an anti-Japan united front, but these proposals also failed to gain acceptance.

The Sian Incident

But it was Chiang Kai-shek himself who unwittingly provided the Communists with an opportunity to secure a powerful leverage for forcing his own hand on the united front issue. Toward the end of 1935 Chiang sent the Northeastern Army under Chang Hsueh-liang to bring about the Communists' extermination in northern Shensi. Chiang apparently had hoped that this assignment for the Northeastern Army would serve two purposes. Not only would it suppress the remaining Red forces, but the Northeastern Army (over 150,000 men), which even after its evacuation from the northeastern provinces in Manchuria in 1931-1932 had retained a semi-autonomous status in relation to the National Government in Nanking, would weaken itself and thereby become more amenable to Nanking. But by this time, however, the Northeastern troops were very homesick. When they came into contact with the Communist forces, they quickly succumbed to the Communist clamor for the cessation of the civil war in favor of a joint resistance against Japan. In June 1936, Chang Hsueh-liang, together with Yang Hu-ch'eng, who was formerly a warlord in the northwest and now the pacification commissioner of Shensi, secretly arranged a truce with the Red Army.

The conspicuous silence that followed on the fronts and the appearance of Communist-front organizations in Sian, where both Chang Hsueh-liang and Yang Hu-ch'eng maintained their headquarters, aroused Nanking's suspicion. In December, Chiang Kai-shek flew to Sian to view the situation firsthand. Chang Hsueh-liang and Yang Hu-ch'eng first briefed him on the growing dissatisfaction

[2] John Israel, *Student Nationalism in China, 1927-1937* (Stanford, Calif.: Stanford University Press, 1966), pp. 111-156.

of their troops with their anti-Communist mission, but without intimating to him the existence of the understanding which they had secretly reached with the Communists several months ago. When Chiang told them to restrain their subordinates and to prosecute the anti-Communist campaign with vigor, Chang and Yang had him seized in the night of December 12. The mutinous generals then presented the so-called Eight Demands to their captive, among them the acceptance of the Communists' proposals for a united front and early resistance to Japan. At first Chiang refused even to discuss matters with Chang and Yang, insisting that his captors repent at once and release him unconditionally or else kill him since he could not negotiate with his subordinates under duress and still expect to function as the commander-in-chief and head of government.

When the news of the kidnapping was out, a wave of shock and deep concern swept across the country. Except for those who had been infected by the united front propaganda, people everywhere quickly voiced their disapproval of the incident and unanimously demanded the immediate release of the Generalissimo, whom they had of late come to regard as indispensable to the nation's survival and rejuvenation. Meanwhile, the Nanking government threatened a punitive military and air attack on Sian to bring the rebels to terms. Mindful that such action would inevitably endanger Chiang's life, Nanking decided to suspend hostilities pending attempts to negotiate a peaceful solution to the crisis. On December 22, Madame Chiang Kai-shek flew to Sian and persuaded her husband to listen to Chang Hsueh-liang and give a hearing to Chou En-lai, a CCP representative. Although Chiang was adamant about giving any written commitment on the Eight Demands, he apparently came to a tacit understanding about terminating the anti-Communist campaign. Chang Hsueh-liang and Yang Hu-ch'eng released Chiang Kai-shek on December 25 on the basis of this understanding and because of Communist insistence that Chiang was essential to the success of the anti-Japanese united front, which alone could effectively weaken the Kuomintang and divert the Japanese threat from Soviet Russian frontiers.

Establishment of the Second United Front

Upon Chiang's release from Sian, military hostilities between the Kuomintang and the Communist troops came to a complete stop, though the basis of a formal truce had yet to be defined. On February 10, 1937, the CCP leaders sent a telegram to the Third Plenum of the Kuomintang Fifth Central Executive Committee at

Nanking calling for an end to all civil wars, the convocation of a National salvation conference, and speedy completion of preparations for resisting Japan. To win popular sympathy and to create favorable conditions for their party to carry on propaganda and organizational activities in the future, they called for improvements in the living conditions of the people and guarantees of the freedoms of speech, assembly, and association. The Communists, in turn, promised to abandon the policy of armed insurrection against the National Government; to stop their program of land confiscation; to change the soviet government into a "special area" government of the Republic of China and the Red Army into a unit of the National Revolutionary Army under the command of the Nanking government; and to enforce in their special area a democratic system based on universal suffrage. In reply, on February 21 the Kuomintang plenum adopted the "Resolution for Complete Eradication of the Red Menace." While reiterating Nanking's determination to eliminate Communism in China, the resolution stated that a reconciliation between the Kuomintang and the CCP could be effected if the latter would abolish the Red Army and the Soviet government, end all Communist propaganda and accept the Three People's Principles, and stop their call for a class struggle. Anxious to formalize the truce and to remove all obstacles to an early resistance war against Japan, the Communists agreed to the conditions laid down by the Kuomintang.

On July 7, 1937, Japanese forces launched an attack at the Marco Polo Bridge near Peking. When the Chinese resisted this thrust, full-scale military hostilities between the two countries ensued. On September 22, the CCP Central Committee issued a statement publicly proclaiming its acceptance of the four conditions for a new Kuomintang-CCP rapprochement. A month earlier, the National Government had reorganized the Red Army in northern Shensi into the Eighth Route Army (later renamed the Eighteenth Group Army, with Chu Teh and P'eng Teh-huai as commander and deputy-commander respectively. This army, composed of some 30,000 men, was organized into three divisions under Lin Piao, Ho Lung, and Liu Po-ch'eng and assigned to the Second War Area under the command of Yen Hsi-shan. Another group of Communist troops, which had managed to survive in Kiangsi and Fukien following the evacuation of the main Red forces from there in 1934, was reorganized into the New Fourth Army, with Yeh T'ing as commander and Hsiang Ying as deputy-commander. This army, consisting of four columns of over 10,000 men, was assigned to the

Third War Area in east China under the command of Ku Chu-t'ung, one of Chiang Kai-shek's most trusted lieutenants. The soviet regime in northern Shensi, with Yenan as its capital, was renamed the Shensi-Kansu-Ninghsia Border Area Government. Lin Tsu-han and Chang Kuo-t'ao served as its chairman and vice-chairman, respectively. Three Communist leaders were also made members of the newly created 24-man National Defense Advisory Council in Nanking, along with some leading intellectuals and representatives of the Kuomintang, the Chinese Youth Party, and the National Socialist Party. Toward the end of 1937, Chou En-lai was appointed a deputy-director of the Political Training Department of the Military Council of the National Government. A few months later in July 1938, when the People's Political Council replaced the National Defense Council as a wartime advisory body to the National Government, seven Communist leaders, including Mao Tse-tung and Teng Ying-ch'ao (Madame Chou En-lai), became members of the new organization. Finally the new rapprochement between the Kuomintang and the CCP permitted the latter to publish a newspaper first in Wuhan and then at Chungking, the wartime capital of China.

Wartime Expansion

Although the CCP's call for an early war against Japan stemmed mainly from patriotic considerations, it was also designed to weaken the Kuomintang and to give their own party an opportunity to recuperate and expand. Even though the CCP leaders carefully concealed their secondary purpose from the public, they freely spoke of it to the rank and file of their party and even some trusted friends outside the party. According to the American correspondent Edgar Snow, Chou En-lai told him in northern Shensi in 1936 that although the Communists wanted to end the civil war and unite with the Kuomintang to resist Japan, they had no intention of abandoning the revolution, but rather hoped to advance it, saying, "The first day of the anti-Japanese war will mean the beginning of the end for Chiang Kai-shek." [3]

In the beginning of the war, Chang Kuo-t'ao seemed to be the only one in the high party councils who seriously took exception to the policy of exploiting the resistance war for Communist purposes. At an enlarged meeting of the Politburo held on August 25, 1937 at Lochuan near Yenan, Chang advocated sincere cooperation

[3] Snow, *The Other Side of the River*, p. 76.

with the Kuomintang with the hope that "through a sincere alliance, the Communists might lead the Kuomintang and other non-Communist groups along a more progressive path than they had followed in the past." [4] But Chang's proposal only prompted Mao Tse-tung to accuse him of betraying Communism (Chang defected to the Kuomintang in 1938). Endorsing Mao's grand strategy for expansion, the conference at Lochuan formally decided that the CCP's main objective was to augment its military and political strength in preparation for an eventual showdown with the Kuomintang, which it considered unfit to save China from foreign encroachment and internal decay. Specifically, the party was to maintain its independence and autonomy within the anti-Japanese united front; to develop its own military force independently; to establish guerrilla bases; and to agitate for a pro-Communist mass movement in all Kuomintang-held areas with such high-sounding slogans as those contained in the "The 10-Point Program for Anti-Japanese Resistance and National Salvation" as the battle cry.[5]

Despite this basic strategy, the Communists showed considerable self-restraint in dealing with the Kuomintang in the first three months of the war. While sparing no effort and missing no opportunity to represent themselves to the Chinese public as the most energetic anti-Japanese force, they usually refrained from criticizing the National Government directly. In fact, they even accommodated the National Government by agreeing to abolish the political commissar system in the Eighteenth Group Army. In the Second War Area in northern Shansi, the Eighteenth Group Army also showed some willingness to coordinate its operations with other Chinese troops. Lin Piao's forces even fought a pitched battle against several thousand Japanese invaders at P'inghsingkuan in September 1937.

Still the spirit of self-restraint and accommodation quickly evaporated after the Japanese capture of Shanghai and Taiyuan in November 1937—an event that was accompanied by a serious depletion of the Kuomintang military power. Believing that the Kuomintang would thereafter be incapable of taking any effective action against his party, Mao Tse-tung decreed a policy of an all-out expansion for the Communists, while continuing to advocate the

[4] North, *Moscow and Chinese Communism*, p. 180.

[5] The 10-point program demanded among other things total mobilization of the country, democratization of the government, improvement of the welfare of the people, and abolition of all laws and regulations curtailing freedom of speech, assembly, and association. An English text of the document is in Brandt *et al., A Documentary History of Chinese Communism*, pp. 242-245.

facade of the anti-Japanese united front.[6] The new line was first reflected by a hardening of the Communist attitude toward the Kuomintang: Communists in charge of liaison work with the National Government were now told to rectify their tendency of accommodation. Efforts to organize mass movements in the Kuomintang-held areas were intensified, and the political commissar system in the Communist forces was revived in violation of the interdictions of the National Government. The National Government's request to appoint its officers as cadres of the Eighteenth Group Army was firmly rejected; indeed, the CCP's exclusive control of the Eighteenth Group Army and the New Fourth Army was maintained with greater determination. Communist publications grew bolder in their criticism of the Kuomintang regime and demands for a greater Communist voice in the formulation of national policies.

Communist intransigency soon revived such open recriminations and conflicts between the Kuomintang and the CCP itself that in August 1938, just one year after the outbreak of the resistance war, the National Government deemed it necessary to outlaw Communist-sponsored mass organizations in Wuhan and other areas under its control. As the Communists became more stubborn after the Japanese occupation of Wuhan and Canton in October 1938, the National Government threw a cordon of troops around the Communist base in northern Shensi. But what strained the united front most was Communist expansion behind the Japanese lines, which began after the Japanese seizure of Shanghai and Taiyuan in October 1937. By the end of 1937 Communist forces had infiltrated the mountainous areas in northern and eastern Shansi, southern Suiyuan and Chahar, and central and southern Hopei, and in the following spring, detachments of the Eighteenth Group Army entered western Shantung. Everywhere the Eighteenth Group Army went it overpowered local self-defense corps and anti-Japanese partisans and added them to its own members. Since regular Kuomintang troops were also operating in some of the areas penetrated by the Eighteenth Group Army, a struggle developed between the Kuomintang and the Communist forces for territory.

With their skill at guerrilla warfare, the Communists usually emerged victorious from contests in the field, gaining exclusive control of the disputed areas and capturing large quantities of arms and munitions from their defeated competitors. They then used the

[6] See his "The Situation and Tasks in the Anti-Japanese War after the Fall of Shanghai and Taiyuan," in *Selected Works* (Peking: Foreign Languages Press, 1965), II, 61-74.

captured weapons and equipment to arm the local peasants who had been mobilized to form guerrilla bands or to augment the ranks of the Eighteenth Group Army itself. The Communists were so successful in expanding their military force in this fashion that by the time the resistance war was a year old the combined strength of the Eighteenth Group Army and the New Fourth Army had grown from the original 40,000 men to 180,000. In the same period, the Kuomintang army, which bore the brunt of the Japanese assault, lost more than one million men.

Wherever Communist troops won control, they set up a border region government. The first two border region governments were formally launched early in 1939, one on the Shansi-Hopei-Chahar border and the other on the Shansi-Hopei-Shantung-Honan border. With their new moderate land policy the Communists gained the support of large portions of the rural population of the border regions.[7] Under this policy only the land of landlords who had become collaborators or who had stayed in the Japanese-controlled cities was expropriated and redistributed; all other landlords were permitted to retain their land on the condition that the rent not exceed 37.5 per cent of the main crop. In March 1940, in a further attempt to gain maximum popular support, the Communists introduced the "Three-Thirds" system. This system provided that elective posts were to be filled one third by Communists, one third by non-party leftist progressives, and one third by middle-of-the-roaders.

With the establishment of the new bases on the strategic Shansi-Hopei-Chahar and Shansi-Hopei-Shantung-Honan borders, the Communists became even more intransigent. In April 1939, Communist troops in western Shantung attacked Kuomintang forces in eastern Shantung and northern Kiangsu. Two months later, Communist troops in Hopei surrounded and defeated Kuomintang forces under Chang Ying-wu at Poshan. In December 1939, Po I-po and other Communists who had infiltrated into General Yen Hsi-shan's troops in Shansi persuaded more than 30,000 men known as the Dare-to-Die Corps to go over to the Communist side. Early in 1940, three Kuomintang divisions on the Taihang mountains were ambushed by the Communists, and other Kuomintang forces in the same region were forced to evacuate. In Shantung, Communist troops invaded eastern Honan and northern Anhwei in an obvious attempt to link up with units of the New Fourth Army, which had been

[7] For an interpretation of the wartime rural policy of the CCP, see Chalmers A. Johnson, *Peasant Nationalism and Communist Power: The Emergence of Revolutionary China, 1937-1945* (Stanford, Calif.: Stanford University Press, 1962).

expanding their fields of operation northward from south of the Yangtze River.

On January 6, 1941 occurred the so-called New Fourth Army Incident when General Ku Chu-t'ung, Commander of the Third War Area, took "disciplinary action" against the Communist forces in southern Anhwei for their expansionist policy and refusal to move to areas north of the Yellow River, as ordered by Chiang Kai-shek. An armed clash lasted for eight days and resulted in the killing of 2000 New Fourth Army men and the wounding of between 3000 and 4000 others. Yeh T'ing, commander of the New Fourth Army, was taken prisoner by the Kuomintang troops, and Hsiang Ying, the deputy-commander, was killed in action. On January 17, the National Government ordered the disbandment of the New Fourth Army, whose remnants escaped into northern Kiangsu and Shantung. Although the CCP reacted indignantly to the forcible action taken by the National Government against the New Fourth Army, the German invasion of the Soviet Union in June 1941 caused the Chinese Communist leaders to adopt a more cautious policy toward the National Government, lest Chiang Kai-shek seek a rapprochement with the Japanese which might incline the latter to attack the "fatherland of socialism" from the east. Thus, from this time until the end of 1942, Communist forces seldom clashed with the Kuomintang troops, although they continued to extend their influence in the areas behind the Japanese lines where there were no Kuomintang troops.

In the beginning of 1943, Russian troops were clearing the Caucasus of the German forces, and the fortunes of war were beginning to turn in Russia's favor. The Chinese Communists once again became aggressive and attacked smaller and exposed Kuomintang units. Minor clashes over territory continued to occur periodically in the remaining years of the resistance war, with the Communists often the victor. Consequently, when the Japanese surrendered in August 1945, the Communists were in control of 19 "liberated areas" in 19 provinces, with a total population of 100 million. At the same time, they had a regular army of a million men and a people's militia of 2.2 million men.[8] In the last years of the resistance war, the Communists also gained considerable political ground in Kuomintang territory. Mindful of the growing popular discontent resulting from the wartime inflation and official corruption and cognizant of the continued political frustration of the

[8] Mao Tse-tung, *Selected Works* (Peking: Foreign Languages Press, 1961), IV, 35.

intelligentsia and the minor parties under the Kuomintang political tutelage, the Communists clamored for a coalition or "New Democratic" government of "all revolutionary classes" and "all progressive political parties." Economically, they called for the nationalization of the big banks, big industry, and big business and for confiscation and distribution of the land of the big landlords, while promising protection for all other forms of private property. They further stated that the system of a mixed economy and a coalition government might continue for a long time before the country would be ready for a socialist revolution. First expounded by Mao Tse-tung in a pamphlet entitled *The New Democracy* in 1940, this program proved to be an effective blueprint for power, for it induced most of the minor parties and some intellectuals to cooperate with the Communists and neutralized the opposition of many businessmen and other social elements.[9]

Another great accomplishment of the Communists during the war was the expansion of the party apparatus and the strengthening of its unity and discipline. Shortly after the outbreak of the war in 1937, the Communists launched a campaign to attract educated youths into their fold. Large numbers of college and secondary school students, especially those from the Japanese-occupied areas, flocked to Yenan, where they attended the Anti-Japanese University, the North Shensi Academy, and the Lu Hsun College of Arts. Later, additional youth training centers were established in various guerrilla bases. These institutions subjected their trainees to rigid discipline and intensive political indoctrination. Upon their graduation, most of the young men and young women became dedicated Communists, serving as cadres in rapidly expanding border regions and the armed forces. With these cadres as a nucleus, the CCP grew from 40,000 members in 1937 to 1,210,000 in 1945.

The party also strengthened its unity and discipline as a result of Mao Tse-tung's consolidation of his personal leadership. As noted above, at the Lochuan Conference of the Politburo in August 1937, Mao successfully defended his wartime expansion policy in the face of Chang Kuo-t'ao's challenge. A year later, at the Sixth Plenum of the Sixth Central Committee held in Yenan, Mao had another challenger to his authority officially repudiated and his own leadership reaffirmed. Ch'en Shao-yü, the challenger, had previously been accused by Mao of committing "leftist adventurism" during his tenure as general secretary of the party in the early 1930's. He

[9] A text of the pamphlet is in *Ibid.*, II, 339-384.

was now charged with pursuing a "rightist opportunist line" because of his misgivings that Mao's bold expansionism might prematurely jeopardize the united front. Since Ch'en had been the most influential leader of the Returned Student Clique, his new disgrace further discredited that clique as a whole. While consolidating his political leadership in the party, Mao also established himself as the chief interpreter of Marxism-Leninism in China. His writings such as *On the New Democracy, On Contradiction, On Practice,* and *Talks at the Yenan Forum on Literature and Art,* were hailed as new contributions to "Marxist-Leninist theory" and as creative interpretations of "the historical peculiarities of the Chinese revolution," even though they did not contain any substantially new theoretical concepts. Mao's assumption of the role as the source and arbiter of all doctrine in the Chinese Communist movement, which was officially acknowledged by his party in its new constitution adopted at the Seventh National Congress in 1945, enabled him to exercise virtually unlimited authority. Anyone who espoused a line different from his own was a deviationist and therefore wrong. In the first *Cheng-feng* or party rectification campaign (1942-1943) the rightist and leftist deviationists within the party were weeded out or brought into line; thus Mao's monolithic control was firmly consolidated, and the party became a well-disciplined organization of professional revolutionaries. During the rectification campaign, the CCP perfected the indoctrination techniques of self-criticism, mutual criticism, intensive study, and public confession meetings, which it has since used effectively as instruments of mass control.

Debilitation of the Kuomintang during the War

While the resistance war afforded the Communists a splendid opportunity to strengthen themselves, it had devastating effects on the Kuomintang regime, already beset in the prewar years (1928-1937) by many problems, including such subjective shortcomings as factionalism, ideological confusion, and a growing propensity to eschew basic socio-economic reforms. First of all, the Japanese invasion undermined the foundation of the National Government by destroying the flower of Chiang Kai-shek's painstakingly built armies, which bore the brunt of the invaders' assaults in the first phase of the war. During the remaining years of the war the Kuomintang regime was unable to rebuild an effective fighting force due to lack of equipment, and the quality of the Kuomintang armies continued to deteriorate as the war dragged on. Whenever a new battle was fought, more equipment and trained men were lost, with the depleted ranks usually replenished by inadequately trained recruits. The Kuomintang armies were further weakened by a serious deterioration in morale and lowered standards of honesty and efficiency among officers, which stemmed from the government's failure to check the demoralizing effects of an increasing scarcity of provisions and clothing and mounting inflation beginning in 1939. Some American military equipment did arrive in China at long last in 1945 but failed to bolster the strength of the Kuomintang army significantly, for most of the soldiers continued to be poorly fed and clad as corruption and the ruinous inflation persisted. Inasmuch as the civil war after V-J Day was ultimately decided in the battlefield, this military enfeeblement of the Kuomintang regime during the resistance war and the simultaneous expansion of the Communist armed forces were developments of great significance.

The war also weakened the Kuomintang regime economically. The Japanese occupation of the seaports during the first year of the war deprived the Kuomintang government of its most important sources of revenue. In the years preceding the invasion, the Kuomintang government derived more than 40 per cent of its annual income from customs duties, about 20 per cent from the salt tax, and about another 20 per cent from the consolidated excise taxes. As a result of the Japanese occupation of coastal provinces, where virtually all the customs duties and most of the salt and consolidated excise taxes had been collected, the National Government lost the greater part of its ordinary financial resources. Thanks to the beneficial effects of the currency reform in 1935 and the successful issuance of internal loans in the first two years of the war, there was no alarming budget deficit until the fall of 1939. Thereafter, the financial strains caused by the war began to manifest themselves. On the one hand, the expenditures of the government mounted as the war went on; on the other, the government failed to find adequate substitutes for the ordinary sources of revenue which had been lost. Taxes on excess profit and inheritance were introduced in 1939, but the excessive fragmentation of the Chinese social and economic fabric imposed a heavy burden on the machinery of tax collection, which had not been characterized by efficiency or honesty.

In 1941, the government took measures to open up new sources of revenue. One of these was the inauguration of government monopolies on the wholesale of certain daily necessities, such as salt, sugar, tobacco, wine, matches and tea, which as a whole yielded about 25 per cent of the revenue in the last years of the war. A more important measure was the land tax reform: the central government declared that the land tax, which had been a source of local finance from the early years of the Republic, was now a national revenue to be collected in kind. During the subsequent years this tax became the principal source of income, yielding as much as 45 per cent of the total revenue. Despite these new sources of revenue, the government's income continued to lag far behind its expenditures. It has been estimated that at no time did all the tax revenues account for more than 30 per cent of the annual total governmental expenditure in the period 1941 to 1945.

The financial problems were aggravated by tax evasion, graft, and speculation. To meet the mounting deficit, the government resorted to the printing press. Together with the shortage of goods of all kinds, reliance on note issue for financing the war quickly brought about inflation. The immediate result of the inflation was an uninterrupted and rapid rise of prices, which, in turn, provided a fertile field for speculation, facilitated official corruption, accentuated administrative inefficiency, and caused serious hardships to the fixed-income groups, such as the bureaucracy, men in uniform, and intellectuals. The demoralization of the civil administration and the men in uniform weakened the government directly, while the impoverishment of intellectuals alienated the government from the people who traditionally had been the principal molders of public opinion in China. The estranged intellectuals became increasingly critical of the government as the military, economic, and administrative deterioration worsened; they vehemently attacked the government for its shortcomings, especially its failure to curb the self-enriching practices of certain high officials, and soon demanded the immediate substitution of a representative government for the Kuomintang political tutelage. Some of them even colluded with the Communists in instigating the formation of anti-government groups among university students. When secret police agents and the San-min Chu-i [the Three People's Principles] Youth Corps used repressive measures on the campuses to intimidate opposition, the intellectuals were only further embittered and thus became more responsive to the Communist call for a united front against the government.

In addition to demoralizing administrative and military personnel and ailenating intellectuals, the economic and financial difficulties caused by the Japanese invasion led the government to adopt policies that alienated it from certain business groups. Among the unpopular economic policies were the inauguration of government monopolies and the creation of other types of government-operated enterprises. These latter were regarded by interested private industrialists and merchants as unwarranted infringements on their interests, and the business groups became all the more resentful when the management of the official enterprises was plagued with corruption and inefficiency. The relationship between the government and the business community did not improve after V-J Day: rather it deteriorated because the government extended rather than retracted its role in the economic field. It took over all the industrial plants formerly owned by the Japanese and ran them as state enterprises. Since state enterprises enjoyed substantial privileges denied to private industry, they offered serious competition to the latter. Embittered, many industrialists became indifferent to the outcome of the civil war, while others even cast their lot with the Communists, whose leaders, as already noted, had promised to establish a New Democratic economy under which the Kuomintang "bureaucratic capitalism" would be overthrown and legitimate private enterprises would be protected and encouraged.

V

The Final Conquest of Power: 1945-1949

Postwar CCP-Kuomintang Peace Negotiations

At the time of Japan's collapse in August 1945, the CCP was a greatly expanded, perfectly disciplined, and highly efficient organization commanding a seasoned army and holding vast stretches of strategically located territory. It was ready to vie with the exhausted and demoralized Kuomintang for supreme power.

The postwar clash between the two parties began with a struggle for the control of the territory, arms, and supplies that the Japanese armies were to surrender. Chiang Kai-shek succeeded in having all but a small fraction (about 30,000 men) of the Japanese troops (1,283,200 men) in China proper, Taiwan, and northern Indochina surrender to the Kuomintang armies. But, over a quarter of a million Communist troops in north China swarmed into Manchuria where they received enormous stockpiles of weapons and ammunition, which the Russian army had captured from the Japanese Kwantung Army following the Soviet Union's declaration of war on Japan on August 8, 1945. In North China, Communist troops taking advantage of their strategic locations endeavored to prevent Kuomintang forces from entering Chahar, Hopei (including the Peiping-Tientsin-Paoting area), eastern Suiyuan, the greater part of Shansi, and the central and eastern parts of Shantung. In east China, the Communists also attempted to seize Nanking and Shanghai from the Japanese immediately after Japan's declaration of surrender. Military hostilities over the control of Nanking, Shanghai, Tsingtao and the Peiping-Tientsin-Paoting area along the coast were temporarily averted as

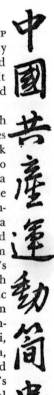

中國共產運動簡史

Kuomintang troops circumvented the intervening Communist ground forces by reaching those places from southwestern China in American airplanes and warships (among other things, this American assistance to the Kuomintang seems to have incurred lasting CCP hatred of American "imperialism"); however, Communist and Kuomintang troops elsewhere in north and central China fought fierce battles in their race to take over from the Japanese.

While these military developments were taking place, both sides expressed the desire to find a peaceful solution to their differences, indulging in this duplicity for the following reasons: First, fully aware of the Chinese people's weariness of the eight arduous years of war against Japan, each party wanted to elicit popular sympathy and support by representing itself as the reasonable, conciliatory, and peace-loving faction, while maneuvering the other side into a position where it would be held responsible for initiating another full-scale war. Second, in the first few months of the postwar period, neither side was in a position to embark on a full-fledged conflict —the Kuomintang needed time to move its troops from the remote southwest to some of the areas evacuated by the Japanese in the east and north and to consolidate these newly acquired positions; the Communists needed time to train the troops that had rushed into Manchuria after the Japanese surrender in the use of Japanese weapons, especially heavy artillery and automatic arms, which they had never before possessed. Third, since the American government was trying to prevent a civil war in China, both the Kuomintang and the CCP saw the wisdom of making the pretense of pursuing peace inasmuch as the U. S. was capable of exerting a tremendous influence on the outcome of a civil war that occurred against its wishes. The Kuomintang was fearful of incurring the displeasure of the United States by refusing to enter into negotiations with the Communists, since it might lose the American support it would need to defeat its foe in a military contest. The CCP did not expect to win any active support for its cause in a civil war even if it could convince the United States with manifestations of peaceful intentions that it was not the culprit. It did hope, however, that if the United States could be led to blame the Kuomintang for starting what was actually an unavoidable strife, then that powerful country would be at least less inclined to intervene in favor of the guilty faction. The Communist leaders apparently believed that the Kuomintang would become highly vulnerable in the absence of American assistance. Moreover, the Communist leaders, confident that their followers were completely cognizant of revolutionary objectives and capable of adapting themselves to the ever-changing party lines and tactics, probably thought that by holding peace negotiations on the political level while carrying on armed struggles in the field they might confuse and bewilder the poorly disciplined and indoctrinated rank and file of the Kuomintang and thus undermine their fighting spirit without sapping the energy or dampening the ardor of their own rank and file.[1]

Regardless of their real motives, the Kuomintang and the CCP began to hold discussions for a political solution of their conflict shortly after the Japanese offered to surrender. The first round of postwar negotiations took place in Chungking with Mao Tse-tung at the head of a Communist delegation. At the invitation of Chiang Kai-shek, Mao flew to Chungking on August 27, 1945 in the company of the American Ambassador, Patrick J. Hurley. During the next 41 days, Mao held informal talks with Chiang Kai-shek and other top Kuomintang leaders, and Mao's aides held five formal meetings with representatives of the National Government. On October 10, Mao returned to Yenan. On the day of his departure from Chungking, the two sides issued a joint statement pledging themselves to make concerted efforts to avoid civil war and ensure peace, democracy, solidarity, and unity. But these encouraging words were belied by the increasing number of military clashes in various areas in China proper and by the Chinese Communists' collusion with the Soviet army in Manchuria in an attempt to prevent Kuomintang troops from entering that important industrial area, which the Soviet government, in the Sino-Soviet Treaty of Friendship and Alliance of August 14, 1945 and its related documents, had promised to return to the control of the Chinese National Government after the defeat of the Japanese Kwantung Army.

The warring factions resumed their negotiations soon after the arrival of General George C. Marshall, who had been sent by President Truman on a special mission to try to end the military conflict and to induce the various Chinese political parties to work together in a coalition government. Through General Marshall's efforts, the National Government and the Communists signed a cease-fire agreement on January 10, 1946. On the next day a Political Consultative Conference was convened in Chungking to arrange a political settlement of China's internal conflict. It consisted of eight delegates from the National Government, seven from the CCP, eleven from

[1] See Mao Tse-tung, "On Peace Negotiations with the Kuomintang," *Selected Works,* IV, 47-51.

third parties, and nine nonpartisan leaders. After 21 days of deliberation with General Marshall serving as a mediator, the Political Consultative Conference reached agreement on the reorganization of the National Government, the program or policies of the reorganized government, the nationalization of the armed forces, the revision of the Draft Constitution of 1936, and the organization and convocation of a constituent national assembly. The proposed reorganized National Government was to serve as a coalition interim regime pending the establishment of a constitutional government, which, in turn, was supposed to be facilitated by the accord on the revision of the Draft Constitution of 1935 (prepared by the Kuomintang) and by that on a constituent national assembly.

No sooner had these agreements been announced than it became apparent that neither the Kuomintang nor the CCP had any intention to abide by them. The two sides not only continued to smear each other but became deadlocked over the implementation of certain features of the political settlement such as the division of provincial offices in the areas contested between the Kuomintang and the CCP and the exact allotment of Communist representatives on the State Council of the future reorganized National Government. The greatest problem, however, was the continued recurrence of military hostilities despite the cease-fire agreement.

"The Third Revolutionary Civil War"

In Manchuria, where the cease-fire agreement was not applicable from the outset, heavy fighting took place at Szepingchieh in May 1946 as Communist troops under Lin Piao attempted to block Kuomintang troops moving northward from Mukden on take-over duties. In addition, Communist forces in north and east China attacked and seized several score cities and counties. In July, Kuomintang troops mounted an offensive against the Communists in several provinces. The growing conflict soon led General Marshall to recognize the futility of continuing his mediation mission. After his departure from China in January 1947, the two warring Chinese factions quickly dropped all pretense of seeking a reconciliation, and an open break came with the expulsion of the Communist delegation from Nanking in February 1947. The CCP today calls this duel with the Kuomintang "the Third Revolutionary Civil War."

For a year (July 1946 to July 1947) the Kuomintang forces seemed to have an advantage over their foe. Late in 1946 they dislodged the Communists from numerous cities and towns, including Kalgan and Chengteh. On March 17, 1947, they managed to cap their territorial gains with the capture of Yenan, forcing Mao Tse-tung and his associates to flee from their old lair. But these victories were only superficial, for they involved no reduction of the Communists' fighting strength and entailed heavy losses of Kuomintang manpower and equipment. This situation arose from the fact that the Kuomintang troops preferred to seize and hold as many cities and towns as possible rather than seek out the Communist forces and destroy them, while the Communists adhered to Mao Tse-tung's policy of annihilating the enemy's manpower through concentrated and surprise attacks rather than capturing or defending a place.

During the Kuomintang offensive the Communists not only managed to wear down the strength of their opponent, but also greatly augmented their own power by equipping the peasants with captured arms and by reinforcing their ranks with reindoctrinated prisoners-of-war. In July 1947, the Chinese People's Liberation Army (as the Communist forces were now styled) began to launch a massive nationwide offensive. As usual the military struggle was supplemented by a political campaign. To discredit the Kuomintang regime, the Communists characterized its officials as "bureaucratic capitalists" who were bent upon self-enrichment in collusion with domestic "feudalists" and foreign imperialists. The appearance of Ch'en Po-ta's (Deputy-Director of the CCP Propaganda Department) pamphlet entitled *The Four Big Families* (*Ssu-ta Chia-tsu*) proved particularly damaging to the public image of Chiang Kai-shek and some of his principal associates. In an effort to ward off American intervention in the Chinese civil war, a mass campaign was engineered in the Kuomintang-held large cities, demanding the immediate withdrawal of American troops from China and opposing American aid to Chiang Kai-shek. The Communists touched off this popular outburst in December 1946 by exploiting in their propaganda a scandal in Peiping involving a Chinese girl student supposedly assaulted by an American soldier. This and other maneuvers apparently increased the American government's desire to extricate itself from the internal conflict of China after the failure of General Marshall's mission. Early in 1947, American troops in China began to withdraw gradually and American military aid to the National Government came to a complete stop. Another Communist-inspired mass movement that exacerbated the demoralization of the Kuomintang regime was the anti-starvation, anti-civil war, and anti-persecution student demonstrations which raged in the country from

May 1947 to the collapse of the Kuomintang rule on the mainland.

On October 10, 1947, the Communists issued a formal declaration, calling upon the nation to overthrow Chiang Kai-shek and promising a "democratic coalition government" with such perquisites as freedom of speech, of the press, of assembly and of association.[2] On May 4, 1946, to arouse the peasants to join the People's Liberation Army and render other forms of support, the CCP Central Committee had issued a "Directive on the Land Question," substituting the policy of confiscating the landlord's land and redistributing it among the peasants for the moderate wartime program calling only for the reduction of rent and interest. This new land reform program had been put into effect only in the old Communist strongholds, and nothing had been said about its applicability in other parts of the country. In a document known as "the Outline of Agrarian Law," the CCP now put forward the same agrarian policy for the nation as a whole. The enactment of this policy gained more rural support for the Communists, thereby greatly facilitating their prosecution of the civil war. While marching on the Kuomintang-held urban centers, the Communists pursued another policy which proved equally effective for lessening resistance and winning support. In sharp contrast to the practice of the Kuomintang carpetbaggers on their return to the places evacuated by the Japanese after V-J Day, Communist troops conducted the take-over of the cities in a systematic, benevolent, and dedicated manner, without looting, extortion, or pillage during or after the capture of an area. Both administrative officials and troops behaved with extreme politeness and self-discipline, endeavoring to foster good relations with the local population and encouraging them to go about their normal business. In establishing transitional administrations in the newly captured cities, the Communists made extensive use of local talent, including those Kuomintang personnel who were not actively involved in "counterrevolutionary activities."[3] Although this policy of not disturbing the normal life of the urban centers was abandoned soon after the consolidation of Communist power on the mainland, its implementation in the midst of the civil war apparently inclined many residents in the cities and towns yet to be "liberated" to view the surging Communist tide with increasing equanimity or even enthusiasm.

With large segments of the population being won over or

[2] An English text of the declaration is in *Ibid.*, IV, 147-153.

[3] See H. Arthur Steiner, "Chinese Communist Urban Poilcy," *The American Political Science Review*, XLIV (March 1950), 47-63.

neutralized and the steady deterioration of the morale of the Kuomintang troops under the impact of repeated setbacks and worsening inflation, the Communist forces were able to make more rapid advances in 1948 and 1949. On April 22, 1948, P'eng Teh-huai's troops recovered Yenan. In May, Mao Tse-tung and the headquarters of the CCP Central Committee moved from northern Shensi to Hsipaipo Village, Pingshan Hsien, Hopei Province in anticipation of an early nationwide victory. During the remainder of the civil war the People's Liberation Army crushed the Kuomintang armies with even greater swiftness and ease. In the campaign between Mukden and Chinchow in the fall of 1948, the Communists reportedly annihilated over 400,000 Kuomintang troops within less than eight weeks. This spectacular victory immediately placed Manchuria under complete Communist control, and made the position of the Kuomintang forces in North China untenable. On January 22, 1949, General Fu Tso-i surrendered Peking and its garrison of over 200,000 troops, after he had recently lost an approximately equal number of men in Tientsin, Kalgan, and elsewhere. While the Communists were still besieging Peking and Tientsin, forces under Ch'en I and Liu Po-ch'eng mounted a gigantic offensive in central China. In the battle of Hsuchow from November 7, 1948 to January 10, 1949, they wiped out over half a million Kuomintang troops, the cream of Chiang Kai-shek's remaining army, with which he had hoped to stem the tide of the Communist forces moving down toward Nanking and Shanghai.

Yielding to a strong pressure from some influential Kuomintang leaders who demanded negotiations with the CCP, Chiang Kai-shek stepped aside from the presidency on January 21, 1949. In his capacity as Acting President, Vice President Li Tsung-jen offered to arrange a peaceful settlement of the civil war. To this end he sent a five-man delegation to Peking on April 1, 1949, but the Communists demanded virtual surrender by the National Government. Immediately after Acting President Li rejected the demand, the Communists renewed their attack. On April 21, 1949, their forces swept across the Yangtze River virtually unopposed; on April 23, they captured Nanking and then spread like a raging flood over the vast territory of south and west China.

The National Government first took refuge in Canton. After the fall of that southern city on October 14, 1949, it retreated to Chungking and then Chengtu. Toward the end of December 1949, the top leaders of the harassed government finally fled the mainland for Taipei, Taiwan. The Communists completed their conquest of mainland China in the summer of 1951 when units of the People's Liberation Army marched into Tibet, following the conclusion of an agreement between the newly established Central People's Government in Peking and the Tibetan local authorities concerning measures for the "peaceful liberation" of that remote region.

Establishment of the People's Republic of China

As the People's Liberation Army was winning one victory after another following the commencement of its nationwide offensive in July 1947, the CCP began to anticipate an early collapse of the Kuomintang regime and therefore set out to make necessary political preparations for the establishment of a new regime that would ensure Communist hegemony but would possess the facade of a broad united front. The first call for the creation of such a government was made in a May Day slogan in 1948.[4] Based on a resolution of the Politburo of April 30, 1948, it proposed that "all democratic parties and groups, people's organizations, and social luminaries, speedily convene a political consultative conference, discuss, and carry out the convening of a people's congress and the formation of a democratic coalition government." This proposal evoked an immediate and enthusiastic response from eight anti-Chiang groups and associated nonpartisans in Hong Kong.[5] Leaders of these dissident groups began to return from exile to "liberated" China in the summer of 1948. At the Harbin Conference of November 25, 1948, they agreed with the CCP that a Preparatory Committee for the new Political Consultative Conference should be established. This committee, composed of 134 delegates from 23 organizations supporting May Day slogans, held two meetings in Peiping, one on June 15-21, 1949 and the other on September 17. To avoid confusion with the Political Consultative Conference previously held in Chungking under the auspices of the Kuomintang regime, the Preparatory Committee decided to designate the proposed new conference as the Chinese People's Political Consultative Conference (CPPCC)—a title having the merit of incorporating the people's terminology on which Mao Tse-tung's latest doctrinal system relies so heavily[6]—and drew up three basic documents to be submitted to the CPPCC:

[4] *China Digest* (Hong Kong), IV (May 18, 1948), 9-10.

[5] *Ibid.*, IV (May 18, 1948), 11.

[6] H. Arthur Steiner, "The People's Democratic Dictatorship in China," *Western Political Quarterly*, IV (March 1950), 38-51.

1. the Common Program of the CPPCC
2. the Organic Law of the CPPCC
3. the Organic Law of the Central People's Government.

In an article written to commemorate the twenty-eighth anniversary of the CCP on July 1, 1949, Mao Tse-tung undertook to sketch in more current and in sharper terms the theoretical foundations of the proposed new state.[7] Revising his earlier concepts somewhat, he now supplemented the New Democracy with a "People's democratic dictatorship," defined as an alliance of four classes: workers, peasants, the petty bourgeoisie, and the national bourgeoisie, who together made up the "people." [8] The dictatorship was to be based mainly on the alliance of workers and peasants. The "people" were to exercise their dictatorship over the "reactionaries" —the lackeys of imperialism, landlords, bureaucratic capitalists, and the "reactionary clique" of the Kuomintang. The "people" were to have the right to vote or voice their opinions, and the "reactionaries" were to be suppressed. This policy, according to Mao, would result in "democracy for the people and dictatorship for the reactionaries," which when combined, constituted the "people's democratic dictatorship."

Mao repeated the Marxist view of the eventual abolition of state power but added, "we cannot afford to abolish state power just now because imperialism, domestic reactionaries, and classes still exist." In keeping with the Marxist tradition, Mao declared: "Such state apparatus as the army, the police and the courts are instruments by which one class oppresses another." He stated: "Our present task is to strengthen the people's state apparatus" so as to prevent the "people's" rule from being overthrown by "domestic and foreign reactionaries." Recognizing that "reactionary influences" were still very strong among the "people," Mao called for the use of democratic methods of persuasion to reform bad habits and thoughts among the "people," but prescribed "compulsory" reform for the "reactionaries."

The necessity of resisting imperialist oppression and the backward nature of China's economy made it desirable for the new regime to work with the national bourgeoisie. "Our present policy,"

[7] Mao Tse-tung, "On the People's Democratic Dictatorship," *Selected Works*, IV, 411-424.

[8] The national bourgeoisie was defined by the CCP as merchants and industrialists who were untainted by foreign imperialism and had operated independently of "bureaucratic capitalists" (i.e., Kuomintang officials who ran state-owned economic enterprises as if they were their personal possessions).

Mao stated, "is to regulate capitalism, not to destroy it." The national bourgeoisie was not to occupy a position of primacy in state administration because of its weakness and the limited nature of its progressive tendency. However, Mao said: "When the time comes to nationalize private enterprise, they, too, would be further educated and remolded." With a view to warning the national bourgeoisie against any tendency toward incompliance, he stated: "The people have a powerful state apparatus in their hands—there is no need to fear rebellion by the national bourgeoisie." According to one of Mao's aides, it was the continued existence of the national bourgeoisie in the People's Republic of China that made the "People's Democracy" in that country different from the "people's democracies" in eastern Europe.[9] Together with a policy of "leaning to one side" diplomatically (i. e., the socialist front headed by the Soviet Union), this state system, Mao concluded, would enable China to "develop from an agricultural into an industrial society, eliminating classes and realizing universal harmony."

With Mao's article as its general guide and with its groundwork already laid by the Preparatory Committee, the CPPCC convened in Peiping on September 21, 1949. There were 588 voting delegates and 77 nonvoting alternates—a total of 662—some of whom, however, were not in actual attendance. Of the 585 voting delegates, 102 represented nine geographical regions; 60 represented the People's Liberation Army; 142 represented 14 political parties and groups, including 16 each from the CCP, the Kuomintang Revolutionary Committee, and the Democratic League; 206 represented 16 newly formed "people's organizations" such as the All-China Federation of Trade Unions, the All-China Federation of Democratic Women, and youth, overseas Chinese, industrial and commercial, and religious groups; and 75 were "specially invited democratic personages." Since most of these delegates were either members of the CCP (the CCP controlled the "liberated areas," the People's Liberation Army, and most of the "people's organizations") or had pledged support of its current "New Democratic" objectives, throughout the entire session of the CPPCC they accepted the leadership of the CCP. At no time was there any outward difference of opinion over alternative programs, and all decisions were made by unanimous vote.

The conference approved the three basic documents drafted by

[9] Hu, *Thirty Years of the Communist Party of China,* p. 80.

the Preparatory Committee.[10] The Organic Law of the Central People's Government, which most closely resembled a provisional constitution, set up the central governmental structure and defined the functions of the various state organs and their relationship to one another. The Organic Law of the CPPCC defined the structure, powers and functions of the body that was to exercise the powers and functions of the conference until the election of a National People's Congress on the basis of "universal suffrage." The Common Program of the CPPCC, a 60-article manifesto, gave the guiding principles of the new state in the period of the "people's democratic dictatorship," and included detailed declarations of policy in all fields—political, military, and economic affiairs; culture, education, national minorities; and foreign affairs. As stated in its preamble, the Common Program was to "be jointly observed by all units participating in the CPPCC, by the people's governments at all levels, and by the people of the whole country." Representing nothing more than the "minimum program" of the CCP for the immediate future, the policies outlined in the Common Program were characterized by a spirit of relative moderation, even though provisions were made for the eradication of "imperialism, feudalism, and bureaucratic capitalism" and the suppression of "reactionary elements in general."

Following the adoption of the three basic documents, the CPPCC elected the Central People's Government Council as well as its own National Committee. Scheduled to meet semiannually and composed of 180 members with Mao Tse-tung as its chairman, the National Committee of the CPPCC was to "supervise the execution of the resolutions" of the CPPCC, whose plenary sessions were normally to meet only triennially. Formally designed as the supreme policy-making organ of the state when the CPPCC was not in session, the Central People's Government Council had a chairman, six vice-chairmen, and 56 members. Mao Tse-tung was made chairman. To keep up the appearance of a coalition, only three of the six vice-chairmanships went to Communists (Chu Teh, Liu Shao-ch'i, and Kao Kang); the other three were bestowed on Soong Ching-ling, widow of Dr. Sun Yat-sen, Li Chi-shen, chairman of the Kuomintang Revolutionary Committee, and Chang Lan, the aged head of the Democratic League. For the same reason, 28 of the other 56 seats

[10] For their texts, see the *Important Documents of the First Plenary Session of the Chinese People's Political Consultative Conference* (Peking: Foreign Languages Press, 1949).

on the Central People's Government Council were filled with non-Communist luminaries. Before its adjournment on September 30, the CPPCC designated Peking, called Peiping when the Kuomintang had their capital at Nanking, as the national capital, adopted a temporary national anthem, and selected a new national flag. Finally on October 1, 1949, the People's Republic of China was formally proclaimed in Peking.

VI

Ideology and Organization of the Chinese Communist Party

Since the establishment of the People's Republic of China in 1949, the CCP has been the leader and center of both the state and society on the mainland. It exercises such extensive, undisputed control over all institutions and regulates every aspect of the country's life that the formal governmental apparatus, the armed forces, and the organizations in other fields are, in effect, mere instruments by which the CCP maintains its hegemony, enacts its programs and policies, and realizes its ideals. The CCP not only determines the goals for and assigns functions to these instruments, but also prescribes, often in minute detail, the ways and means of attaining the goals and performing the functions. Besides this, its omnipresent members frequently take personal command of the organizations in various fields and provide direct leadership for the masses. The CCP today is truly the heart and the head of the nation, despite the fact the Great Proletarian Cultural Revolution (GPCR), which began in 1966, once shattered much of the party's formal structure and brought an inordinate number of men and women in uniform into positions of leadership both inside and outside the party. Its paramount position in the country's life requires that a survey of its policies since its seizure of nationwide power begin with a study of its ideology and organization.

The Role of Ideology

While the CCP is the heart and the head of the nation, Marxist-Leninist ideology, in turn, is the soul and guide of the CCP. Though Marxism-Leninism does not solely determine the thought and action of the CCP, inasmuch as exigencies of circumstance, personal traits of its leaders, and a host of other factors help mold its outlook and behavior, the CCP owes much of its militancy, discipline, and dynamism to it.

First, Marxist-Leninist ideology defines the ultimate purposes of the CCP:

1. The complete abolition of class distinction;
2. The withering away of the state;
3. The establishment of a Communist society in which social wealth is distributed in accordance with the principle "from each according to his ability, to each according to his needs" and in which human nature is characterized by mutual assistance and love instead of selfishness, deception, and antagonism.

This high idealism gives the CCP a tremendous moral appeal and makes it an all-inclusive "faith movement" that demands total commitment from its adherents and aims at a complete transformation of society and man instead of exclusively emphasizing day-by-day interests of expediency. The CCP's ultimate purposes give the party an international outlook. It considers its own revolutionary work in China to be an integral part of the worldwide movement for the realization of socialism and Communism and takes a keen interest in the development of that movement everywhere on the globe.

Second, Marxist-Leninist ideology imbues the CCP with the absolute certitude of self-righteousness. Believing that Communism is the greatest cause in human history and insisting that their party is the most devout, selfless, and far-sighted champion of that cause, the Chinese Communists, like Communists elsewhere, consider themselves the guarantors of the future and the agents of history. They think that whatever they do deserves the wholehearted support of society and that opposition to their programs or rejection of their leadership can only impede the construction of the promised paradise. Since opposition is considered counterrevolutionary and intolerable, they have a natural urge to transform or destroy all political forces and social institutions that obstruct the realization of their "sacred" goals. Because of its self-righteousness, Communist ideology has become quite rigid in its long-range aims, although the party may make compromises for tactical expediency. Communist self-righteousness condones the use of any means to seize and preserve the power it believes necessary to attain its goals. Communists are never inhibited by traditional moral concepts or legal injunctions, which they regard as mere instruments used by the dominating classes to subject the exploited. The present regime in Peking therefore enjoys far more freedom of action in its exercise of power than previous Chinese governments, which often acknowledged, in varying degrees, moral and customary limits to their choice of alternatives in means as well as ends.

Third, Marxist-Leninist ideology provides the Communists with a general perspective as well as specific methods by which to view the course of history, analyze socio-political problems, and decide upon organizational and tactical measures. As a guide to action it may at times prove to be grossly inaccurate and disastrously misleading, but it has been of great use to the Communist movement. For one thing, the Marxist-Leninist concept of society has made the Communists more inclined to look at social problems from an overall rather than an isolated point of view; to regard social phenomena as living, conditional, and changeable rather than dead and immutable; and to seek comprehensive solutions to the problems of society rather than piecemeal remedies for what are actually interconnected social ills. Despite its many pitfalls and impracticalities, this strong propensity to approach problems comprehensively and dialectically has enabled the Communists to perceive the intricacies of socio-political dynamics more shrewdly and to manipulate them more skillfully than those who use other approaches. Furthermore, the Communists' seemingly systematic diagnosis of the ills of antecedent societies and their ostentatious prescription for a complete reconstruction of the social order and man have a special appeal to the desperate and impatient in societies where there is great dislocation and frustration.

Additional roles played by the Marxist-Leninist ideology in the Chinese Communist movement will be discussed below, but one more point should be mentioned here: the insemination of the Communist's mind with an unshakable sense of confidence in the ultimate triumph of the revolutionary cause. This ideology proceeds from the premise that changes in the means of production inevitably bring changes in the mode of production, in the relations of production, and ultimately in the whole process of social, political, and intellectual life. Marx's historical materialism holds that the locomotive of history moves irreversibly toward socialism, because the social character of the production process in the industrial age is bound to give rise to the social ownership of the means of production. Despite its oversimplification of the law of social development, or perhaps because of it, this philosophy of history has led the Communists to believe that Communism is the wave of the future and that even the most formidable obstacles can only temporarily retard or divert it from reaching its final destination. This optimism about the future of the movement gives Communists a resilience in withstanding adversity and persisting in their revolutionary mission.

The Thought of Mao Tse-tung

Though the CCP takes Marxism-Leninism as its guide to action, it has often boasted of its unflagging efforts to uphold the principle of synthesizing the universal truth of Marxism-Leninism with the practice of the Chinese revolution. In its Constitution adopted on June 11, 1945,[1] the party expressly defined this principle of synthesis as the "Thought of Mao Tse-tung." Although the Constitution of the CCP, adopted on September 26, 1956,[2] no longer made any direct reference to the "Thought of Mao Tse-tung," it nevertheless reiterated the necessity of applying the principles of Marxism-Leninism in a flexible and creative way. Thus the 1956 charter implicitly recognized the continued sanctity of the "Thought of Mao Tse-tung." Some of Mao's ardent supporters during the GPCR alleged that the deletion was the result of an anti-Mao conspiracy perpetrated by Liu Shao-ch'i and other top party leaders who subsequently became major targets of the GPCR; it was actually done in deference to the Soviet campaign against "the cult of the individual" launched at the Twentieth Congress of the Communist Party of the Soviet Union in February 1956, and Mao himself reportedly endorsed the action.[3] To be sure, the economic setbacks resulting from the ill-fated Great Leap Forward and the Commune Movement, which Mao personally launched in 1958, caused many of his erstwhile supporters such as Liu Shao-ch'i to circumscribe his authority by quietly discouraging the invocation of his Thought. But no sooner had this devious effort begun than the fourth volume of Mao's *Selected Works* appeared in September 1960. Meanwhile, Lin Piao, who had become Minister of National Defense a year earlier and who was to be Mao's most powerful supporter in the CCP in the next decade and more, unfolded a new campaign within the armed forces to exalt the "Thought of Mao Tse-tung" with unprecedented vigor. Before long the party apparatus deemed it wise to follow suit despite its domination at that time by Liu Shao-ch'i

[1] An English text of the Constitution can be found in Liu Shao-ch'i, *On the Party* (Peking: Foreign Languages Press, 1954), pp. 155–204.

[2] An English text of this Constitution is given in *The Eighth National Congress of the Communist Party of China* (Peking: Foreign Languages Press, 1956), II, 137–168.

[3] See Ch'en I's remarks on the matter in *SCMM*, No. 635 (December 2, 1968), p. 14.

and other incipient "revisionists." The campaign gained further momentum during the GPCR. Needless to say, the party Constitution, adopted by the triumphant pro-Mao forces on April 14, 1969, at the end of the GPCR,[4] explicitly reaffirmed Mao's Thought along with Marxism-Leninism as the theoretical basis guiding the CCP's thinking.

In addition to hailing the "Thought of Mao Tse-tung" as a theory that unites Marxism-Leninism with the practice of the Chinese revolution, Chinese Communist spokesmen as well as the new party Constitution have asserted that it is a further development of Marxism-Leninism now that imperialism is approaching complete collapse and socialism is advancing to victory all over the world, and that it is living Marxism-Leninism at its highest.[5] Mao has been exalted as not only the most outstanding revolutionary theoretician, statesman, poet, and scientist in China, but also "the greatest Marxist-Leninist of contemporary time."[6] Among Mao's alleged contributions to Marxism-Leninism are his pronouncements on the theory of knowledge, the theory of contradiction, and such policies and tactics as the question of leadership in a bourgeois democratic revolution, the revolutionary role of the peasantry, contradictions within socialist society, peaceful transformation of the bourgeoisie, party rectification, the people's democratic dictatorship, armed struggle, the mass line, and the theory of continuing the revolution under the dictatorship of the proletariat.[7]

Although some of the claims of Mao's originality are exaggerated, he must be credited with more explicit and cogent expositions of certain Marxist-Leninist tenets, such as the theory of contradiction in socialist society, that have made them more serviceable to the Communist movement. The Marxist-Leninist "science of revolution" certainly has been enriched by Mao's advocacy of a protracted revolutionary war from self-sustained rural bases, by his use of guerrilla and guerrilla-type mobile warfare against overwhelmingly superior forces of the enemy, and by his integration of these two measures with an appeal to the proprietary instincts of

[4] An English text of this Constitution is given in *Peking Review*, No. 18 (April 30, 1969), pp. 36–39.

[5] "Long Live Mao Tse-tung's Thought," editorial in *People's Daily,** July 1, 1966.

[6] *Ibid.* See also T'ao Chu's article in *Nan-fang Daily,** April 4, 1964.

[7] There has been a divergence of views on Mao's originality among Western scholars on China. See, for example, Arthur Cohen, *The Communism of Mao Tse-tung* (Chicago: University of Chicago Press, 1964); and Stuart R. Schram, *The Political Thought of Mao Tse-tung* (New York: Frederick A. Praeger, Inc., 1967).

the landless inhabitants in the countryside. While the Communist world is plagued with "revisionism," the Thought of Mao Tse-tung, which calls for resolute and unremitting struggle against attempts to adulterate orthodox Marxism-Leninism, has become the principal embodiment of revolutionary socialism and an important source of inspiration for many revolutionary forces throughout the world. Hoping to remedy some of the common ills of the age of "specialization," "elitism," and "social alienation," Mao has fought against "bureaucratism," called for mass participation in the administration of public affairs, and insisted on "serving the people" and subordinating particularized interests or purely technical points of view to the requirements of the overall situation. This last tenet has been officially expressed in the much-repeated slogan "Politics Takes Command," although quite a few Western observers have often misunderstood the true meaning of the metaphor.

Mao's skillful application of Marxism-Leninism to the Chinese Communist movement has been generally recognized as his greatest theoretical and practical contribution to revolutionary "science." Without his judicious determination of such delicate questions as to when, where, and how a given concept or policy of Marxism-Leninism is to be applied, the Chinese Communist movement since the mid-1930's could not have been as successful as it has been. Marx, Engels, Lenin, and Stalin did not always provide the CCP with a detailed and precise operational code for the implementation of programs in China and, in certain situations, prescribed alternative and even conflicting recipes. The failure of the Comintern and the CCP leadership to adopt proper measures at the proper time in accordance with the general theories of Marxism-Leninism contributed greatly to the catastrophic setbacks of the CCP between 1926 and 1935. The theoretical significance of Mao's application of Marxism-Leninism lies in his verification of the efficacy of some of its untested concepts and strategies. A notable example is the Leninist-Stalinist postulation that a Communist movement can triumph even if it has to derive its strength mainly from the peasantry instead of the urban proletariat. By proving for the first time the validity of such theories with concrete deeds, Mao gave them real meaning and reinforced their appeal to revolutionaries elsewhere. In view of the traditional Communist emphasis on the dependence of theory on practice, Mao's feat is certainly as important a contribution to the Marxist-Leninist "science of revolution" as any "new" theory might have been.

Regardless of the exact nature of Mao's contributions to Marxism-Leninism, the Chinese effort to glorify him has not been a senseless undertaking, but on the contrary, has been of great service to the CCP itself. First, crediting Mao with developing the theories of Marx, Engels, Lenin, and Stalin has the psychological effect of Sinifying these alien doctrines, thus facilitating their acceptance by the Chinese people. Moreover, by fostering the image of its leader as the foremost theorist as well as the most resourceful statesman of the contemporary world Communist movement—probably a valid claim—the CCP has managed to endow him with such great prestige that millions of Chinese have come to regard him as the source of all wisdom and the infallible guardian of the party and of the country. His writings have assumed the sanctity of holy canons, and his commands almost always elicit zealous compliance—all of which cannot but serve to maximize the unity and effectiveness of the CCP. Perhaps Lin Piao's letter, dated March 11, 1966, concerning the study and application of Mao's works to industry and communications gives the most succinct official exposition of their importance to China at her present stage of development. The letter reads in part: "China is a great socialist state of the dictatorship of the proletariat and has a population of 700 million. It needs unified thinking, revolutionary thinking, and correct thinking. That is Mao Tse-tung's thinking." The aspects of Mao's Thought that transcend ideological differences and that have been particularly useful to China's nation-building efforts are the extolment of hard work, plain living, self-reliance, inventiveness, and fearlessness before difficulties and danger.

Organizational Principles of the CCP

With Marxist-Leninist-Maoist ideology as its basis, the CCP derives much of its strength from a tightly knit and disciplined organization. Interdependent and mutually supplementary, ideology and organization are indeed the two pillars of the party. The CCP has obviously appreciated Lenin's dictum that the working class can and will inevitably be an all-conquering force if its ideological unity is strengthened by an efficient organization.[8] In line with Lenin's teachings, the CCP's structure is nationwide and arranged pyramidically, roughly resembling the territorial tiers of the state administrative hierarchy. At the base of the pyramid lie the primary organizations in factories, mines, enterprises, neighborhoods, governmental offices, schools, military units, communes, production brigades, and production teams. The fledgling party member must usually belong to and work in one of these primary party organ-

[8] V. I. Lenin, *One Step Forward, Two Steps Back* (London: Lawrence and Wishart, 1948), pp. 114–115.

izations. Together these become county or city organizations, which, in turn, become provincial, regional, and special municipal organizations. (Some cities are directly controlled by the central authority in Peking.) At the summit of the pyramid are the central or national party organs that control the entire structure and determine both general line and specific courses of action for the entire party (Figure 1).

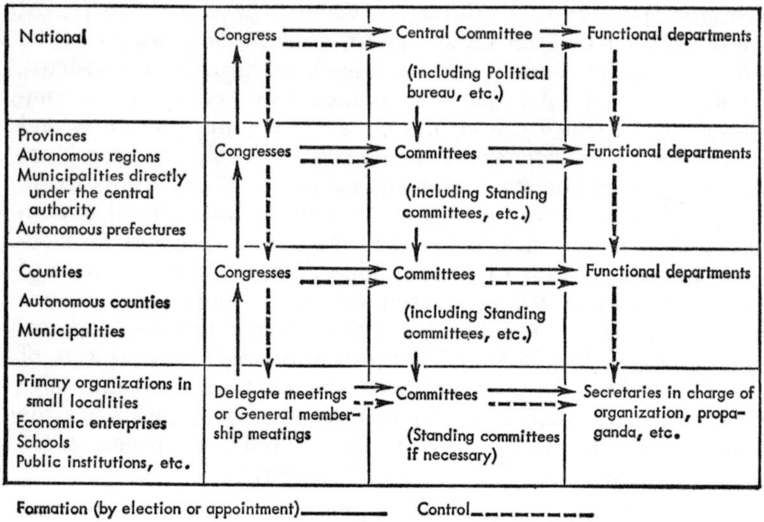

FIGURE 1. *The Chinese Communist Party Structure.*

The organization and operation of the CCP are supposedly based on "democratic centralism," which, as defined in the party Constitution of 1945, originally consisted of the following principles:

1. The leading bodies at all levels of the party must be elected;
2. The leading bodies at all levels must submit reports at fixed intervals to the lower party organizations that elected them;
3. Each individual party member must submit to the decisions of the party organization to which he belongs; minorities must submit to the majority; the lower party organizations must submit to the higher party organizations; and all constituent party organizations must submit to the Central Committee;
4. Party discipline must be strictly observed and party decisions carried out unconditionally.

However, these principles do not accurately indicate how the party then actually worked. Generally speaking, the CCP was highly conscious of the importance of promoting internal democracy and definitely recognized the need to curb the tendencies of "subjectivism" and "commandism" and to develop "positivism" and "creativity" on the part of individual party members and local party organizations. In the meantime, however, the party clearly emphasized centralist more than democratic principles because of its belief that a hierarchical and strictly disciplined organization was necessary for the strength and maneuverability needed to fulfill the herculean tasks of revolution and reconstruction. For this reason, the election of important officials of any party organization could be valid only upon ratification by the party organization at a higher level, and the executives could appoint, dismiss, or transfer subordinate officials when lower congresses were in recess. The now-famous reorganization of the Peking CCP Municipal Committee in June 1966, involving the dismissal of P'eng Chen as its First Secretary, was done by the Central Committee in accordance with this usage.

To check the increased bureaucratism since it had come to national power, the CCP, in September 1956, decided to enlarge somewhat the democratic dimension of the organizational principle by stipulating in its new Constitution the following additional rules:

1. The leading bodies at higher levels must give careful consideration to the suggestions or requests of those at lower levels; and
2. The party organizations at all levels must combine individual responsibility with collective leadership.

Despite these provisions, bureaucratization of the CCP continued in the ensuing years. This prompted Mao and his loyal supporters at the Ninth National Party Congress in April 1969 to go still further in fostering a genuine measure of democracy that, they hoped, would really complement the party's continuing stress on discipline. This they did by inserting several truly novel provisions into Article 5 of the present party Constitution, which defines the meaning of democratic centralism. The first of these new stipulations enjoins the leading bodies of the party at all levels to "listen to the opinions of the masses both inside and outside the party" and, more important, to "accept their supervision." Although the exact scope and procedures of mass supervision of party organizations remain to be delineated in detail, the sheer proclamation of the new injunction certainly marked a significant departure from the Bolshevik tradition which emphasizes the party's role as the vanguard of the proletariat and brooks no interference with party affairs by the popular masses, whose political consciousness is perceived to be too low for that weighty task. There is also the provision that "party members have the right to criticize party organizations and leading members at all levels and make proposals to them." In view of the sacredness of Marxism-Leninism and Mao's Thought, it is safe to assume that neither the right to criticize nor the privilege to supervise party organizations permits anyone to undermine that ideology or any of the basic socio-political programs based on it. However, people of the rank and file today seem to be genuinely encouraged to speak their minds and even to take issue with party organizations if it will better serve the cause of the party and the country. To encourage legitimate dissent and to authorize subordinates to expose political deviations and other wrong-doings of their superiors, Article 5 also states that if "a party member holds different views with regard to the decisions or directives of the party organizations, he is allowed to reserve his views and has the right to bypass the immediate leadership and report directly to higher levels, up to and including the Central Committee and the Chairman of the Central Committee."

The National Party Congress. In theory, the supreme body within the powerful central organization is the National Party Congress. The Eighth National Party Congress was composed of about 1000 delegates elected in 1956 by congresses in the provinces, autonomous regions, the cities of Peking, Shanghai, and Tientsin, the organs of the central party headquarters and People's Liberation Army, and the agencies of the Central People's Government. The delegates were chosen by their respective units under the careful guidance of the controlling party bureaucrats as in virtually all the other elections both in the party and the country. Prior to 1956, the successive national party congresses held only one session each, with delegates elected anew each time. However, the 1956 revision of the party Constitution introduced a five-year term for the National Party Congress and the congresses at the provincial and county levels. In reality, the term of that particular congress did not expire until the Ninth National Party Congress met on April 1, 1969. As the CCP then was still in the process of rebuilding itself on the ruins of the GPCR (during which the party structure below the national level was deliberately scrapped), the procedures for selecting the more than 1500 delegates to the Ninth National Party Congress could not but be different from those adopted for the Eighth National Party Congress. There is no detailed information on how they actually differed; the official press communique on the opening of the Ninth National Party Congress merely reported that the delegates to the Congress "were unanimously chosen in accordance with the decision of the enlarged 12th plenum of the Eighth Central Committee of the party through full democratic consultation by party organizations at various levels and after seeking the opinions of the broad masses." However, the solicitation of opinions from the broad masses on the selection of delegates was an unprecedented process in the party's history, and its adoption reflected Mao's determination to prevent his party from degenerating into an organization totally controlled by self-interested functionaries.

According to the party Constitution of 1956, the Central Committee was supposed to convene the National Party Congress at least once a year under normal circumstances. The same document also authorized the Central Committee to advance or postpone a regular session of the Congress if "extraordinary conditions" existed. Consequently, after the adjournment of its first session, the Eighth National Party Congress held only one other brief session in May 1958. Far more realistic, the present party Constitution no longer calls for annual meetings of the Congress. Instead, the current charter states that the Congress shall be convened by the Central Committee every five years and that, under "special conditions," it may be convened before its due date or postponed.

The following powers and functions are customarily assigned to the National Party Congress:

1. To hear and examine the reports of the Central Committee and other central organs.
2. To determine the party's line and policy.
3. To amend the party Constitution.
4. To elect the Central Committee.

In reality, however, the Congress, handicapped as it is by an unwieldy membership and by infrequent and often brief sessions, is not in a position to exercise these powers. As the records of the two sessions of the Eighth National Party Congress and that of the first and only session of the Ninth National Party Congress show, the actions of the assembled delegates were essentially formalistic: they heard and "studied" reports on various phases of the work of the party, held discussions on programs for future action, gave approval to what had been done or was anticipated, and elected members of the Central Committee nominated by the top party leadership "in consultation with" the delegates themselves, though perhaps the consultation was conducted somewhat more earnestly at the Ninth National Party Congress than on earlier occasions.

A major function of the National Party Congress is to focus the attention of the whole party on the new programs and policies unveiled at its meetings and whip up enthusiasm in the rank and file for their implementation. These meetings are held with great fanfare, the top leaders appearing in full force to add glamour to the proceedings. The delegates themselves, especially those who are relatively obscure, can participate physically and emotionally in the high drama of "intraparty democracy" with such dignitaries as Chairman Mao Tse-tung and Premier Chou En-lai. Here they have a chance to sit and identify with the men they have long adulated. They not only achieve distinction but also find the excitement that deepens their commitment to the party and reinforces their bond with the leaders.

The Central Committee. A far more important agency of the CCP is the Central Committee, and within it, the Politburo, the ruling organ of China. According to the party Constitution, the Central Committee creates and supervises the operational agencies of the party and decides all major policy matters in the intervals between Congresses. The Central Committee elects the members of the Politburo, the Standing Committee of the Politburo, as well as the chairman and vice-chairman of the Central Committee. It is also charged with guiding the work of the central state organs, the People's Liberation Army, and the people's organizations through "leading party members' groups" within them.

The party Constitution of 1956 required the Central Committee to hold at least two plenary sessions a year. In practice, the Eighth Central Committee, which was in office from September 1956 to March 1969, held only twelve plenums; and most of the sessions were short, three of them lasting for only one day each. In another manifestation of great realism, the present party Constitution refrains from specifying any number of plenary sessions of the Central Committee in a given period of time, but authorizes the Politburo to convene the plenums of the Central Committee at its discretion. As of June 1973, the Ninth Central Committee had met in two plenary sessions. Held on the afternoon of April 28, 1969, immediately upon the adjournment of the Ninth National Party Congress, the first plenum devoted itself almost exclusively to the election of the chairman and vice-chairman of the Central Committee and to the election of a Politburo, including the latter's

Standing Committee. The second plenum met from August 24 to September 6, 1970. It apparently had a much broader agenda. The proceedings of all the plenums are closed, but reports are given out on at least some of the matters discussed, and formal announcements are made on the important actions taken. It is difficult to obtain a clear picture of the actual work of the plenums, but from all indications the Politburo always determines the agenda of the plenums and controls their final actions, even though in some recent plenums there has been a candid and serious exchange of views on important party and state matters.

Until 1969 the Central Committee was an assembly of the most powerful Chinese Communists who, even at the time of their election to that body, were already holding multiple strategic positions in the party, government, armed forces, and people's organizations and who, of course, continued to hold important offices after their election to the Committee. In 1969, a sizeable number of genuine workers, peasants, and soldiers found their way to the Ninth Central Committee as beneficiaries of Mao's policy of elevating exemplary people of the rank and file to the high councils of the party. But since only the most celebrated model workers, peasants, and soldiers received this extraordinary recognition and since many of them have subsequently been given positions of considerable responsibility in addition to their original work, their presence on the Central Committee does not really alter its elitist nature. Thus, the importance of the Central Committee continues to lie not so much in what it formally does at its plenums as in the authority that its members individually wield in their fields of operation and the influence committeemen exert on the Politburo by virtue of their relatively easy access to the members of this exclusive club. In fact, the members of the Politburo are invariably selected from the Central Committee and retain their Committee memberships after having been elected. Viewed in this context, the role of the Central Committee closely resembles the "establishment" of a Western country.

The Central Committee has both full and alternate members. Full members are entitled to vote, while alternate members are only entitled to take part in discussions. There has been a steady trend to enlarge the size of the Central Committee because of the need to give recognition to a growing number of men and women who have rendered much meritorious service to the party. Specifically, whereas only 44 full members and 24 alternates were elected in 1945 to the Seventh Central Committee, the Eighth Central Committee, as first elected in 1956, consisted of 97 full members and 73 alternates. Then in May 1958, the Second Session of the Eighth National Party Congress elected 25 additional alternate members to the Eighth Central Committee. In April 1969, at the end of the GPCR, the Ninth Central Committee came into being with as many as 170 full members and 109 alternates. This further increase in the Central Committee's size enabled the victorious Mao-Lin leadership to place on that body "all of the new proletarian fighters who had come forth during the GPCR" as well as those veteran leaders of the party who had survived. In contrast to the remarkable continuity in membership between the Seventh and the Eighth Central Committees[9] more than two-thirds of the full and alternate members of the outgoing Eighth Central Committee were dropped from the Ninth Central Committee after having been denounced as "capitalist roaders." This difference, in turn, reflected the basic stability and cohesion of the Chinese Communist elite in earlier years and the discord and schisms that had begun to beset the party since the late 1950's. On the other hand, the policy of rehabilitating all erring comrades who have turned over a new leaf was reflected in the reelection to the Ninth Central Committee of several men who had fallen from political favor prior to the GPCR. Of equal significance was the election to the Central Committee of such preeminent scholars and scientists as Kuo Mo-jo, Li Ssu-kuang, and Ch'ien Hsueh-sen. Undoubtedly, the Maoist leadership hoped by this gesture to bring home the point that, despite the fact that one of the major thrusts of the GPCR was to criticize and repudiate the "bourgeois reactionary academic authorities," those scholars and scientists who dedicated their knowledge and talents to the construction of socialism not only need not fear harassment but might even receive political recognition.

Some foreign observers have called attention to the large number of military men and political commissars of military units among the full and alternate members of the Ninth Central Committee. It is true that men in uniform account for as many as roughly 40 per cent of the regular members and 35 per cent of the alternate members, clearly attesting to the enormous role that the army has played since the GPCR. But these percentages are not unprecedented in the history of the party. For example, of the 97 full members of the Eighth Central Committee, 66 per cent of them had spent most of their party life as military commanders or senior political commissars. Military commanders and political commissars

[9] Franklin W. Houn, "The Eighth Central Committee of the Chinese Communist Party: A Study of an Elite," *American Political Science Review,* LI (June 1957), 392–404.

also accounted for a large percentage of the alternate members of the Eighth Central Committee. Not only is it not unprecedented, it also does not signify military domination of the party. First, most senior officers of the People's Liberation Army have been primarily loyal to the party rather than the army. After all, the overwhelming majority of them began their careers in the army only after they had first joined the party. Second, the army does not have a monolithic officer corps who could challenge Mao's leadership, although some key personalities in the army have disagreed with Mao in their capacity as senior party leaders. Third, with some exceptions, the army has been the most faithful implementor of Mao's policies. Instead of degenerating into a hotbed of warlordism, it now best exemplifies the Maoist style of work and organization. The Maoist leadership's determination to ensure the loyalty of the army and its ability to rid the army of both actual and potential dissidents during the GPCR were evidenced by the apparent ease with which it dismissed Chief of the General Staff Lo Jui-ch'ing, Marshal Ho Lung, Acting Chief of the General Staff Yang Ch'eng-wu, and many other senior officers, including the commanders of six of the thirteen military regions. The resolve and ability was even more dramatically demonstrated in September 1971 when Lin Piao was purged, along with five of his proteges in the CCP Politburo and an undisclosed number of senior officers in the army.

The Politburo and its Standing Committee. Long the center of authority, the Politburo is authorized by the party Constitution to exercise the powers and functions of the Central Committee between plenums. This is in accord with the principle of centralism, which calls for vesting the ultimate decision-making power in a small group of leaders at the zenith of the hierarchy. The Politburo meets frequently, on occasion several times a week, and the meetings usually take place in Peking, though a few have been held elsewhere. An air of informality presumably permeates the proceedings. In its deliberations, it probably tries to arrive at a consensus by discussion instead of a mere show of hands. For all practical purposes, the power and jurisdiction of the Politburo is transcendent and boundless: it determines the general line and the concrete policy for all matters of national importance by arrogating to itself most of the substantive functions that belong to other organs of the party and state, such as the National Party Congress, the National People's Congress, and the State Council. It converts these organs into mere tools for imparting formal legitimacy to its acts and decisions and for enacting them. Furthermore, the Politburo unifies and directs the vast, multifarious activities in all realms of national life. Finally, it selects and controls the high-echelon personnel of the party, government, armed forces, and other public organizations. However, like all other ruling bodies throughout the world, the Politburo is not omnipotent. Apart from the social, economic, and technological constraints upon its choice of policy alternatives, the nature and quality of its decisions are conditioned by the information that it receives from the men in charge of the various subordinated agencies. The enforcement of its decisions is also affected by the attitude, skill, experience, and enthusiasm of the personnel at the operational level.[10] Moreover, serious dissensions within the Politburo, even if carefully camouflaged (such as those which occurred in the years preceding the GPCR), can prevent it from acting decisively for a time.

Membership in the Politburo is the most exalted and powerful position in the CCP hierarchy. Since Mao's ascendancy, the task of determining its membership has become, in effect, his personal prerogative, though the Central Committee still retains its formal authority in the matter. In exercising this prerogative in the three decades prior to the GPCR, Mao was consistently guided by three major considerations: (1) the candidates' seniority in the party; (2) their contributions to his rise to power and the success of the CCP; and (3) their current usefulness and faithfulness to him and the party. Since Mao appointed only individuals who could satisfy all or nearly all of these requirements, his appointees were invariably persons of the greatest prestige and influence, and were selected from among the more important members of the Central Committee. Although the Politburo elected in April 1969 at the end of the GPCR consisted of several persons whose seniority in the party had not been particularly high by CCP standards and who had been relatively obscure in the Chinese Communist movement until the outbreak of the GPCR, their prominent roles during that momentous struggle against "revisionism" certainly gave them special claims to membership afterward. Appendix I shows the evolution of the membership of the Politburo since 1949.

The Politburo contains an inner circle known as the Standing Committee. This small group of preeminent leaders plays a more important role in initiating and deliberating policies than the Politburo as a whole, and on occasion even makes decisions in the name of the Politburo without consulting the other members. The

[10] See, for example, Michael C. Oksenberg, "Policy Making Under Mao, 1949–68: An Overview," in John H. Lindbeck, ed., *China: Management of a Revolutionary Society* (Seattle, Wash.: University of Washington Press, 1971), pp. 79–115.

party Constitution also authorizes the Standing Committee to "exercise the powers and functions of the Central Committee when the latter is not in session." To emphasize the exalted position of the Standing Committee in the party hierarchy, it is elected not by the Politburo but by the Central Committee at its plenary session. Prior to its reorganization in August 1966, the Standing Committee consisted of Mao Tse-tung, Liu Shao-ch'i, Chou En-lai, Chu Teh, Ch'en Yun, Lin Piao, and Teng Hsiao-p'ing. As a result of the reorganization the Standing Committee was enlarged, and the rankings of the individual members were arranged in this order: Mao Tse-tung, Lin Piao, Chou En-lai, T'ao Chu, Ch'en Po-ta, Teng Hsiao-p'ing, K'ang Sheng, Liu Shao-ch'i, Chu Teh, Li Fu-ch'un, and Ch'en Yun.[11] As noted in Appendix I, shortly after the reorganization, T'ao Chu, Teng Hsiao-p'ing, and Liu Shao-ch'i fell from favor completely. Thus from the fall of 1966 to the spring of 1969, the actual membership of the Standing Committee comprised only Mao Tse-tung, Lin Piao, Chou En-lai, Ch'en Po-ta, K'ang Sheng, Chu Teh, Li Fu-ch'un, and Ch'en Yun, although throughout that period Chu Teh and Ch'en Yun never were as active in party affairs as the others, and Li Fu-ch'un's role also began to diminish after 1967. By then, Mao's informal "proletarian headquarters," consisting of Mao himself, Lin Piao, Chou En-lai, Ch'en Po-ta, K'ang Sheng, and Chiang Ch'ing, had become the interim supreme policy-making body of the party, pending a complete overhaul of the CCP machinery at the end of the GPCR. This reorganization took place in April 1969. On April 29, the newly elected Ninth Central Committee elected a new Politburo and designated Mao Tse-tung, Lin Piao, Chou En-lai, Ch'en Po-ta, and K'ang Sheng as members of the Standing Committee. Upon the "purge" of Ch'en Po-ta[12] and Lin Piao, only Mao Tse-tung, Chou En-lai, and the ailing K'ang Sheng remained on the Committee. As of June 1973, the seats vacated by Lin Piao and Ch'en Po-ta had not been formally reassigned. But the added prominence in party and state affairs that Chiang Ch'ing and Yeh Chien-ying had enjoyed since September 1971 suggested that they had possibly joined Mao and Chou in the inner circle of the Politburo on a de facto basis.

The Chairman and Vice-Chairman of the Central Committee and the rise and fall of Lin Piao as Mao's potential successor. Created in 1945, the chairmanship of the Central Committee is unquestionably the prime seat of political power, overshadowing

[11] For an account of this rearrangement, see Appendix I.
[12] For an account of Ch'en Po-ta's disgrace, see Appendix I.

all the other offices in the party and the government. Serving concurrently as chairman of the Politburo, Mao Tse-tung has held this post since its inception. It is from him rather than anybody else that the ultimate and most authoritative statements of policy and doctrine are expected. He is the personification of the whole party and nation, even though his only official post in the government since April 1959 is a seat in what is essentially an ornamental organ —the National People's Congress. During the GPCR he was hailed by his ardent followers as "our great teacher, great leader, great supreme commander, and great helmsman." Then in October 1971, he was given a new title—Supreme Commander of the Whole Nation and the Whole Army—in official news reports of the observances in Peking of the twenty-first anniversary of the People's Republic of China.

The primacy of Mao's position as chairman of the Central Committee is not the result of any specific provisions in the party Constitution; rather it reflects his accomplishments and the Communist principle that within the party the leader occupies a place of special importance by virtue of his being "the most authoritative, influential, and experienced" individual. So far Mao's preponderant influence in the party has not resulted in any personal tyranny akin to that of Stalin. Unlike Stalin, who willfully liquidated many prominent leaders of his party, Mao has not resorted to physical violence against his opponents. Indeed, men like Ch'en Shao-yü, Li Li-san, and Chang Kuo-t'ao, who fought Mao for years, are still alive. Their past records are still denounced in the historical literature of the party, but Mao has treated them with considerable leniency. Ch'en Shao-yü and Li Li-san were made members of the Central Committee in 1945 and again in 1956. In 1949 Mao gave both men important posts in the newly organized Central People's Government. In the early 1960's the press identified Li as a secretary of the CCP's North China Bureau. Although Ch'en went to the Soviet Union in 1956 for "a rest" and then refused to return to China, his action appeared to have been caused by political frustration rather than fear of any danger to his life if he did go back to Peking. The exclusion of Li and Ch'en from the Ninth Central Committee in 1969 was due to Li's complicity in the "conspiracy to sabotage" Mao's policies on the heels of the Great Leap Forward and Ch'en's denunciation of the GPCR while in exile in Russia. Although Chang Kuo-t'ao was expelled from the party after his defection in 1938 and is now in exile in Hong Kong, Mao nevertheless has shown an apparent solicitude for his personal welfare.[13]

[13] Snow, *The Other Side of the River*, p. 149.

Although the purge of Kao Kang and Jao Shu-shih in the mid-1950's resulted in the alleged suicide of Kao and the imprisonment of Jao, these tragedies should not be blamed primarily on Mao, for he seemed to have no compelling reason to treat the victims harshly; their alleged antiparty activities posed no challenge to his own position, despite a contrary allegation made during the GPCR. However, there is every reason to believe that Liu Shao-ch'i and, to a lesser extent, Chou En-lai insisted on stern punishment of Kao and Jao, because Jao sought to dislodge Liu from his vice-chairmanship of the Central Committee and Chou from his premiership of the State Council, and to make Kao, the senior partner of the "antiparty alliance," Mao's heir-apparent—a position for which Liu had been groomed from 1945 on. At the time of the purge, Kao's position in the CCP was just below those occupied by Liu Shao-ch'i and Chou En-lai (and possibly Ch'en Yun). In 1959, the policy of eschewing extreme penalties against close associates in error was applied to Marshal P'eng Teh-huai. Although he was dismissed as Minister of National Defense that year over serious policy disagreements, his name was kept on the roster of the Politburo until August 1966. His "crime" was not openly mentioned in the official press until May 1967, during the peak of the GPCR. Together with his towering accomplishments, Mao's apparent benignity seems to have greatly endeared him to many of his followers, creating a fatherly image of him and evoking a degree of respect, affection, and devotion not to be found in political associations based solely on fear or expediency.

Mao's attitude toward the problem of succession also differs greatly from those of many other modern dictators. Unafraid that the fostering of a successor may unintentionally bring forth a challenger to his own position and cognizant of the merit of making early preparations for a smooth transfer of power at the time of his retirement or death, Mao began to groom Liu Shao-ch'i as his heir-apparent at least as early as 1945. In that year he had Liu elected the sole vice-chairman of the Seventh Central Committee of the party even though the party Constitution did not then provide such a post. In September 1956, the Eighth Central Committee reaffirmed Liu's preeminence among Mao's "close comrades" by making him the first of its four (later five) vice-chairmen, taking precedence over Chou En-lai, Chu Teh, and Ch'en Yun. Two years later, Mao enhanced Liu's prestige further by dividing the Standing Committee of the Politburo into "the first and second fronts," with Liu heading the first front, which was to play a more active role in party affairs, while Mao himself voluntarily receded to the second front where he and the other unidentified party leaders no longer concerned themselves with "routine matters." [14] In April 1959, Mao again raised Liu's prestige and authority by relinquishing the chairmanship of the state to him.[15] Until his replacement by Lin Piao as heir-apparent, Liu had been Mao's closest associate throughout the preceding twenty years or more, often appearing as if he were Mao's other self. It was generally agreed that he contributed the most to Mao's consolidation of power in the party during the Yenan period (1937–1947). Besides attending to doctrinal and organizational affairs of the party on behalf of Mao, Liu brought into the party, whose cadres had been depleted during the Long March, many of the politically gifted and relatively well-educated young men and women who after 1949 were to play increasingly important leadership roles in the party and the state. Liu had been the principal "talent scout" for the party in Peking and other centers of learning in the Kuomintang-controlled areas when he was the CCP's leading underground agent from 1936 to 1937.

Liu Shao-ch'i was replaced by Lin Piao as Mao's potential successor at the eleventh plenum of the Eighth Central Committee, held in August 1966 during the GPCR. The plenum reduced the number of vice-chairmanships of the Central Committee from five to one and elected Lin Piao to the post. Although the communique of the plenum did not mention this important change in the party's top leadership, Lin's new role in the CCP immediately became known to the whole world a few days later on August 18 when he stood next to Mao Tse-tung on the Heavenly Peace Gate rostrum during the first mass rally of the Red Guards. He occupied the same prominent place at seven additional rallies between August 30 and No-

[14] This arrangement was first disclosed by Mao on October 24, 1966, at a work conference of the CCP Central Committee. See *Current Background* (hereafter cited as *CB*), No. 891 (October 8, 1969), pp. 71, 75.

[15] Mao's relinquishment of the chairmanship of the state in 1959 was officially explained at the time as a measure to enable Mao to devote all his time to party policy and ideology. Non-Communist observers generally thought that Mao did it to groom Liu Shao-ch'i as his future successor. Then, early in January 1967, Red Guard wall posters in Peking quoted Mao as having told the party Central Committee in October 1966 that his action in 1959 was not voluntary but was forced upon him by Liu Shao-ch'i and Teng Hsiao-p'ing. The posters further quoted Mao as stating that on that occasion Liu Shao-ch'i and Teng Hsiao-p'ing "treated me as if I were their dead parent at a funeral" and thereafter "never bothered to consult me on vital matters." The accuracy of these quotations is open to question, however, in view of the fact that the communiqué of the eleventh plenum of the Eighth Central Committee issued on August 12, 1966, attributed authorship to and praised Mao for many important policies in the preceding years. For a text of the communiqué, see *Peking Review,* No. 34 (August 19, 1966), pp. 4–8.

vember 26. On January 28, 1967, the official press at long last explicitly identified Lin as the sole vice-chairman of the CCP Central Committee. The New China News Agency released the text of a message of respect to Chairman Mao and Vice-Chairman Lin sent by the People's Liberation Army units stationed in Shansi Province in the wake of the pro-Mao "revolutionary rebels' " seizure of power there from those in the provincial party committee and people's government "who had taken the road of capitalism." In the meantime, Hsiao Hua, Director of the General Political Department of the People's Liberation Army, referred to Lin as "Chairman Mao's closest comrade-in-arms, his best student, and the best example in creatively studying and applying Chairman Mao's works." Shedding light on one of the most important reasons for Lin's designation as Mao's new potential successor, Hsiao Hua stated: "Comrade Lin Piao has always implemented Mao Tse-tung's thought and carried out his correct lines most faithfully, firmly, and thoroughly. At every crucial turn in the history of the Chinese revolution, Comrade Lin Piao has resolutely taken his stand on the side of Chairman Mao and carried out uncompromising struggle against every kind of 'left' and right erroneous line and has courageously safeguarded Mao Tse-tung's thought." [16]

Liu Shao-ch'i, on the other hand, soon became the principal target of Red Guard wall posters in Peking and elsewhere, and was condemned for sabotaging the GPCR and for being the backstage boss of P'eng Chen and other "bourgeois counterrevolutionaries who had usurped power in the party and the government and who were plotting to restore capitalism in China." According to dispatches from Peking by Japanese and other foreign correspondents, on December 27, 1966, Liu Shao-ch'i and Teng Hsiao-p'ing (General Secretary of the CCP Central Committee) were brought to a mass rally in Peking, where they were denounced for their opposition to Mao Tse-tung and Mao's Thought. In April 1967, the official press joined forces with the Red Guard wall posters in the "struggle" against Liu Shao-ch'i. Obliquely identifying Liu as "the top party person in authority taking the capitalist road," the press characterized him as China's Khrushchev and "the chief representative of the bourgeoisie inside the apparatus of the proletarian dictatorship." The press attack quickly ignited a nationwide mass campaign "to criticize and repudiate Liu and the bourgeois reactionary line that he put forward." The tenor of the charges against him made it plain that Liu's political guilt stemmed mainly from

[16] "Hsiao Hua's Talks to a Meeting of Cadres of the Air Force," *ibid.*, No. 42 (October 14, 1966), pp. 6–8.

his attempt since the ill-fated Great Leap Forward in 1958–59 to circumvent a wide range of Mao's policies; he was also accused of using his large personal following in the party and the government to frustrate Mao's effort to build up Lin Piao as the party's future leader. The building up of Lin probably began with his appointment as Minister of National Defense in August 1959 and was followed by: the launching of the campaign to emulate the People's Liberation Army in December 1963; the establishment of political departments in the governmental ministries, educational institutions, and business enterprises in 1964; and his appointment in December of that year as the ranking vice-premier of the State Council. These measures enhanced the prestige of Lin and the military establishments under his control, and permitted pro-Lin political commissars to secure footholds in various important nonmilitary organizations, which until then had been largely manned by Liu Shao-ch'i's protégés.

In view of the great trust that Mao had placed in Liu in the years preceding the Great Leap Forward, Liu's subsequent infidelities to Mao and his "revolutionary line" must have been most disturbing to Mao and his followers. The denunciation of Liu was particularly bitter, and his history of error was extended back not only to 1949, when the CCP seized power, but all the way back to the mid-1930's when he was in charge of the party's underground operations in the Peking area. (Some denunciatory articles traced Liu's "infamous deeds" even further back to the early 1920's when Liu first joined the CCP.) Perhaps the editorial in the *Liberation Army Daily* on April 11, 1967, most succinctly summed up the main charges against Liu:

> The top Party person in authority taking the capitalist road, obstinately taking a reactionary stand, opposes the Party, socialism, and Mao Tse-tung's thought. In the period of the democratic revolution, time and again he pursued the line of capitulation to the bourgeoisie. As early as on the eve of the War of Resistance Against Japan, he vociferously propagated the philosophy of survival above all, and of the turncoat, ordering some "Communists" in jail to surrender to the class enemy. Later, he shielded them, recruiting deserters and accepting traitors and forming cliques for the pursuit of his own selfish interests. He allowed them to steal their way into important positions. After victory in the War of Resistance Against Japan, he loudly advertised the "new stage of peace and democracy," preparing to go down on his knees and capitulate to U.S. imperialism and the Kuomintang. Following the liberation of the whole country and the seizure of state power by the proletariat, he did his utmost to oppose the socialist revolution and advocated putting capitalism into operation. In 1949, he put forward the idea of welcoming capitalist

exploitation and developing capitalism. In 1950, he called the traitorous reactionary film "Inside Story of the Ching Court" "patriotic"; he advocated vigorous efforts to foster the type of rich peasant "who owns three horses, a plough, and a cart" and opposed labour-exchange teams, mutual-aid teams, and the development of the collective economy, raising a cry for "the consolidation of the New Democratic order." In 1951 and 1952, he advocated the development of a rich-peasant economy and capitalism and the "four freedoms" (freedom of usury, of hiring labour, land sale, and private enterprise). Later, he also opposed the socialist transformation of capitalist industry and commerce, opposed agricultural co-operation, and slashed the number of agricultural co-operatives. In 1956, accommodating himself to the international revisionist trend of thought, he wildly talked about the dying out of class struggle. In 1962, he energetically publicized the idea of individual peasant farms, advocated the "extension of plots for private use and of free markets, the increase of small enterprises with sole responsibility for their own profits or losses, the fixing of output quotas based on the household," and "the liquidation of struggle in our relations with imperialism, the reactionaries and modern revisionism, and reduction of assistance and support to the revolutionary struggle of other peoples," and opposed the general line for building socialism, the great leap forward, and the people's communes, while publishing and putting on sale large numbers of his book on self-cultivation. In 1964, pursuing an opportunist line which was "Left" in form but Right in essence, he sabotaged the socialist education movement. During the great proletarian cultural revolution, he advanced and pursued the bourgeois reactionary line in collusion with another top Party person in authority taking the capitalist road. All this fully shows that over a long period of time he has opposed Mao Tse-tung's thought and the proletarian revolutionary line represented by Chairman Mao, and that he is not a Marxist at all. He is the most important representative of the bourgeoisie within our Party, a Khrushchev lying right beside us.[17]

While Liu might have occasionally advanced views different from Mao's in the two decades before the Great Leap Forward, in the end he probably always deferred to Mao's position. Otherwise, it would be difficult to explain why he was allowed to be the second man in command in the party throughout those years. The extension of Liu's history of guilt to the mid-1930's then would seem to have been designed to completely discredit him and thoroughly eradicate his influence. In October 1968, the CCP formally decided to strip Liu of all his titles and expel him from the party. This was followed by the adoption in April 1969 of a new party Consti-

[17] "Fight for the Thorough Criticism and Repudiation of the Top Party Person in Authority Taking the Capitalist Road," *Liberation Army Daily,** April 11, 1967. The quoted passages were taken from an abridged English translation of the editorial given in *Peking Review,* No. 16 (April 14, 1967), p. 8.

tution that expressly designated Lin Piao as Mao's political heir.

This new line of succession was shortly upset, however. Last seen in public on June 3, 1971, at Mao's reception for President Ceausescu of Romania, Lin's political and physical demise apparently occurred in the following September amid a number of unusual developments, including the sudden disappearance from public view of all his proteges on the CCP Politburo, the dropping from public mention of Lin's own name, the abrupt ending of preparations for the traditional National Day parade which Mao and Lin had always reviewed together in Peking since 1966, and the crash of a Chinese airplane in Outer Mongolia on September 12 while apparently heading for the Soviet Union. Although for nearly a year thereafter Lin was not openly charged with any wrongdoings, there was a stream of articles and broadcasts obliquely attacking him for, among other things, his duplicity, his sectarianism, his improper exaltation of Mao's image and Thought, and his policy differences with Mao. With regard to duplicity, an article in the March 27, 1972, issue of the *Kuang-ming Daily* (Peking), while ostensibly recalling the late Lu Hsun's struggle against "counterrevolutionary double-dealers" on the literary front in the 1930's, characterized Lin by implication as one of the "false Marxist political swindlers today who wave a 'red flag' against the red flag, who say all good things but do everything evil, and whose mouth is honeyed but whose belly conceals a sword." Obviously taking cognizance of the deference that Lin had always shown to Mao in public, the same article went on to say: "The characteristic of counterrevolutionary double-dealers is their outward obeisance but inward contravention, open agreement but secret disagreement, and saying gratifying things to your face but making trouble behind your back." With regard to sectarianism, Lin was accused of having paid lip service to Mao's policy of "narrowing the target of attack" during the GPCR while actually seeking to usurp party power by getting rid of the majority of "the revolutionary cadres, particularly those revolutionary leading cadres who have devoted themselves to the party cause for years and persisted in carrying out Chairman Mao's revolutionary line." [18] At least some of these veteran Communists who fell into oblivion during the GPCR but who have reappeared in public since Lin's downfall could have been among the victims of this particular phase of Lin's sectarianism. Lin's factionalism also allegedly manifested itself in "sinister 'small group' schemes" and "cliquish splittism." Vague as these charges were, they

[18] "Unity of Revolutionary Cadres: A Guarantee of Victory," *ibid.*, No. 27 (July 7, 1972), p. 7.

referred to Lin's efforts to place an inordinate number of his military proteges in strategic positions in the party and government and to the serious devisive effect that his action might have had. Still another allusion to Lin's sectarianism accused him of attempting to contact and win over Communists who had made mistakes so as to enlist their services for his factional activities; Ch'en Po-ta reportedly was one of these persons. With regard to improper exaltation of Mao's image and Thought, Lin was subtly accused of having represented Mao before the Chinese people as a prophet and superman and promoted the concept that geniuses, heroes, persons of superior intelligence, spiritual force, and innate knowledge make history and lead the masses. Labeling Lin's viewpoints as metaphysical and therefore non-Marxist, an article in *Red Flag* quoted Mao as having said: "The People and the people alone are the motive force in the making of world history." [19] The article again quoted the Chinese leader: "When we say that Marxism is correct, it is certainly not because Marx was a prophet but because his theory has been proven correct in our practice and in our struggle. No such formalistic and mystical notion as that of prophecy ever enters our minds." [20] The official press also attacked Lin with characteristic subtlety for making Mao's Thought absolute and for precluding the possibility that Mao's Thought can develop continuously. "The greatness of Chairman Mao," argued one writer, "lies precisely in the fact that he always stands in the van of history and continuously makes his thought and practice advance together. Making Mao Tse-tung Thought absolute and solidified in itself is counter to Mao Tse-tung Thought. Marxism-Leninism-Mao Tse-tung Thought has in no way exhausted truth but ceaselessly opens up roads to the knowledge of truth in the course of practice." [21] The critics then concluded that Lin's extollment of Mao was merely a smoke screen behind which he was actually promoting his own interests, including "the establishment of his own absolute authority."

Although these errors on Lin's part unquestionably undermined his continuing fitness as Mao's potential successor, the most important development that ultimately forced the issue seemed to be a serious discord between the two leaders over policy. For a time the official mass communications media were the least explicit on this aspect of the Lin Piao affair, but the timing of Lin's eclipse

[19] "A Critique of Liu Shao-ch'i's Reactionary Theory of Human Nature," *Red Flag,** No. 242 (October 1, 1971), p. 38.

[20] *Ibid.*, p. 37.

[21] Wang Che, "How Engels Criticized Duhring's Apriorism: Notes on Studying Anti-Duhring," *Peking Review,* No. 10 (March 10, 1972), p. 9.

and a terse reference in a joint *People's Daily–Red Flag–Liberation Army Daily* editorial on January 1, 1972, to "political swindlers who had illicit relations with foreign countries" quickly led most foreign observers to believe that Lin had headed a faction that opposed the new policy of contact with the U.S. Lin and his supporters might have felt that settling the existing disputes with Moscow would better serve Chinese interests in the long run than a detente with Washington. They probably argued that given their geographical proximity China and Russia must somehow find a way to live in peace lest they become mortal enemies to the detriment of both sides. Lin's opposition to Mao's response to President Nixon's friendly overtures also might have been caused by a strong disbelief in the President's sincerity.

Another important area of disagreement between Mao and Lin was agricultural policy. An article in the December 1971 issue of *Red Flag* apparently alluded to this when it attacked those who attempted to interfere with Mao's agricultural policies from the Right and the "Left." [22] Interference from the Right was clearly identified as that from the Liu Shao-ch'i faction mainly prior to the GPCR. Though interference from the "Left" was not explicitly attributed to any particular person or faction, the article did date the occurrence of the "Leftist" line after the great victory of the GPCR. This, coupled with some other subtle references in the article, seemed to lay the blame for such interference at the door of Lin Piao and possibly Ch'en Po-ta as well. The ultra-leftist line, according to the article, sought to alter the policy of three-level ownership with the production team as the foundation for the rural people's communes which had been in force since the early 1960's, the policy of distributing commune income on the basis of "from each according to his ability and to each according to his work," the policy of trading with the communes and commune members "at equal value," and the policy of allowing commune members to operate small private plots and have a family side-occupation "on condition that the development and absolute superiority of the collective economy are guaranteed." By seeking these changes, Lin and his supporters probably hoped to extract more from the countryside to finance an accelerated program of industrial development for military purposes. Conscious of the limit of the Chinese peasant's socialist consciousness and unwilling to repeat the mistake of over-collectivization made more than a decade ago, Mao and his more pragmatic associates resolutely rejected these proposed changes,

[22] Hsiang Hui, "Conscientiously Implement the Party's Economic Policies for Rural Areas," *Red Flag,** No. 244 (December 4, 1971), pp. 30–34.

which the above-mentioned article characterized as "subjective idealist voluntarism."

While the official mass media were making these indirect attacks, the story of the Lin Piao affair was reportedly told to cadres of all levels in China and through them to the people at small group sessions. In the meantime, however, officials in Peking steadfastly refused to discuss the whereabouts of the 64-year-old Lin. Then on June 28, 1972, the 78-year-old Mao himself broke the official silence on the matter by telling Mrs. Sirimavo Bandaranaike, the Prime Minister of Ceylon, who was visiting Peking, that Lin Piao had been killed in an air crash on September 12, 1971, while fleeing the country after an attempted *coup d'etat*. Within less than two weeks Mao repeated the same story to Maurice Schumann, the French Foreign Minister. In addition to accusing Lin of attempting to usurp the leadership of the party, government, and army by "infiltrating" his partisans into key organizations, Mao confirmed the existence of differences between himself and his one-time heir-designate over a number of domestic and foreign issues, including the decision to seek a normalization of relations with the U.S. Mao was reputed to have said that another policy opposed by Lin was the move to rebuild the CCP apparatus in the wake of the GPCR. The implication, left moot by the Chairman, was that Lin saw the rebuilding of the party as a threat to his power which had been based mainly on the considerable number of military units under the command of his proteges, many of whose associations with him dated back to the late 1920's when he was the commander of the First Army Corps of the Chinese Workers' and Peasants' Red Army. But Mao's version of Lin's story was not made known to the world at large until about a month later. Then, on July 28, the Chinese Embassy in Algiers, in response to questions from two reporters of the Algerian government newspaper *El Moudjahid,* issued a statement publicly confirming Lin's death.[23] After Lin's initial attempts to usurp power had been "unmasked," the statement asserted, Mao had tried to rehabilitate him, but Lin "did not change his perverse nature one iota." Lin, added the statement, subsequently led an unsuccessful plot to overthrow and assassinate Mao and was killed in the manner that Mao had described to the two foreign dignataries. While no question was raised as to Lin's physical and political demise, many American experts on China strongly doubted that he died in the plane crash. They believed that he either committed suicide, died of natural causes while imprisoned following

[23] For an English text of the statement, see *The New York Times,* July 29, 1972.

his political disgrace, or was shot trying to escape. Those who died in the plane crash probably were some of Lin's supporters, possibly including his son, Li Li-kuo, who was then Deputy Chief of the Operations Department of the Chinese Air Force. American experts also discounted the charge that Lin had conspired to assassinate Mao. Lin, said the experts, unquestionably had conspired against Mao, but murder was never planned because of the turmoil that might have ensued if it had become known in China. By accusing Lin of attempting to murder the immensely popular leader of the new China and by attributing Lin's death to a plane crash while trying to escape to the Soviet Union following his alleged abortive coup, the Peking leadership, in the opinion of some American experts, hoped to arouse popular indignation against Lin, while absolving itself of the responsibility for his sad end. The need to attribute Lin's unexpected demise completely to his own "ignominious" activities was made imperative by the fact that during his long career in the Chinese revolution Lin did, even according to the official statement on his death, "accomplish some useful work," especially in the powerful support he gave Mao during the preparatory and early stages of the GPCR.

Powerful and prestigious as Lin Piao had been, there were, however, no signs of disruption of normal life in China at the time of his demise, indicating that the socio-economic stability that the Maoist leadership has brought about in the nation since 1949 is now durable enough to withstand any top-level shake-ups in the party, government, and army. In particular, Lin Piao's failure to use the army to support his cause demonstrated anew that the bulk of the armed forces were still loyal to Mao's principle that "the party commands the gun and the gun must never be allowed to command the party." Lin's elimination nevertheless did have an unsettling effect on the question of succession. As of 1973, Peking has not yet designated a new heir to Mao. If Premier Chou En-lai, who is 74, outlives Mao, he is the logical choice to hold the reins of the party. Besides his party seniority, governmental experience, political adroitness, and international prestige, Chou is unusually persuasive and has a substantial personal following both inside and outside the CCP. More important, insofar as maintaining party control of the army is concerned, he, while not a professional soldier, has had long experience in military affairs; and many of the senior officers in the army are his personal friends or former lieutenants. Indeed, up to the period of "the second united front" in the late 1930's, Chou's principal activities in his party were in the military field. As noted in Chapter III, he once even headed the CCP Military

Affairs Commission. These qualifications, together with his temperament, make him an ideal man to steer the ship of state after Mao's retirement or death and before the emergence of a younger leader with long-term survival prospects.

If Chou is not to succeed Mao, then the prospects of installing a "collective leadership" at least as an interim device would be very high because there is no one within the present CCP hierarchy with sufficient prestige and power to take Mao's place. If so, the future collective leadership is likely to comprise leading members of the most important but informal factions in the party. Two such factions today are said to be the so-called "Cultural Revolution Group" headed by Chiang Ch'ing, Chang Ch'un-ch'iao, and Yao Wen-yuan; and the "State Council Group" consisting of Premier Chou En-lai's proteges. There are also some veteran party and army leaders who have not been very active of late but whose prestige and support could assure the smooth functioning of a post-Mao regime. Another likely development is that Chiang Ch'ing might inherit the mantle and powers of her illustrious husband. Now in her fifties, Chiang won instant and fervent support of the Chinese youth when she made her political debut at the beginning of the GPCR. Inasmuch as young people account for the overwhelming majority of the Chinese population, this popularity, which stemmed from her staunch defense of Mao's "revolutionary line" and her own "populist" stand against elitism, bureaucracy, and the bourgeois way of life, is a significant political asset. Given the scarcity of prominent leaders after the GPCR and the Lin Piao affair, she now certainly has the political stature and support to be seriously considered a potential claimant to her husband's position, at least in reality if not in name. Needless to say, a dark horse may emerge to lead the party and the nation after Mao's departure. In any event, there is no reason to believe that the eventual transfer of power cannot be peacefully accomplished. A change in leadership will not necessarily usher in drastic changes in either domestic or foreign policy since, on the whole, the present policies have been highly successful and popular.

The Central Secretariat and the functional departments and commissions. From the time when the party Constitution was revised in September 1956 to the fall of 1966, the Central Secretariat was the administrative center of the CCP, "attending to the daily work of the Central Committee under the direction of the Politburo and its Standing Committee." In its operations, the Central Secretariat served as the principal staff agency of the national party leadership. Its members checked and commented on the reports and memoranda from all agencies of the party, government, and various "people's organizations" before they were submitted to the Politburo or its Standing Committee. Instructions from the Politburo or the Standing Committee were also channeled through the Central Secretariat. Members of the Central Secretariat helped the Politburo anticipate problems and formulate contingency plans for coping with them. Secondly, the Central Secretariat supervised the execution and implementation of the party's policies and decisions in administrative, financial, economic, military, social, cultural, and professional institutions at every level throughout the country. Directly under its control were the functional departments and commissions of the central party headquarters. The number of departments and commissions varied from time to time, but as of the fall of 1966 at least eight departments and commissions were known to exist: the Organization Department, Propaganda Department, United Front Work Department, Agriculture and Forestry Political Department, Industry and Communications Political Department, Finance and Trade Political Department, International Liaison Department, Higher Education Department, Women's Work Commission, and Military Affairs Commission.

Virtually paralleling the governmental ministries, these departments and commissions and their generously staffed subdivisions initiated policy in their respective fields for consideration by the Central Secretariat and the Politburo. They also formulated general plans and decided upon a specific course of action for enforcing an approved policy by the appropriate governmental agency, people's organization, or party organization on a lower level. To ensure effective control, the Central Secretariat and the functional departments and commissions issued directives to the various organizations (in the case of nonparty organs, directives were issued through the party cells within them), checked their performances, and determined their key appointments.

The Central Secretariat was second in importance only to the Politburo and its Standing Committee. As of the spring of 1966, the Secretariat was composed of ten secretaries (Teng Hsiao-p'ing, P'eng Chen, Wang Chia-hsiang, T'an Chen-lin, Li Hsueh-feng, Li Fu-ch'un, Li Hsien-nien, Lu Ting-i, K'ang Sheng, and Lo Jui-ch'ing), and three alternate secretaries (Liu Lan-t'ao, Yang Shang-k'un, and Hu Ch'iao-mu). However, Wang Chia-hsiang (because he was against the ideological dispute with Moscow) had been inactive since the early 1960's. He, together with P'eng Chen, Lu Ting-i, Lo Jui-ch'ing, and Yang Shang-k'un (early victims of the GPCR), was formally dropped from the Secretariat at the eleventh plenum of the Eighth Central Committee in August 1966. One month before the plenum met, however, T'ao Chu, Yeh Chien-ying, and Liu Ning-i were identified as new members of the Secretariat. Long active in liaison work with foreign Communist parties and in people's diplomacy in general, Liu had been President of the All-China Federation of Trade Unions since 1958 and Secretary-General of the National People's Congress since 1964. As the GPCR was gathering momentum, Teng Hsiao-p'ing, T'ao Chu, Liu Lan-t'ao, and Hu Ch'iao-mu came under political fire in Red Guard wall posters, from December 1966 on, for their collusion with Liu Shao-ch'i in resisting the movement and "restoring capitalism in China." They were immediately separated from the Secretariat. The same fate befell T'an Chen-lin after May 1, 1967, and Liu Ning-i early in 1968. These purges left the Secretariat with only Li Hsueh-feng, Li Fu-ch'un, Li Hsien-nien, K'ang Sheng, and Yeh Chien-ying. However, even before this the Secretariat had already lost many of its powers and functions to the Central Committee's Group in Charge of the Cultural Revolution. The Secretariat apparently ceased to function altogether sometime in 1968. The party Constitution of 1969 makes no provisions for a new Central Secretariat. With the dissolution of the Group in Charge of the Cultural Revolution following the adoption of the new party Constitution, the functions of the Central Secretariat were probably assigned to a small staff agency of the Politburo. The Politburo could then more easily supervise these functions and they would be less likely to develop into a semi-independent power base, for which the Central Secretariat had been indicted during the GPCR. The present status of the functional departments and commissions is obscured by lack of official information, though the press in recent years has made frequent references to the International Liaison Department, the Military Affairs Commission, the United Front Work, and the General Administrative Office, which seems to be in charge of the housekeeping work of the central party headquarters.

The Military Affairs Commission. The Military Affairs Commission of the party is the principal agency through which the CCP, or more accurately its Politburo, formulates basic military policies, supervises the work of the Ministry of National Defense and the General Political Department, and controls the People's Liberation Army and other armed forces, which are legally under the command of the state chairman. The importance of the Commission is indicated by the fact that Mao Tse-tung personally serves as its chairman, and Lin Piao was his principal deputy when he was Minister of National Defense from 1959 to his downfall in

1971. Since the fall of 1971, former Marshal Yeh Chien-ying has been acting in Lin's place. Former Marshals Liu Po-ch'eng, Hsu Hsiang-ch'ien, and Nieh Jung-chen also are identified as vice-chairmen of the Commission.

The Central Control Commission. Now apparently defunct, the Central Control Commission was the principal guardian of Communist morality and party discipline before the GPCR. The Commission headed a control organization that paralleled the territorial organization of other party organs down to the level of county or city committees. Elected by the Central Committee at its plenum, the Central Control Commission on the eve of the GPCR consisted of sixty full and alternate members, with nearly twelve of them concurrently serving on the Central Committee. Its possible abolition could have been due partly to its failure to check the revisionist activities of the Liu Shao-ch'i faction and partly to Mao's GPCR policy of simplifying party and government organizations.

Regional Bureaus of the Central Committee. To facilitate supervision of the work of the many provincial party organizations, the party Constitution of 1945 empowered the Central Committee to establish regional and subregional bureaus with jurisdiction over several provinces and border areas. From 1949 to 1954, there were six regional and four subregional bureaus. The four subregional bureaus were in effect provincial party organizations, while each of the six regional bureaus supervised the affairs of a number of provinces and metropolitan cities. Acting as field agents of the central party organs and headed by seasoned party members, who, with the exceptions of Kao Kang and Jao Shu-shih, subsequently played prominent roles in Peking until the GPCR, the six regional bureaus wielded enormous power. Not only did they supervise and coordinate the activities of the provincial party organizations, but they also controlled the regional military commands and ran the regional administrations. These administrations were organized and operated as small-scale replicas of the national administration. They were better able than the central party leadership to guide provincial and local functionaries in enforcing party policies, taking into account the regional peculiarities resulting from the size of the country. The regional bureaus rendered valuable services to the central party leadership and contributed much to the smooth and effective functioning of the new regime. In mid-1954, however, all the regional bureaus, governments, and the military commands were abolished following the first oblique disclosure of the purge of Kao Kang and Jao Shu-shih, who were the heads of the Northeast and East China Bureaus respectively. Among other things, they were accused of having been tempted by their enormous powers to seek key positions on the national level while regarding the vast regions under their leadership as "their personal property or independent kingdom."

Although the abolition of regional party bureaus removed a potentially fertile breeding ground for centrifugal tendencies, the central party authorities soon found that it was not easy to supervise the more than twenty provincial party organizations and the other provincial public and semipublic institutions. Thus the 1956 party Constitution contained a provision once again authorizing the Central Committee to establish regional bureaus at its discretion and extending the privilege of creating area (*chuan-ch'ü*) and district (*ch'ü*) bureaus to the provincial and county committees. Despite the new authorization, for several years the Central Committee made no attempt to reestablish any regional bureau (except for a subbureau in Shanghai) apparently because of its continuing apprehension that a revival of powerful regional establishments might again breed centrifugal tendencies. In January 1961, however, the Eighth Central Committee at its ninth plenum resolved to establish six regional bureaus: these were the Northeast, North China, East China, Central-South China, Southwest China, and Northwest China Bureaus, with headquarters located in Mukden, Peking, Shanghai, Canton, Chengtu, and Sian, respectively. Each bureau was under the charge of several secretaries headed by a First Secretary. The subdivisions of the new bureaus were not as elaborate as those of the regional bureaus abolished in 1954. Unlike their predecessors, they did not run any governments or military commands on the regional level. They oversaw the administration of governmental and military affairs in their respective regions only through the provincial party committees and the party committees attached to the several military districts in each region. This significant difference made the bureaus far less inviting bases of power than their predecessors. However, these reconstructed bureaus were swept away again in 1967 by the political storms during the GPCR, as nearly all of the men in charge of them were exposed as agents of Liu Shao-ch'i. Thus far, the Maoist leadership has shown no intention of reestablishing any regional party bureaus.

Party Organizations at the Provincial, Prefectural, and County Levels

All regular party organizations from the provincial level down were temporarily disbanded during the GPCR to prevent them from being utilized by Liu Shao-ch'i's proteges who had been entrenched there. Following the Ninth National Party Congress in April 1969, steps were taken to reestablish regular party organizations at and below the provincial level, with those at the provincial level receiving priority. By August 1971, all twenty-one provinces; the five autonomous regions of Inner Mongolia, Sinkiang, Ninghsia, Kwangsi, and Tibet; and the three special cities of Peking, Shanghai, and Tientsin had rebuilt their provincial-level organizations. Meanwhile, progress was made in rebuilding party apparatus at lower levels. Normally, the local party organizations in the counties, autonomous counties, and cities are below the provincial organizations. However, when an autonomous prefecture (*Tzu-chih-chou*) exists as an intermediate territorial-administrative entity between a provincial government on the one hand and the governments of several counties, autonomous counties, and cities on the other, the normal organizational hierarchy of the party invariably gives way to a prefectural party organization. Patterned after the setup in Peking, each party organization at the provincial, prefectural, and county level has a congress, executive committee, standing committee, secretariat, several functional departments, and a number of field bureaus. The congress and the executive committee delegate much of their authority to the standing committee, the secretariat, or to a single secretary if it is a small county party organization. Secretaries of the provincial and prefectural organizations are, in effect, selected by the central leadership, as are secretaries of some key cities, though since the end of the GPCR more emphasis has been put on "listening to the opinions of the masses."

Each provincial, prefectural, city, or county party secretariat is headed by a First Secretary. The First Secretary constitutes part of the core of the nationwide network of permanent party functionaries, mainly through whom the party controls the myriad governmental, economic, social, cultural, and military institutions and establishments throughout the country. The First Secretary is the single most important person in the area under the jurisdiction of his organization, overshadowing even the highest government official on the corresponding level of the territorial-administrative level. After the GPCR, however, all First Secretaries at the provincial level have been concurrently heading Revolutionary Committees of their respective provinces, which now perform the functions of the previous Provincial People's Governments. Theoretically, the First Secretary is accountable to the party committee on the corresponding level, but since he actually owes his position to the next higher First Secretary in the hierarchy, he tends to look to him for instructions and advice rather than to his own committee, to which he transmits orders from above. To prevent the First Secretary from becoming too autocratic, numerous articles appeared in the official press in the fall of 1971 reminding each First Secretary that, while his role in a party committee resembles that of a "squad leader" in an army, he must avoid becoming the "only voice" of his committee. These articles therefore called for a combination of the First Secretary's special responsibility with the principle of collective leadership.

Party Primary Organization

The party primary organizations are at the bottom of the hierarchy. Formed in public and semipublic institutions at every level of Chinese society and in many residences where there are party members, these organizations are in direct contact with the rank-and-file membership of the party and thus are its basic operational units. Information is lacking on the current number of these units in the country. As of July 1959, they numbered approximately 1,069,000 as compared with only 250,000 in 1951. Besides performing purely intraparty functions such as recruitment, indoctrination, and mobilization of party members, these organizations also "guide and supervise" the administrative bodies and mass organizations of the enterprises or institutions in which they are located. This right is granted them to ensure the energetic fulfillment of the decisions of higher party organizations and state organs. However, they have no control over the principal governmental organs and other major public institutions to which special party committees are attached for maintaining the party's hegemony.

Like the organizations at higher levels, the central figure and director of a primary party organization is the secretary, who has a hand in every activity of his unit and gives the orders. Of special significance is his role as friend, counselor, and guardian of all the people under his jurisdiction. Charged with the responsibility for looking after the welfare of his comrades, the secretary stands ready to render personal services when the need arises. He is to give his comrades hope and encouragement in time of difficulty or despair, and even serves as "father confessor" for their personal moral problems. If a secretary discharges these responsibilities with devotion and competence, he is likely to win the affection as well as respect of his comrades and, increasing his qualifications as their leader, thus enhance his utility to the party. Otherwise, the enormity and directness of his power over the rank and file can easily make the secretary a petty tyrant who is obeyed but intensely hated.

VII

Party Membership, Cadres, and Youth Organizations

Membership

Growth and recruitment of membership. Officially designated as the vanguard of the Chinese working class, the CCP is an elitist organization that recruits only those who are most devoted to its cause and willing and able to accept its discipline. In enforcing this membership policy the CCP put into effect one of Lenin's famous party-building principles: although a Communist party should keep in close touch with the masses it seeks to represent and lead, it must set off its organization sharply from the whole of the masses so as to enable it to maintain exacting demands and enforce rigid discipline. However, the party does not think of itself as a closed shop to protect the vested interests of its members by not accepting newcomers regardless of their personal merits. Realizing the immensity of its tasks and the usefulness of broadening its base, the CCP since the rise of Mao has sought to enlarge its ranks "boldly" while continuously endeavoring to be selective, cohesive, and dynamic. As a result of this policy as well as of the party's successful seizure and retention of power, the membership of the CCP has registered a steady and phenomenal growth in the last two decades (Table I). When the latest official statistics were released on July 1, 1961, the party had 17 million members compared with a little over one million in 1945.

The growth from 1945 to 1961 occurred in waves coincident with the major campaigns of that period: the "Third Revolutionary War" (1945–49); the agrarian reform (1949–50); the Three-Anti and the Five-Anti campaigns; the movement to suppress counterrevolutionaries (1950–

TABLE I. GROWTH OF THE MEMBERSHIP OF THE CHINESE COMMUNIST PARTY: 1921–1961.*

Date	*Approximate Membership (Number of People)*	*Remarks*
1921	50	
1924–1927	59,000	During this period the CCP was allied with the Kuomintang.
1927	10,000	The months following the split between the CCP and the Kuomintang in the middle of the year.
July 1928	40,000	The early period of rural soviets.
1934	300,000	Shortly before the Long March.
1937	40,000	After the Long March but prior to the outbreak of the Sino-Japanese War.
1945	1,210,000	On V-J Day.
1949	4,500,000	When the People's Republic of China was founded in Peking.
December 1950	5,800,000	
February 1954	6,500,000	
February 1956	9,000,000	Prior to the completion of the "socialist transformation of industry, commerce, handicrafts, and agriculture."
September 1956	10,734,385	After the completion of the "socialist transformation."
September 1957	12,720,000	During the Rectification and Anti-Rightist Campaigns.
October 1959	13,960,000	The Tenth Anniversary of the People's Republic of China.
July 1961	17,000,000	During the period of economic readjustment.

* SOURCES: *Current Events Handbook,** No. 16 (June 5, 1951), p. 14; *Eighth National Congress of the CCP*, Vol. I, p. 209; *People's Daily,** October 19, 1957, and July 1, 1961; *Ten Glorious Years: 1949–1959* (Peking: Foreign Languages Press, 1960), p. 283.

52); the movement for socialist transformation of industry, commerce, and agriculture (1955–56); the anti-rightist campaign (1957–58); the Great Leap Forward and the Commune Movement (1958–59); and the economic readjustment campaign (1960–66). These campaigns provided persons aspiring to party membership with splendid opportunities to demonstrate their fidelity and usefulness to the party's causes. From the party's point of view, the qualifications shown by prospective members are a far better indication of their fitness for membership than those revealed in oral professions or by other less demanding tests. Furthermore, by rewarding "activists" with party membership (which today not only confers prestige and status but is also an entree to personal success), the party inspires more people to make greater efforts in major campaigns in the present and future; however, in current Maoist parlance "personal success" does not mean fame, position, and material reward but the opportunity to render more useful service to the revolution and the people.

According to the provisions of the party Constitution of 1969, membership in the party is now open to any Chinese worker, poor or lower middle-class peasant, revolutionary army man, or any other revolutionary worker who has reached the age of eighteen and older, accepts the Constitution of the party, joins a party organization and works actively in it, carries out the party's decisions, observes party discipline, and pays membership dues. His application must include recommendations from two party members and be examined by a party branch, which must seek the opinions of the broad masses inside and outside the party. Application is subject to acceptance by a general meeting of the party branch and approval by the next higher party committee. Unlike several earlier charters, the party Constitution of 1969 no longer requires a one-year probation period for admission. To build the party into a militant and vigorous organization wholeheartedly dedicated to Mao's "proletarian revolutionary line," the new party Constitution specifically states that "proven renegades, enemy agents, absolutely unrepentant persons in power taking the capitalist road, degenerates, and alien class elements must be cleared out of the party and not be readmitted." In addition to these formal requirements, the party has other criteria for recruiting new members, often in order to attract capable persons for the central tasks of a given period and to strengthen certain areas in its organization.

Obligations of party members. Defining itself as a combat organization, the CCP subjects its members to a rigorous system of discipline, self-denial, and service reminiscent of a medieval religious order. Since it considers a party member useless if he merely goes along passively as a believer or sympathizer, the party requires active participation and self-sacrifice of every member in all its struggles and drives. Every member is expected to be faithful to the cause of the party and to set a good example in work and personal conduct not only under close supervision, but also when alone. As part of the effort to keep the CCP from degenerating into a revisionist organization representing the interests of a privileged few, in 1964 Mao elucidated five specific obligations of membership, which are now stipulated in the party Constitution of 1969:

1. Study and apply Marxism-Leninism-Mao Tse-tung Thought in a living way;
2. Work for the interests of the vast majority of the people of China and the world;
3. Be able to unite with the great majority, including those who have wrongly opposed them but are sincerely correcting their mistakes; however, special vigilance must be maintained against careerists, conspirators, and double-dealers so as to prevent these bad elements from usurping the leadership of the party and keep the state in the hands of Marxist revolutionaries.
4. Consult with the masses when problems arise;
5. Be bold in making criticism and self-criticism.

Since solidarity and unity are considered an important source of the party strength, every member is required to safeguard the party's solidarity and consolidate its unity at all times and in all places. Since the GPCR, however, the Maoists have advanced the concept that party unity should be maintained only when it conforms with Mao's Thought and "the interests of the people." In the meantime, they have accused Liu Shao-ch'i of advocating the "erroneous" theory of unconditional subordination of individual party members to the party organization. Although the new concept provides a theoretical justification for factionalism or intra-party struggles in defense of Mao's Thought or the interests of the people, the Maoist doctrine still forbids "unprincipled" or "petty bourgeois" factional activities that violate the laws of the state, the party's political line, or the organizational principles based on Mao's Thought.

The formal obligations of party membership are indeed onerous. Needless to say, not all of them can be faithfully fulfilled by all members at all times. In fact, even the party itself, as will be noted later, has repeatedly admitted serious infractions. Nevertheless, the obligations of membership enumerated in the party Constitution are not empty phrases designed to impress outsiders. On the contrary, the CCP has worked tirelessly to make individual party members fulfill them as thoroughly as possible. Consequently, it now has a membership whose discipline and dedication to the Communist cause are unexcelled by any other political party in the world.

Rewards of party membership. The requirements of party membership are so burdensome and limit the members' personal life so drastically that it may well be asked why anyone would want to join. There are many different motives for becoming a party member, but there is certainly no dearth of candidates. Some of them are fired by a zeal amounting to religious fanaticism. They see in the party a reason for being, an ideological guide that gives purpose to life. Others want to join because they have been impressed by the CCP's determined efforts to modernize China and restore the country to a respectable place in the family of nations after more than a century of foreign oppression and humiliation. Still others are eager to elevate themselves into the elite group which is represented by the party. If one wants to be recognized as a "revolutionary" to whom official ideology has accorded the highest status in Chinese society, he must belong to the party, even if he has to pay a stiff price. Another distinct advantage involves employment; not all the better positions in government and business are held by party members, but they are given preference. These positions confer not only power and prestige but also material benefits, although in recent years there has been a persistent campaign against the idea of "entering the party in order to be an official," and for the idea that a party member should serve others and not himself. The attractiveness of the party also lies in the fact that with the weakening of many traditional social bonds, it is now a magnet for human loyalty; it gives the individual a sense of belonging, and it looks after his legitimate personal interests.

Indoctrination of party members. The CCP maintains a high level of political consciousness and revolutionary competence by indoctrination, which it euphemistically calls *hsueh-hsi,* or training and study. This indoctrination takes different forms. Every literate member is required to study ideology during his spare time. Frequently he must jot down the essence of what he has learned, comment on it, and then submit his notes to a responsible official of his party organization. Illiterate members must attend ideological training classes. Political education is also conducted through group discussion, the press, radio, television, the stage, motion pictures, mass rallies, street demonstrations, "struggle meetings," and "cultural palaces." In addition, party schools at various levels provide more systematic and intensive training to selected rank-and-file members as well as cadres.

The basic contents of inner-party education are threefold. The first part comprises the study of the theoretical concepts, strategies, and tactics of Marxism-Leninism and the Thought of Mao Tse-tung. The second part entails the study of current policies and tasks of the party and the state. The third part is concerned with the individual's moral cultivation. To make these kinds of education more effective in solving actual problems of the party and in the individual's thought and working style, the party seeks to link the subject matter of education closely to current situations, tasks, and ideological trends. For instance, in the early 1960's when self-sacrifice and heroism were required in the face of serious economic disasters, the party launched the "learn from Lei Feng" movement. Lei Feng was depicted as "a great ordinary soldier," who before his heroic death in the course of discharging his duties as a group leader in a military engineering corps, always maintained a work style of hardship and austerity. He found "the significance of life in dedicated service to the people and the party" and always strove to do his best at any post, "whether it was important or not, its condition was good or bad, he liked it or not, or he was familiar with it or not." [1] Hailing Lei as a personification of the true virtues of an "ordinary Communist," the propaganda organs of the party throughout the country exhorted all members, soldiers, the Young Communist League, workers, and peasants to emulate Lei's indomitable revolutionary spirit and inexhaustible enthusiasm for service. Lei Feng's spirit, said the official press, soon became a powerful inspiration for millions. In the meantime, several new heroes at the grass-roots level, including Wang Chieh, Ouyang Hai, Mai Hsien-te, Ch'en Yung-kuei, and Chiao Yü-lu, were singled out as additional examples for the nation to emulate.

The Cadres

The importance of cadres. Cadres are the backbone of the party: they serve as functionaries in the organs of the party and government and in all the other organizations and establishments under the party's control, including communes, factories, schools, the armed forces, and the "people's organizations." [2] They, more than the rank-and-file party members, have therefore been instrumental in projecting the party's influence to every aspect of the national life and in mobilizing and directing the rank-and-file party members and the broad masses in carrying out the party's policies and tasks. In comparison with the rank-and-file members, they are on the whole more resolute in their political stand and better able to be leaders wherever they work.

As of 1960, there were about six million cadres working in various fields. Cadres specialize in organizing within the party, man-

[1] Lo Jui-ch'ing, "Learn from Lei Feng," *SCMM*, No. 358 (August 1, 1963), pp. 1–3.

[2] A. Doak Barnett, *Cadres, Bureaucracy, and Political Power in Communist China* (New York: Columbia University Press, 1967).

aging factories, and administrating communes. What makes them most valuable to the CCP and different from party workers and civil servants in non-Communist countries, however, is their willingness to accept a new assignment even when it entails great personal sacrifice. Indeed this vast, disciplined corps of cadres has enabled the CCP to launch many gigantic mass campaigns and carry out most of its far-reaching reform programs with characteristic thoroughness.

Mao Tse-tung's policy of employing cadres. The existence of a large corps of disciplined, efficient, and devoted cadres is due to Mao's policy on their selection, training, use, and treatment. In the selection of cadres, Mao insists that the party appoint people "on their merit" and not by "favoritism." [3] The "worthy," according to Mao, are persons who combine character and ability. "Character" refers to political attitude, ideology, working style, family background, personal experience, and social relations. "Ability" means cultural standards and professional working ability. In other words, the "worthy" are those who are both "politically red and professionally proficient." For Mao, only these persons can be "resolute in carrying out the party line, observant of party discipline, closely connected with the masses, capable of working independently, active and hard-working, and self-denying." [3]

Mao considers the correct training of cadres absolutely essential if they are to do their work successfully and continuously raise their political and professional qualifications. Thus the CCP systematically organizes cadres to study theories, policies, and current events; to sum up lessons of experience in practical work; and to acquire knowledge of their trade. How to use cadres is another important aspect of Mao's policy. They must be given adequate guidance so that they can perform their tasks in accordance with the party's political line. However, they should be given a free hand on questions of detail and on concrete problems that can be settled in various ways in order to encourage their initiative and creativity. Mao also insists that the cadres' work be checked in a positive spirit and for a positive purpose: upon discovery of defects and mistakes, the party is to help them analyze the cause and find ways to improve; the party will take disciplinary measures only against those who have committed serious mistakes and still resist guidance. Mao also insists that the party organizations should care for their cadres in a motherly way; take an interest in their personal problems; look after their working conditions; and en-

[3] Mao Tse-tung, *Selected Works,* II, 202–203.

able them to "appreciate the warmth of the revolutionary big family" and undertake their assignments with enthusiasm and devotion.

The Young Communist League and the Young Pioneers

With malleable minds and no fixed ideology, youth is regarded by the CCP as most likely to accept Communism wholeheartedly and to work most faithfully for the cause. In addition, the present leaders of the CCP know well that the continuation and ultimate success of their grand experiment will depend on the extent to which they succeed in making the coming generation the willing heirs of the party's ideals and tasks. Thus the CCP attaches great importance to the indoctrination and rallying of youth. Until the emergence of the Red Guards during the GPCR, the principal instruments for achieving these ends had been the Young Communist League and the Young Pioneers. However, as the GPCR was receding, the Maoist leadership began to rebuild the two older youth organizations as the party's principal auxiliaries.

The Young Communist League. The genesis of the Young Communist League (YCL) was the Chinese Socialist Youth Corps, which was formed a year before the CCP itself. The immediate predecessor of the YCL was the New Democratic Youth League, founded in April 1949 as the chief rallying point for young people in mainland China. With the transition from the "New Democracy" to socialism, the New Democratic Youth League changed its name to the YCL in May 1957, but today it is for all practical purposes a continuation of the New Democratic Youth League.

As the regular channel between the party and youth, the YCL is open to any Chinese working boy or girl between the ages of fifteen and twenty-five who accepts its constitution, wishes to join and work in one of its organizations, pledges to carry out its decisions, and pays membership dues. "Working youths" are defined as young people who perform manual and mental labor as well as those who are studying and preparing for work; the term excludes those who are guilty of "exploitation" or who intend to exploit others in the future. Every application for membership must be supported by the recommendation of two YCL members. Although no formal probation period is required, the YCL organizations scrutinize applicants for admission as carefully as the CCP itself, both groups wanting only those "who are most active in actual struggle and show the highest degree of socialist awakening." Like the CCP, the YCL insists on "boldness" as well as "prudence" in recruitment.

Thus, instead of simply waiting for aspiring young people to apply for admission, it charges each of its units and individual members with the responsibility of "actively fostering young activists and regularly arousing, educating, and drawing into the league those who are qualified for membership." [4] As a result of this policy, YCL membership rose from less than 200,000 in April 1949 to some 25 million in May 1959. The current membership probably has exceeded 30 million with the admission of eight and a half million young people into the league in 1965 alone.[5]

Despite official silence on this point, in past years the league tended to make itself the chief rallying point primarily for youths with administrative ability and technical knowledge. In January 1957, its members accounted for 85 per cent of the YCL-age population working in the state organs at various levels and for 50 per cent of those in factories and mines.[6] In 1956, 57 per cent of the total student body in institutions of higher learning were YCL members.[7] As late as April 1964, rural YCL members, by contrast, accounted for only 13 per cent of the total number of rural youths.[8] However, in 1965 the league, under Mao's prodding, made an effort to rectify the situation; and according to an official report, most of the eight and a half million new members admitted into the league in that year were from working-class or former poor peasant families.[9] Officially defined as "a mass organization of the advanced youths of China, a school for studying Communism, and an assistant to the CCP," the YCL is very closely tied to the party. First, the structure is patterned after that of the CCP. The YCL organizes primary units in factories, mines, shops, streets, farms, government offices, schools, and basic units in the armed forces. These units report to county or city organizations and from there to provincial organizations. A national congress of the YCL is supposed to be held once every four years to elect a Central Committee, which in turn elects a Standing Committee and a Central Secretariat headed by a First Secretary. As in the CCP, the backbone of the YCL organization on any level is the secretaries, who receive instructions from the higher YCL headquarters and from the CCP organizations at the corresponding level.

[4] "Lectures on the Constitution of the YCL," *CB,* No. 680 (April 10, 1962), p. 14. See also Li Wen-i, "Show Keen Concern for Young People's Request to Join the League," *The Chinese Youth Daily,** June 29, 1965.

[5] *NCNA,* May 3, 1966.

[6] *The Chinese Youth Daily,** January 18, 1957.

[7] *Kuang-ming Daily,** January 18, 1957.

[8] *The Chinese Youth Daily,** April 2, 1964.

[9] *NCNA,* May 3, 1966.

The league, through its primary units, uses a great variety of means to indoctrinate youth with Communist ideology and cultivate personal characteristics that will make them trustworthy and useful citizens of the new society. To prevent ideological and professional studies from being divorced from practice, the league emphasizes the importance of applying education to actual tasks ("struggles") in the socialist revolution and construction. The Communist leaders consider personal participation an excellent way to imbue young people with patriotism and Communist values. The YCL plays an important role in publicizing and carrying out the lines and policies of the CCP; in mobilizing the broad masses of youth for the central tasks of the party; in promoting production and the values of hard work; and in exposing and eliminating shortcomings and mistakes in work. Like the party, the league looks after its members' personal interests. In addition to instilling a sense of mission in the minds of youth, thus making their life more meaningful, the YCL also renders many practical services to its members. It is concerned with the members' studies, work, leisure, recreation, health, emotional lives, marriages, and families; and loyal members who have problems can often get advice and assistance from the local YCL secretaries. By looking after their welfare, the league seeks to convince young people that it is the place where they can work for the public good while promoting their own interests, thus inclining them to make a total commitment to its cause.

As the most exalted organization next to the CCP, the YCL attracts young people because membership in it is a symbol of considerable achievement; it provides a stepping-stone to party membership and serves as the main recruiting ground for the ruling group, as shown by an official report that between 1949 and 1959 approximately four of every ten new party members came from the YCL.[10] In organizations consisting primarily of young people, YCL members often constitute an even larger percentage of the party's new recruits. For example, over 95 per cent of the newly admitted party members in the army prior to May 1961 were YCL members.[11]

The Young Pioneers. Closely affiliated with the YCL is the Young Pioneers. Officially defined as a mass organization of children and not an organization of *advanced* children, the Young Pioneers draws its membership from children nine to fifteen years old regardless of background. From 1949 to March 1962, the total

[10] *The Chinese Youth Daily,** September 25, 1959.
[11] *Ibid.*, May 3, 1961.

number of children in this organization increased from one-half million to 50 million.[12] To enable children to take active part in the GPCR, the number of Young Pioneers was further increased from a little over 50 million in 1965 to 100 million by June 1, 1966.[13]

The Young Pioneers is organized in groups of seven to thirteen members; two to five groups form a team, and two or more teams form a brigade. Each group has one head and two deputy heads, and each team and brigade has a committee. Each brigade is attached to a primary unit of the YCL, which has a children's committee that has charge of the brigades' activities and appoints "outstanding" YCL members as tutors. Because it operates completely under the direction and supervision of the primary units of the YCL, the Young Pioneers does not have a national administrative hierarchy of its own. Organized primarily in elementary and junior high schools, the Young Pioneers is charged with "enlightening children on Communism and cultivating them to be a new generation that loves the fatherland, the people, labor and science, takes good care of public property, and is healthy, active, courageous, honest, and creative in spirit." Since the CCP began to revive the YCL in the wake of the GPCR, there have been signs that the Young Pioneers may have been renamed "the Red Little Soldiers," although no official pronouncement on the matter has yet been made.

Rectification campaigns. A major device for maintaining a high degree of ideological purity and revolutionary discipline in the party (and at times in the YCL) is the "rectification campaign" or *cheng-feng yun-tung*. A form of intraparty struggle, rectification campaigns have become so important to the party over the years that in January 1961 a member of the Central Control Commission called them "powerful magic weapons." [14] During such a campaign, party members study assigned documents, associate theory with practice, and engage in general and self-directed criticism. Rectification campaigns differ from regular theoretical study in two major aspects. First, rectification campaigns occur sporadically, whereas the theoretical study goes on year in and year out. Second, the participants must make a thoroughgoing study of their errors and attitudes—a process not required by regular theoretical study. Each party member is called upon to examine his thinking and behavior, to criticize others straightforwardly, to accept criticism made

[12] *NCNA*, April 8, 1950; *The Chinese Youth Daily,** March 10, 1962.

[13] *People's Daily,** June 1, 1966.

[14] K'ung Tzu-jung, "Rectification Campaigns Are Powerful Magic Weapons," *Survey of China Mainland Press* (hereafter cited as *SCMP*), No. 2424 (January 25, 1962), p. 5.

of him, and to acknowledge any errors of thought or action by publicly pledging to reform. Anyone who remains silent during a campaign can be accused of being uncooperative, harboring incorrect attitudes, or concealing questionable deeds. Thus a rectification campaign enables the party leadership to detect deviations, shortcomings, disloyalties, or misconduct among the rank and file and to weed out undesirables and recalcitrants.

Although the party insists on "relentless" exposure and "severe" punishment, it is strongly opposed to "excessively harsh struggles" and "merciless blows" during rectification campaigns as well as in routine discipline. The purpose of intraparty struggles, declared Liu Shao-ch'i in 1939, was not to destroy the party, but to increase its unity, improve its discipline, and enhance its prestige.[15] In his lecture "On Intraparty Struggle," delivered in July 1941, Liu cited appropriateness, moderation, sincerity, frankness, positive educational attitudes, and helpfulness as the basic rules governing mutual criticism and more serious intraparty struggles.[16] A little later, Mao Tse-tung vividly expounded this policy as "learning from past mistakes to avoid future ones" and "curing the sickness to save the patient." [17] However, rectification campaigns have not always emphasized positive attitudes, comradely mutual help, and moderation in dealing with shortcomings and errors of party members. But generally the policy has mitigated the demoralizing effect of intraparty struggles while enhancing their usefulness. This must be borne in mind if the function of the CCP's rectification is to be correctly understood.

Several major campaigns have occurred since 1942, as a result of some special political situation or change in party policy. The objectives of each were determined by different situations, and they have ranged from an emphasis on general housecleaning in administrative procedures, as in the campaign of 1952, to an attack on power-hungry high officials, as in 1954. The campaigns are crisis-born; and in addition to educating the party members, they provide an occasional catharsis for the party members. The first rectification campaign was mounted in 1942–43 and, as noted before, had the stated aim of combating "subjectivism, doctrinairism, and sectarianism"; it attempted to accelerate the reform of bourgeois intellectuals who had entered the party without acquiring the neces-

[15] Liu Shao-ch'i, *How to Be a Good Communist* (Peking: Foreign Languages Press, 1952), p. 98.

[16] Liu Shao-ch'i, *On Intra-party Struggles* (Peking: Foreign Languages Press, 1950), pp. 30ff.

[17] Mao Tse-tung, *Selected Works,* III, 50.

sary proletarian world view. The second occurred in 1947. By this time party membership had reached 2.7 million and reportedly included a number of landlords, rich peasants, and other undesirables who had managed to gain control of local party organizations, and the 1947 campaign was largely directed against them. In June 1950, following their full assumption of power, the Communists initiated a third rectification campaign designed to raise the theoretical and political level of party members in general and new recruits in particular. It was also designed to put party members newly transferred from rural to urban districts through a special reorientation program in which they would sum up their new experience and study new policies and regulations.

The 1952 rectification campaign—the Three-Anti Campaign—involved a general overhaul of all branch organizations as well as a complete reexamination of the qualifications of individual party members. Its targets were waste, corruption, and bureaucratism—three major evils that had plagued the party since it had seized power a few years before. In 1954, following the purge of Kao Kang and Jao Shu-shih, the party launched another rectification campaign against complacency and personal empire-building among high-ranking officials.

In the spring of 1957, in the midst of widespread popular discontent and dissatisfaction, many party members, having been in power for about eight years, had come to feel they belonged to a privileged class, and were as a result self-centered, conceited, and contemptuous of nonmembers. Zealously craving luxuries, honors, and rank, these Communists were said to have formed cliques and carried on factional struggles, to have acted arbitrarily and capriciously, and to have lost concern for the interests and aspirations of ordinary people. In response to these abuses, the CCP Central Committee called for another rectification campaign on April 27, 1957. Singling out "bureaucratism, sectarianism, and subjectivism" as the chief evils, or what Mao Tse-tung called "contradictions among the people," the party leaders said that this campaign, unlike previous ones, "must be carried out seriously but as gently as a breeze or a mild rain." There was a guarantee that no one would be held responsible for anything he might say in the course of the campaign. The call for a candid and thoroughgoing examination of the party's handling of public affairs led a considerable number of party members to criticize the inadequacies and shortcomings of various functionaries and agencies. They were joined by members of the minor parties and prominent independents, whom the leadership of the CCP had asked to "assist" the party in its efforts at self-purification. Encouraged by the daring spirit of the ordinary party members and nonmembers, Communist officials also voiced dissatisfaction; among them were the First Secretary of the Honan provincial party committee, the governors of Chekiang, Chinghai, Shantung, and Liaoning, and more than a score of vice-governors and members of provincial party secretariats. Some indigenous provincial party leaders, especially those of minority nationalities, criticized the national party leadership for appointing too many outsiders to important posts in their own provinces. Others accused the party of favoring individuals who had participated in military struggles. Still others questioned basic party policies such as thought control, the absolute subordination of governmental agencies to the party, compulsory grain delivery, economic collectivization, and suppression of "counterrevolutionaries."

Shocked by these unrestrained criticisms from inside and out, the national party leadership began to strike back early in June. It converted what was originally intended as a gentle campaign into a fierce, nationwide struggle against "rightists," "localists," "nationalists," and "right-opportunists." For weeks, culprits were violently denounced at public meetings and in the press. As for critics within the party, countless intraparty struggles were waged to expose their "mistakes" and "antiparty activities." This turbulent campaign did not end until the famous Great Leap Forward movement was about to begin early in 1958.

Another rectification campaign was launched in 1960 in the aftermath of the disastrous Great Leap Forward and the Commune Movement. Blaming the failure of its policies on incorrect implementation by the cadres, the party leadership chastised many highly placed members for failing to understand the true meanings of the policies. Cadres were condemned for ignoring the policies and taking things into their own hands. Other cadres were criticized for trying to enforce party policies without explaining their merits to the masses and enlisting their willing support. In the meantime, the party made special efforts to rectify the work style of cadres in rural communes. Mindful that the widespread disaffection caused by the commune system had been aggravated by the arbitrariness and arrogance of rural functionaries, the party exhorted them to practice "four togethernesses"—to eat, live, work, and consult with commune members.

Meanwhile, the party initiated an intensive ideological reorientation program for the armed forces to reaffirm the correctness of Mao Tse-tung's doctrines on the primacy of men and policies in war and the importance of ideological work and dynamic thinking. This reaffirmation was prompted by Marshal P'eng Teh-huai's "undue" stress on the importance of weapons and equipment and his contention that political indoctrination and civilian labor had been overemphasized at the expense of regular military training. The ideological reorientation in the armed forces was also designed to halt a serious deterioration in troop morale caused by an acute shortage of provisions and new equipment after the collapse of the Great Leap Forward and the loss of Soviet military aid.

Toward the end of 1962, another rectification campaign, the "socialist education" movement, was under way in the countryside. All available evidence indicates that this campaign, unlike many others, was conducted purely by means of persuasion. Aiming at rectifying the inclination of peasants in and out of the party toward individual farming, profit-making, feudalistic exploitation, and extravagant living, the campaign laid special emphasis on socialism, collectivism, patriotism, and internationalism. Cadres and ordinary commune members alike were exhorted to run communes and conduct family affairs industriously and thriftily and join their fellow countrymen in all walks of life in carrying out "the class struggle, struggle for production, and scientific experiment." The campaign also stressed self-reliance and dedicated service to the collective, the country, and mankind.

As the socialist education movement was underway, a rift grew between the upper echelons of the party which was carefully concealed from the outside world until several years later. A faction headed by Mao Tse-tung insisted that the principal contradiction to be resolved in the socialist education movement was the one between capitalism and socialism, and that the main emphasis should be on the fight against capitalism among those in authority. Liu Shao-ch'i, who after the collapse of the Commune Movement and the Great Leap Forward, became increasingly more concerned with production than with collectivization, headed another faction which, while overtly supporting Mao's policy, covertly maneuvered to steer the party toward a more pragmatic course in various fields. By this Liu hoped to achieve economic recovery and development, stimulate intellectual creativity, and relax social and political tension.

According to the official revelations in 1967, for a short period in 1964 Liu went so far as to put forward "an opportunist line for the movement that was Left in form but Right in essence" to sabotage the socialist education movement. He allegedly asserted that the movement should center on the contradiction between being "clean" or "unclean" on four questions—accounts, warehouse inventories, public property, and work points. Instead of stressing the fight against capitalist tendencies, Liu was said to have let his wife, Wang Kuang-mei, spearhead an indiscriminate attack on the basic-level cadres and the masses. "In this way, they covered up the sharp struggle between the two classes—the proletariat and the bourgeoisie, and between the two roads—the socialist and the capitalist, switched the general orientation set for the socialist education movement, and hit hard at many to protect a handful of party persons in authority taking the capitalist road." Moreover, from November 1963 to April 1964, Liu, in order to bolster his wife's authority, sent her to direct the socialist education movement in the Taoyuan Brigade of the Luwangchuang Commune in Funing County, Hopei Province. Later, Liu and his wife "peddled the so-called Taoyuan experience in Peking, Tientsin, and many other cities and provinces, with the sinister aim of making the Taoyuan Brigade a national model in opposition to Chairman Mao's call: 'In Agriculture, Learn from Tachai.'" (The Tachai Brigade of the Tachai Commune in Siyang County, Shansi Province, had for many years been a national pace-setter in transforming nature and expanding agriculture through hard work and self-reliance. See p. 163.) Liu's maneuver prompted Mao to give his personal attention to the course of the socialist education movement. Soon the party adopted a 23-article document entitled "The Current Problems Raised in the Socialist Education Movement." Drawn up under Mao's direct guidance, the document widened the orientation of the "Four Clean-Ups Movement" to rectifying politics, ideology, organization, and economy. This campaign reportedly "mobilized the broad masses of the people in the communes, factories, mines, enterprises, and other undertakings to drag out the handful of persons in the party who were in charge of these establishments and were taking the capitalist road, dismissed them from office, and dealt severe blows to those [former] rich peasants and rightists who clung to a counterrevolutionary stand."[18]

The most far-reaching rectification campaign was the GPCR, which will be discussed in Chapter XIII.

[18] *Red Flag** commentator, "Defend the Great Achievements of the Four Clean-Ups Movement," *Peking Review*, No. 11 (March 10, 1967), pp. 15–16; "The Crimes of China's Khrushchev in the Socialist Education Movement," *ibid.*, No. 38 (September 15, 1967), pp. 25–27; Richard Baum and Frederick C. Teiwes, *Ssu-Ch'ing: The Socialist Education Movement of 1962–1966* (Berkeley: Center for Chinese Studies at the University of California, 1968).

VIII

The Development of Administrative, Control, and Defense Mechanisms

In Chapter VI it was stated that the CCP is the leader and hard core of the state while the government, the armed forces, and the "people's organizations" are but tools by which the CCP controls the national life of China. The kinds of tools that the CCP has developed in the last 24 years and the ways in which it has used them have had a considerable bearing on its ability to administer the affairs of the nation, to keep dissident elements under control, and to protect the nation against foreign enemies. In addition, the CCP's political style has been molded greatly by its development and use of these tools.

Development of Formal Governing Mechanisms Since 1949

The formal machinery used by the CCP for governing the country has undergone a process of repeated modification in response to changing conditions and ideological requirements. The administrative machinery that the CCP initially established in a newly "liberated" urban district in the late 1940's was "the military control commission." Appointed by the local commands of the People's Liberation Army, the military control commissions in various localities served as interim governments for the areas concerned during the takeover period. Among the major responsibilities of these commissions were the restoration and maintenance of order; the arrest, punishment, and custody of those former Kuomintang officials who had committed "crimes against the people" in the past and who might engage in sabotage and other counterrevolutionary activities in the future; the takeover and protection of archives and properties left behind by the agencies of the

中國共產運動簡史

former regime; the screening of former Kuomintang personnel who had severed their ties with the Kuomintang and who wished to work for "the people"; and the execution of emergency economic measures aimed at halting the runaway inflation left over by the Kuomintang government and ensuring adequate supply of foods and other daily necessities for residents in war-torn cities and towns. Military control commissions were also charged with the primary responsibility for organizing local "people's governments," which were to replace the commissions themselves as local administrative bodies. Displaying the discipline of the People's Liberation Army, scrupulously adhering to the CCP's policy on governing "newly liberated areas," and owing their effectiveness to meticulous planning by the party prior to the final collapse of the Kuomintang, the military control commissions contributed much to the orderliness of the initial phase of the Communist takeover, and this orderliness, in turn, helped the new regime win the respect, if not support, of a considerable segment of the population.

In the rural areas "people's governments" at the village, district (*ch'ü*), and county levels were established immediately after their "liberation." Like the people's governments in the urban areas, principal offices in the rural people's governments were filled with cadres of the People's Liberation Army who had had administrative experience in the "old liberated areas" or who had recently received special training for their new duties. Also like the urban people's governments, the new governing bodies in most of the rural areas saw fit to retain the services of some former Kuomintang personnel whose talents were sorely needed and who were willing to cooperate. Meanwhile, the CCP organized people's governments at the provincial level. The provincial governments were, among other things, to supervise the people's governments of the counties and cities in their respective provinces. To facilitate this supervisory task, the provincial people's governments stationed administrative commissioners in the administrative prefectures (*chuan-ch'ü*), which usually comprised some 20 counties each. As noted in Chapter VI, in the early years of the People's Republic there were also regional administrations acting essentially as agents of the central government in directing the work of the provincial governments under their jurisdictions and carrying out central government decisions and orders in their respective regions. The heads of all the regional, provincial, county, city, district, and village people's governments at first were appointed officials, responsible only to the CCP committees on corresponding levels and to the people's governments at higher levels.

In order to give some substance to the democratic aspect of the official doctrine on "people's democratic dictatorship" and to create a sharp contrast between the "People's Republic" and the former Kuomintang regime, which for many years made no provisions for popular representation in government, the Central People's Government in Peking early in December 1949 called for the establishment of "all-circle people's representatives conferences" at the county, municipal, and provincial levels. As a sort of provisional legislatures, these conferences were empowered to "gradually exercise the rights and functions of the envisioned people's congresses. Specifically, they were to hear and examine the work reports of the provincial, municipal, and county people's governments; to examine and pass provincial, municipal, and county budgets; to submit proposals and resolutions on the politics of the people's governments concerned; and to elect people's government councils at corresponding levels. By March 1950 an overwhelming majority of the provinces, cities, and counties were said to have convened all-circle people's representatives conferences; and the conferences in 10 of the 27 provinces had already exercised the right to elect provincial government councils including governors and vice governors. Most of the members of the conferences were "elected" by various "people's organizations" in the areas concerned. Among the participating people's organizations were those of women, youth, peasants, merchants and industrialists, writers and educators, and national minorities. Some provincial and municipal all-circle people's representatives conferences also provided representation for minor political parties and "independent personages."

Toward the end of 1950, the provisional system of "popular representation" was extended to the district (*ch'ü*) and village levels. Together with the efforts to eliminate the gentry's hold on local governments and to destroy all the other traditional centers of political influence, the creation of the provisional system of "popular representation" was officially described as "the Campaign for the Establishment of People's Democratic Political Power." In practice, the all-circle people's representatives conferences provided an effective means of mobilizing the broad masses of people to assist the government in implementing revolutionary and construction work. They served as a formal channel for the new regime to communicate with large numbers of political activists, who tended to develop a sense of self-significance after having acquired membership in one of these conferences and thus become all the more enthusiastic about the new order. Furthermore, the convening of the conferences was, in effect, a dress rehearsal for the people's congresses that were to make their appearance a few years later as "full-fledged" representative bodies.

By the end of 1952 the Campaign for the Establishment of People's Democratic Political Power and "the people's democratic revolution" in the social, cultural, and economic fields (to be discussed later) had been basically completed. "To consolidate and legalize the achievements" of the initial phase of the People's Republic and to open an era of transition to socialism, the CCP-dominated Central People's Government Council on January 13, 1953 decided to enact a constitution for the country. As part of the process for establishing a "constitutional government," the Council also called for the convocation of a National People's Congress and local people's congresses at various levels. On March 1, 1953, the Council promulgated a law governing the election of deputies to the people's congresses. In accordance with this law qualified citizens in the basic-level units (i.e., administrative *hsiang* or villages, towns, and wards within cities) held elections in 1953 and early 1954 for deputies to the basic-level people's congresses. These congresses soon elected deputies to the county and city people's congresses, and in June and July 1954 the county and city people's congresses met. Among other things, they elected deputies to the provincial people's congresses. In the following month, the provincial people's congresses and the People's Liberation Army elected deputies to the National People's Congress.

On March 23, 1954, Mao Tse-tung, on behalf of the Central Committee of the CCP, submitted a "preliminary draft" of the national constitution to a 26-member Constitution-Drafting Committee headed by himself. After "consulting" more than 8000 persons from all walks of life, the Committee accepted the draft on June 11, and immediately submitted it to the Central People's Government Council for action. Three days later the Council decided by unanimous vote to publish this draft "so that the people throughout the country can discuss it and make suggestions for its improvement." For more than two months, over 150 million persons took part in the nationwide debate, lending their "support" to the draft constitution and suggesting "many amendments and addenda." After considering these suggestions, none of which contradicted the basic spirit and provisions of the draft, the Constitution-Drafting Committee presented a slightly revised draft to the Central People's Government Council. On September 9, the Council resolved to submit it to the first session of the First National People's Congress for final examination and adoption. On September 20, the 1197 recently elected deputies gave unanimous approval to the document without proposing any change whatsoever.

Although it replaced the Common Program of the Chinese People's Political Consultative Conference and the Organic Law of the Central People's Government as the supreme law of the land, the new Constitution reaffirmed the hegemony of the CCP in the state. Structurally, the Constitution preserved the dual hierarchy of party and governmental organs with pyramidal arrangement of the party organization paralleling the territorial tiers of the governmental hierarchy and with the governmental organs at each level of the hierarchy operating under the dual direction of the party committee on the corresponding level and governmental organs on the next higher level. Structural changes introduced by the Constitution were confined to a few areas. First, the Constitution contained no provision for the establishment of superministerial committees in the State Council as the provisional constitution did. This was designed to secure administrative efficiency. Except that the State Council is now theoretically accountable to the National People's Congress or to its Standing Committee during its recess, whereas the former Government Administrative Council was legally responsible to the Central People's Government Council or, when the latter stood adjourned, to the chairman of the Republic, the State Council now has about the same status and functions as its predecessor. Neither of them was intended to be a body capable of carrying out its own policies, for in either case they were required by unwritten law and open injunctions to be extremely alert to the contours and oscillations of the line of the CCP. Ministers of the State Council, like the members of the former Government Administrative Council, appear to be merely high technical advisers and administrators—executors of the will of the Politburo of the CCP. They undoubtedly have plenty of opportunities to render expert advice, draw up initial plans, suggest policies that may be adopted, and administer their execution, but the definite word on all fundamental courses of action still lies with the central authority of the CCP, and Mao Tse-tung transcends them all.

The Constitution transferred some of the powers formerly exercised by the chairman of the Republic to the Standing Committee of the National People's Congress, but the chairmanship of the Republic under the new Constitution remains nonetheless a highly important office as shown by the fact that Mao Tse-tung personally held the post from its inception in September 1954 to April 1959 and then had his heir apparent at the time, Liu Shao-ch'i, elected to it.

Besides legalizing the new order created after October 1949 and introducing certain changes in governmental machinery, the Constitution provided a legal basis for the forthcoming socialist transformation of the national economy, the nationalization of natural resources, and centralized planning. It prescribed certain basic rules governing social and institutional behavior and expressed the normative goals and aspirations of the state. The reorganization of the government at various levels that took place immediately after the adoption of the Constitution gave the CCP a convenient opportunity to place more of its own members in important offices of the government and reduce the minor parties' share of such offices, although care was taken to preserve the facade of the united front. Insofar as enlisting popular support was concerned, the holding of general elections, particularly those on the grass-roots level in which hundreds of millions of people took part, and the election of millions of deputies to the people's congresses at various levels apparently imbued many of the participants with a sense of involvement in the affairs of the state, despite the omnipresence of the CCP's strong guiding hand.[1] At least some of those who were elected as deputies were apt to be susceptible to such additional influences as the prestige and material perquisites accruing to their status. Since the deputies were leaders or model workers in various fields, their closer identification with the regime could only strengthen the latter's hold on the nation, and periodical elections and convening of the people's congresses make it possible for the CCP to derive this benefit continuously. That political activists indeed prize membership in the people's congresses can be seen from the fact that in 1963 the regime decided to expand the congresses at all levels. The Third National People's Congress elected in 1964, for example, was more than twice as large as its two predecessors elected in 1954 and 1959.

People's Organizations as an Instrument of Mobilization and Control

Seeking to effect a thoroughgoing transformation of the Chinese society, the CCP leaders are never content to use only formal governmental institutions for carrying out their programs and policies. Rather Mao and his associates always insist on awakening the masses and setting them in motion in all revolutionary struggles. Professing a belief that the masses are the real makers of history, Mao Tse-tung

[1] During the 1953 elections, 278,093,100 or 85.88 per cent of the registered voters went to the polls to elect 5,669,144 deputies to the basic-level people's congresses. See Teng Hsiao-p'ing's report on these elections, *Kuang-ming Daily,** June 20, 1954.

once said: "As long as we rely upon the masses, firmly believe in the infinite creative power of the people, and therefore have confidence in them, and unite as one with them, then we will be able to overcome any difficulty, no matter how serious it may be, and no enemy will be able to overwhelm us but will be overwhelmed by us." [2] Without forsaking the use of coercion, the CCP leaders appear to believe that mass support for their policies can be best achieved by enlightening and heightening the consciousness of the masses, involving them in the work of the party and the government, and maintaining close contact with them. Thus the people's organizations in the last 24 years have devoted much of their energy to assisting the party and the government in explaining official policies to individuals within their respective groups, in remolding the ideology of their members, and in rousing their members to collective action for the construction of a socialist new China.

As affiliates or auxiliaries of the CCP, the people's organizations serve as the party's eyes and ears, reporting to the party on the sentiments and behavior of their members and assisting the party in suppressing dissident elements. Some of these organizations have played even more direct roles in the political and administrative processes. The peasants' associations, for example, were assigned the task of organizing "struggle meetings" against the landlords and local "bullies" in the vast countryside and redistributing land, and the trade unions once had the primary responsibility of ensuring the private industrialists' compliance with the government's regulations and directives concerning labor protection, labor insurance, wage standards, factory hygiene and safety devices, and other matters. More recently, the Red Guards spearheaded the campaign against "those people in power who have taken the road of capitalism."

Most of the people's organizations draw their memberships from distinct occupational groups such as workers, peasants, industrialists and merchants, writers and artists, and scientists and engineers. Other organizations direct their attention to youth, women, religious groups, and the like. There are no up-to-date statistics on the memberships of the various people's organizations, though it is generally believed that the majority of the adult people and school-age children on mainland China today belong to one or more of these organizations. Through these groups the CCP is able to bring the largest number of individuals into its direct organizational control, thus maximizing its ability to persuade, mobilize, and coerce

[2] Mao Tse-tung, *On Coalition Government* (Yenan: The New China News Agency, 1945), p. 145.

the Chinese masses. An official spokesman has said: "If the party were taken as a generator, then the various people's organizations would be the lathes which link in motion the generator and the machines of different workshops. The people's organizations are considered an indispensable link between the party and the masses just because short of these organizations it would be difficult for the party to contact the broad masses." [3]

No discussion of the people's organizations as instruments of mass control and mobilization would be complete without mentioning the crucial role played in this regard since 1954 by the "urban inhabitants' committees." [4] A successor to the now defunct "security preservation committees," which made their appearance in the cities and towns in the wake of the Campaign for Suppressing Counter-revolutionaries in 1952, the urban inhabitants' committees are neighborhood organizations working among all the inhabitants of the various residential districts in each city without regard to occupational and other differences. There is an inhabitants' committee for every 100 to 600 households. To facilitate the committee's work, the households under its jurisdiction are organized into several "groups" with each group comprising 15 to 40 households. A "household group" usually has a leader and a deputy leader. Each of the "household groups" under the jurisdiction of an inhabitants' committee elects a representative to serve on that committee, and the committee elects its own chairman and a number of vice-chairmen. Needless to say, the elections are always carefully guided by the local organizations of the CCP, and those who are elected to leadership positions are usually political activists.

Although their main functions are the detection of subversive activities and the mobilization of local inhabitants for participating in officially sponsored drives and campaigns, the committees are also concerned with neighborhood disputes and welfare programs. Furthermore, they are charged with keeping the local authorities informed of the inhabitants' state of mind and aspirations, a function which, if faithfully carried out, can be of great service to the regime. The inhabitants' committees operate under the close supervision of the local party and government organizations, especially "the street committees," which act as a sort of "field offices" of the city governments concerned. However, the inhabitants' committees are not considered part of the city government. Coupled with the

[3] *Extracts from China Mainland Magazines* (Hereafter cited as *ECMM*), No. 60 (December 10, 1956), p. 8.

[4] See "Regulations on the Organization of Urban Inhabitants' Committees," *Kuang-ming Daily,** January 1, 1955.

fact that their members are "elected" by the local residents from among themselves, the unofficial nature of the inhabitants' committees is believed to be better able to bring the enthusiasm and initiative of the masses fully into play in undertaking projects of local and/or national significance.

Minor Parties and the "People's Democratic United Front"

The people's democratic united front is another mechanism through which the CCP seeks to influence, control, and mobilize the Chinese population. Aside from the workers and peasants, which the CCP claims to represent, the major components of this united front are the eight minor parties that the CCP has officially characterized as "democratic parties of a bourgeois nature." These political groups are the Kuomintang Revolutionary Committee, the China Democratic League, the China Democratic National Construction Association, the China Association for Promoting Democracy, the Chinese Peasants and Workers Party, the Chiu San Society, the Chih Kung T'ang, and the Taiwan Democratic Self-Government League.

The feasibility of tolerating the continuing existence of bourgeois parties after China has supposedly entered the era of socialist revolution and socialist construction, which the bourgeoisie normally cannot be expected to accept, rests on the following assumptions:[5] first, after having supported the CCP in bringing the "people's democratic revolution" to a successful conclusion, many bourgeois elements have become genuinely convinced that only by continuing to accept the leadership of the CCP can their parties make further contributions to the noble task of building a united, prosperous, and powerful new China; second, with the CCP firmly in control of the powerful state apparatus, those bourgeois elements who otherwise might have been reluctant to follow the CCP in the march toward socialism have recognized the expediency of accepting socialism and supporting the CCP continuously; third, since the petty bourgeoisie, the national bourgeoisie, and the political parties that represent them have a "dual character" politically, it is possible for the CCP to help them develop their progressive tendencies and rectify their reactionary inclinations, thus ensuring their willingness to remain in the united front in the era of socialism. The CCP has sought to give its "help" to the minor parties by pursuing a policy of "winning over" and political re-education.

The CCP also emphasizes the desirability of preserving the non-Communist parties in the era of socialism. First, because of the

[5] See Chang Chih-i, *A Preliminary Study of the Chinese People's Democratic United Front** (Peking: People's Press, 1958).

immensity of the tasks of realizing socialism on the one hand and the shortage of professionally proficient men and women on the other, it is wise for the CCP to continue to pursue a policy of uniting with all that can be united so that all available talents can be placed in the service of the "great" cause. Second, because of their social and ideological affinity with the petty bourgeoisie and the national bourgeoisie in the country at large, the "democratic parties" can be particularly effective in persuading those social elements to accept socialism and to undergo thought reform, which the CCP deems essential if the bourgeoisie are to become wholehearted supporters of the new order. Third, as long as the "democratic parties" are willing to assist the CCP in building a socialist new China, they can serve as a useful safety valve, calling the People's Government's attention to the legitimate grievances of the social elements they represent and advising the government on ways and means of improving administrative inadequacies and shortcomings. With their help the CCP can be better able to resolve "contradictions among the people," which, according to Mao Tse-tung, are likely to exist even in a socialist state.[6] Fourth, the continuing existence of the "democratic parties" in China in the era of socialism, the CCP hopes, will have a favorable impact on the future development of the world Communist movement. Specifically, the CCP hopes to use this "tolerant" policy to allay the universal fear that a Communist victory anywhere in the world will inevitably entail the destruction of all the non-Communist parties in the country concerned. Once this fear is allayed, the CCP believes, Communists in non-Communist countries will be less handicapped in organizing broad united fronts with other revolutionary and "progressive" forces for joint struggles against the socio-political status quo in their lands, thus facilitating the triumph of socialism and communism.

In accordance with the principle of division of labor, which is designed in part to restrict their mass base, all the "democratic parties" today carry on mobilization and re-education work only among social groups that the CCP has assigned to them. The Kuomintang Revolutionary Committee, for example, confines its operations to former Kuomintang members on the mainland and present Kuomintang members on Taiwan and elsewhere, and the China Democratic League works among certain sections of the politically active intelligentsia.

In line with the united front ideology and desirous of supplementing persuasion and coercion with tangible rewards, the newly

[6] Mao Tse-tung, "On the Correct Handling of Contradictions among the People," *CB*, No. 458 (June 20, 1957), pp. 1–26.

founded People's Government in 1949 filled many of its exalted positions with members of the "democratic parties." Despite a slight reduction of their share of such positions after the adoption of the new national Constitution in 1954, the minor parties continued to hold a disproportionate number of high offices in the following years. In 1956 the CCP even spoke of "long-term coexistence and mutual supervision" as a principle governing its relations with the "democratic parties." However, it was brought to light during the "One Hundred Flowers Campaign" in 1957 that many leaders of the "democratic parties," instead of being steadily attracted to communism as a result of their participation in the People's Government, had actually become disenchanted with the CCP. Besides their abhorrence of certain Communist "excesses" in collectivization, thought reform, and the treatment of "counterrevolutionaries," the non-Communist politicians' dissatisfaction with their role in the government apparently was a major contributing factor to the disenchantment. Many of them charged during the campaign that although they had been given high positions in the government, they were never permitted to exercise the authority that their offices supposedly possessed. Some outspoken members of the minor parties even characterized the People's Government as a "party empire" in which there were "high walls and deep ditches" between members of the CCP and the non-Communist people. A few critics went so far as to say that the state of affairs in the country was worse than the days of the Kuomintang and that "some top-ranking Communists in Peking should alight from their sedan-chairs and some should even be removed from office." [7] Like critics in other quarters, the disenchanted members of the minor parties were quickly subjected to a fierce counterattack by the CCP. Dubbed "rightists," they were severely condemned in the press and at "struggle" meetings staged by their respective party organizations. This anti-rightist campaign, which began on June 8, soon compelled the culprits to make public confessions of their anti-socialist and anti-CCP errors. It also led to the dismissal of many critics from their positions in the government, various people's organizations, and their own parties, and for some time these critics dropped completely out of sight.

The banishment of the "rightists" was followed by a Communist demand that all minor parties undergo a thorough remolding so as to discard their bourgeois attitudes and acquire the socialist outlook. On February 27, 1958 all the "democratic parties" launched

[7] For information on the subject see Roderick MacFarquhar, *The Hundred Flowers Campaign and the Chinese Intellectuals* (New York: Frederick A. Praeger, Inc., 1960).

a self-reform campaign, which culminated on March 16 in a spectacular joint rally of over ten thousand prominent members of minor parties and independents. At the rally, held at the Heavenly Peace Gate Square in Peking, the participants pledged to "dedicate their hearts" to socialism and to the CCP. Accepting this outward submission as a suitable cause for showing forgiveness and recognizing the continued utility of the united front in a period of serious economic dislocation caused by the collapse of the Great Leap Forward, the intensifying dispute with Moscow, and natural calamities, the CCP in April 1959 reinstated some of the disgraced non-Communist politicians in their parties and in the government, but in a lesser capacity than before.

At the same time steps were taken to strengthen the CPPCC. Having ceased to be the highest organ of state power ever since the inauguration of the National People's Congress in 1954, the CPPCC was now to become the principal organization for consolidating and developing the Chinese people's united front. One of the measures taken to strengthen the CPPCC was the expansion of its National Committee from 726 to 1071 members, enabling the CCP to give national recognition to a larger number of men and women in all walks of life, especially those in the minor parties and some independents. Such recognition, it was hoped, would cement the bond between the CCP and the various social elements involved. Another step was to give the CPPCC considerable vitality by establishing some 300 new local committees at various levels. The political significance of these two measures was enhanced in the spring of 1960 when members of the national, provincial, municipal, and county committees of the CPPCC were given the privilege of attending the sessions of the people's congresses on corresponding levels as observers. This arrangement enabled members of the CPPCC committees to acquire practically the same political prerogatives and material perquisites as those accorded the regular deputies to the people's congresses; the only exception was the right to vote—a matter of little significance since voting at the people's congresses has always been a formality. To make the committees of the CPPCC at various levels still more useful vehicles for increasing the opportunities of non-Communist elements for political participation while preserving its hegemony, the CCP initiated the practice in 1962 of having the plenary sessions of the National Committee of the CPPCC attended not only by its regular members but also by over 800 observers—in very much the same way and for the same purposes as members of the National Committee of the CPPCC would attend the meetings of the National People's Congress.

Such efforts to solidify and develop the united front may still fall short of achieving total success inasmuch as some non-Communist people of great ambitions are unlikely to be satisfied with the limited political roles that these measures provide for them. But the prominent and ambitious non-Communist politicians are aging, and the CCP's measures are apt to have an increasingly mollifying effect on them as their ages keep advancing. In any event, the main objective of the CCP's adherence to the policy of the united front at the present time is no longer, it would seem, the mobilization and re-education of the "democratic parties," whose ranks have dwindled due to lack of replacements for deceased members. Rather, it is the much-desired "peaceful liberation of Taiwan" that calls for the continuation of the policy. Should the Kuomintang leaders on Taiwan ever feel that their position on the island is seriously threatened either locally or by a foreign power, the CCP's continuing pursuance of the united front policy could be a great inducement for them to give up their long-held anti-Communist stand in favor of a policy of reconciliation with the Peking regime. The return of Li Tsung-jen, former Acting President of the Kuomintang regime, to mainland China from New York in the summer of 1965 seems to have given the CCP some encouragement for such a prospect.

Building the Armed Forces

Influenced by Lenin's dictum that even a proletarian dictatorship must sustain itself by violence as well as by persuasion and remembering the fact that foreign invasions of China in modern times were the direct result of her military weakness, the CCP has made the development of a mighty military establishment one of its principal tasks ever since its assumption of power. Today the regular military establishment, known as the People's Liberation Army (PLA), consists of an army, a navy, an air force, and specialized units—the three last-mentioned forces products of the post-1949 era—and is believed to have a total strength of 3.3 million. Even though in view of the total Chinese population this is a relatively modest size, it is the third largest military establishment in the world, ranking only after those of the United States and the Soviet Union. Of the total, some 2.3 million men are in the army, which is larger than the ground forces of any other nation.

Unlike the pre-1949 era, when the Communist army did not have sufficient quantities of even obsolete small arms, the ground forces of mainland China now are well equipped with rifles, machine guns, automatic and semiautomatic weapons, mortars, light rocket launchers, recoilless rifles, and light and medium artillery. Although much of the limited quantities of heavy equipment, such as tanks and self-propelled guns, was provided by the Soviet Union prior to 1961, the light and medium weapons are manufactured by Chinese arsenals, thanks to earlier Soviet technical assistance and the CCP's determined efforts in recent years to attain self-reliance in national defense as well as in all other fields. The Chinese air force, once severely impaired by the loss of Soviet equipment and spare parts, is estimated to have about 3600 combat aircraft, 440 bombers, 300 helicopters, 2900 fighters, and 400 transports. Among the fighters are estimated 1700 MIG-17's and 100 subsonic MIG-15's. There are some 1000 MIG-19's and 15 to 30 MIG-21's. Because of her recent advances in military technology and the development of a petroleum industry, China's ability to breathe new life into her air force should not be underestimated. A case in point is the new supersonic jet fighter F-9, which can fly at speeds up to roughly twice the speed of sound, or 1000 miles an hour. Eighty of these new jets were believed operational by January 1972.[8] The navy has always been the weakest of the Communist Chinese armed forces. Essentially a coastal defense force, it has a few destroyer escorts, about 40 minesweepers, 25 subchasers, 30 submarines of which about two dozen are of the long-range type. It also reportedly has a few submarines with launching tubes capable of firing three nuclear-tipped missiles with a range of 300 to 400 miles. All the units of the PLA are controlled by the Ministry of National Defense, which in turn operates under the direction and supervision of the Military Affairs Commission of the CCP Central Committee.

The PLA is supplemented by the Public Security Forces (or People's Police) and the militia. Numbering half a million men, the Public Security Forces have the primary responsibility of preserving internal order and combating sabotage and other subversive activities. They are controlled by the Ministry of Public Security, which like the Ministry of National Defense works under the direct guidance of the party's Military Affairs Commission. The militia has been an important adjunct to the regular Chinese Communist army ever since Mao Tse-tung first founded a military base on Chingkangshan in 1927. In 1950 when the party had been in power for only one year there were some 5.5 million men in the militia. In 1958, the CCP decided to expand the already sizeable militia still further by launching the "Everyone a Soldier" movement. In addition to strengthening China's ability to wage a people's war against an invading force equipped with superior weapons, the movement also

[8] *The New York Times,* January 30, 1972; February 1, 1972; and November 8, 1972.

had important political and economic implications. Economically, it was designed to enable the CCP to utilize the organization and discipline of the militia to more effectively control and mobilize the masses for production. Indeed, the movement began amid the Great Leap Forward and the drive to establish communes. Politically, the expanded militia organizations were used to intensify the political indoctrination of the masses and thereby militarize and collectivize their lives. Finally, the militia was to provide physical training for the masses with a view to improving the physique of the Chinese people.[9]

The militia is divided into two principal types, the "ordinary" and the "basic." The ordinary militia, whose members receive only rudimentary military training during non-working hours, is intended to perform such duties as guarding granaries, factories, and communications lines rather than engaging in active combat. The "basic" units are the backbone of the militia. Consisting of ex-servicemen from the PLA and activists in other walks of life, the "basic" units receive military training on a regular schedule. Since 1961 special emphasis has been placed on the development of this type of militia, for it will be called up to reinforce the PLA in time of war. Because of its apprehension that the continuing escalation of the war in Vietnam might eventually lead to an American attack on China, Peking has lately stepped up the training of the militia, especially in night and close fighting, which according to CCP strategists will make it impossible for the United States to make good use of its air superiority and tactical nuclear weapons.

Parallel with the intensified training of the militia have been the efforts to strengthen the capabilities of the PLA and to place it on a war footing. To improve the professional competence of military personnel, the Peking government in January 1965 amended the Conscription Law of 1955 extending the service of non-commissioned officers and enlisted men in the various branches of the PLA from three to five years to four to six years. A top priority in recent years has been to prepare the PLA psychologically for war against the U. S. and the U.S.S.R. with their formidable nuclear arsenals and advanced conventional armaments by instilling in military personnel and the Chinese people as a whole an unshakable self-confidence. A technique used in this undertaking is to give prominence to Mao's slogans: "The Imperialists and All Reactionaries Are Paper Tigers," and "Despise the Enemy Strategically and

[9] Ralph L. Powell, "Everyone a Soldier: The Communist Chinese Militia," *Foreign Affairs* (October 1960), pp. 100–111.

Take Good Account of Him Tactically." Another technique is to stress the primacy of the human factor in war. At the PLA senior officers' conference in October 1960 Lin Piao made this Maoist concept the first of four cardinal principles of army building; the other three are that politics should take command, that ideological work should take precedence over administrative work, and that dynamic thinking is better than ideas in books.

A corollary of the "human factor first" concept is the importance attached to the raising of man's political consciousness and the cultivation and development of man's courage and spirit of sacrifice. Mao's stress on political and ideological work is geared to these ends. Mao and his associates believe that the display by the Chinese armed forces of a high degree of valor and initiative will aid the country to overcome many difficulties that she would inevitably face in a war against an enemy with more sophisticated weapons. An important device used by the PLA to attain this objective is the launching of successive drives to emulate revolutionary heroes, such as Lei Feng, Wang Hsieh, Mai Hsien-te, and others, who as ordinary soldiers reportedly risked their own lives "serving the people," displayed "the dauntless spirit of defying heaven and earth in fighting against the enemy," and "were always determined to overcome whatever hardships that they were experiencing in their work." Another concomitant of the "human factor first" concept is the endeavor to preserve and develop a close and cordial relationship between officers and soldiers with the objective of heightening the morale of the ranks, enhancing the latter's initiative, strengthening the unity between soldiers and officers, and ultimately improving the fighting power and cohesion of the army so that it can withstand the greatest adversities. Since 1958 the PLA has put into effect a system whereby commanding generals, senior political commissars, and other high-ranking officers will serve for one month each year as common soldiers at the company level. On May 24, 1965, the 10-year-old system of military ranks was abolished to "help eliminate certain objective factors contributing to breeding rank consciousness and ideas to gain fame and wealth and to help the officers more consciously place themselves in the position of ordinary soldiers and ordinary workers, thus making the officers and soldiers more intimate comrades-in-arms and class brothers." The abolition of military ranks was followed by a drive to promote the "triple democracy" that the PLA had practiced during the civil war.[10] Under

[10] Ho Lung, "The Democratic Tradition of the PLA," *Liberation Army Journal,** July 31, 1965.

this system soldiers have the right to offer opinions and suggestions concerning political work, military tactics and techniques, and living arrangements. The CCP has claimed that when applied under the "centralized guidance" of the party committees in the army this system of triple democracy can be highly effective in raising the revolutionary consciousness and sense of dedication of the masses of soldiers, in curbing arbitrariness on the part of officers as well as in promoting internal unity.

Not only does the CCP seek to strengthen the unity between officers and soldiers but it is also conscious of the importance of achieving unity between the army and the people—a prerequisite to the ability to wage a "people's war." To accomplish this the CCP now continues to require thorough observance by all military personnel of "The Three Rules of Discipline and Eight Points for Attention," a set of norms of behavior laid down by Mao Tse-tung for the Communist army during the civil war. Among other things, these norms enjoin members of the PLA to speak politely to civilians and to pay for what they buy—behavior seldom seen among Chinese troops in the recent past. For their part, the Chinese people have been taught to change their conception of an army—not to fear the troops but to befriend them, not to regard soldiers as "the most terrible people" but to regard them as "the most beloved people," not to fear or refuse to serve in the army but to compete and take the lead in joining it, not to think that "good men never become soldiers" but to realize that "good men must become soldiers." Another important facet of the CCP policy of army building in the post-1949 era has been a continuing adherence to the Maoist concept that "the PLA is forever a combat unit; and in the meantime, it is also a working unit" that engages in economic production and mass campaigns. By charging the army with nonmilitary tasks the CCP not only seeks to utilize the vast manpower, skills, and organization of the army for the advancement of its multifarious goals, but also hopes to have the army gain the experience and attitude necessary for joining civilians in agricultural production, manufacturing, and other chores that a people's war would necessitate. Moreover, the party probably believes that the nonmilitary chores may help prevent the men in uniform from developing a purely professional outlook, which is regarded as a potential threat to the preservation of the party's absolute leadership in the army. The CCP's determination to forestall a situation in which (to use a Maoist expression) the party can no longer direct the guns but is forced to allow the guns to direct the party seems to have been strengthened by its recollection of the state of affairs that existed in China only a few decades ago and by its knowledge of the many military *coups d'état* that have taken place in recent years in emerging nations. Thus far the CCP has maintained its absolute leadership in the army by subjecting men in uniform to regular and intensive indoctrination and by having a pyramid of party committees in the army lead and supervise the work of military units at every level. Today the PLA is considered the model of political orientation, plain living, and hard struggle, and the whole nation has been exhorted to emulate it.

Though Communist China's army building has been done in accordance with Mao Tse-tung's ideas, from time to time some of his top lieutenants in the army have questioned the continuing soundness of certain tenets of his military doctrine.[11] According to a recent official account,[12] there have been three attempts to modify this doctrine since the party seized power 24 years ago. The first was made shortly after the Korean War: "Under the signboard of 'regularization' and 'modernization,'" the official account alleged, "a handful of representatives of the bourgeois military line at the time, making a complete carbon copy of foreign practice, vainly tried to negate our army's historical experience and fine tradition and to lead our army onto the road followed by bourgeois armies." "Responding to Mao's call 'Down with the slave mentality, let's bury dogmatism,'" the 1958 enlarged session of the CCP Military Affairs Commission "smashed the frantic attack of the representatives of the bourgeois military line" and defended Mao's thinking on army building. The second attempt occurred in 1959, and, as noted in the Appendix, was spearheaded by the then Defense Minister P'eng Teh-huai, although his name was not identified with this episode until 1967. According to the account cited above, in that year "a right opportunist antiparty clique made a great effort to do away with the party's absolute leadership over the army, to abolish political work, to abolish the tasks which the army has of participating in socialist construction and doing mass work, and to abolish the local armed forces and the militia; in this way they tried completely to negate Chairman Mao's ideas on the people's army and people's war."

Judging from other fragmentary official revelations on the matter, it seems quite clear that what prompted the "right opportunists" to advocate a new approach to army building was not a desire to free

[11] See Alice L. Hsieh, *Communist China's Strategy in the Nuclear Era* (Englewood Cliffs, N. J.: Prentice-Hall, Inc., 1962).

[12] Editorial in *Liberation Army Journal,** August 1, 1966.

the army completely from party control as the official indictment alleged but rather reflected a concern that in the age of professional specialization continued insistence on the PLA's participation in non-military tasks might jeopardize its military training, and that the policy of placing equal emphasis on the development of the PLA, the Public Security Forces, and the militia might divert the already limited resources of the nation from the PLA to whose further modernization they attached the greatest importance. It was the party's view, however, that the proposed changes, if implemented, would lead to a steady erosion of the party character of the army, even though that might not have been the intention of the champions of reform. Perhaps the party's imputation of antiparty motives in the case resulted from the reformers' failure to cease advocating their views after the party had already rejected them. In any event, in August 1959 the party's Military Affairs Commission "thoroughly settled accounts" with P'eng Teh-huai and a few other "right opportunists" and dismissed them from office. Upon the dismissal of P'eng, Lin Piao was put in actual charge of the CCP Military Affairs Commission while concurrently serving as Minister of Defense. He immediately made a thorough and resolute enforcement of Mao's ideas on army building the sacred mission of the armed forces. Before long however Lo Tui-ch'ing, the PLA's new Chief of Staff, had the same misgivings about the Maoist military line expressed by P'eng Teh-huai. According to the above-mentioned official account (which consistently adhered to the policy of not identifying erring veteran Communists by name), while serving as Chief of Staff, Lo and some other officers sharing his views were guilty of overtly agreeing to but covertly opposing Mao's thought and Lin Piao's directives on putting politics in the forefront, and of talking about putting politics in command but in practice giving first consideration to military affairs, technique, and specialized work. Since November 1965 Lo has not been seen in public. The party now calls this episode "the third big struggle between the proletarian and bourgeois lines of army building since the founding of the People's Republic."

The above account of the CCP's emphasis on the primacy of man and politics in army building does not warrant the inference, however, that Mao Tse-tung, Lin Piao, and others presently in charge of the party and the army do not have an adequate appreciation of the role of weaponry in war. Earlier we have mentioned Peking's growing capability for manufacturing tanks, rockets, jet fighters, and submarines. But the most unmistakable evidence of the Chinese leaders' recognition of the importance of modern weaponry is their determination to develop nuclear weapons and ballistic missiles, despite the great strain on the country's material and scientific resources that the development of such weapons will incur.

Communist China exploded her first atomic "device" on October 16, 1964, and the second and third test shots were announced on May 14, 1965 and May 9, 1966. After each of these tests scientists and military experts in the non-Communist world initially underestimated the scientific and technical ability and potential that the Communist Chinese had attained in the nuclear field and later were forced to upgrade their estimates. Yet the most dramatic revelation of the pace and vigor with which the Communist Chinese had been developing nuclear and missile capabilities occurred on October 27, 1966 when Peking announced that China had just exploded on target a nuclear weapon carried by a guided missile, which the Atomic Energy Commission of the United States believed to have traveled in the air for some 400 miles. In contrast to the three previous occasions, observers throughout the world immediately responded to the news with remarks like "the test marked a giant Chinese stride toward operational capability" and "Peking had progressed faster than was generally predicted." [13] This new appraisal proved to be highly accurate; on June 17, 1967, the Chinese exploded a hydrogen bomb after having conducted their fifth atomic test December 28, 1966. By March 1972 she had conducted 13 known nuclear tests in the atmosphere and one known underground test. On April 24, 1970, China also became the fifth member of the international space club by successfully launching her first space satellite, weighing 380 pounds. This represented a major advance in her capacity in rocket and general space technology. Meanwhile, she was believed to have developed an intermediate missile with a 1000-mile range. Experts also expect her to be in a position to deploy 15 to 20 ICBM's by about 1975.

China's growing nuclear armament will steadily increase her overall military strength, bolster her diplomatic influence, and thus deepen the world's concern over her future course of action in the international arena. It seems unnecessary, however, to view her acquisition of these dangerous weapons with undue alarm. First, despite the remarkable advances that she has already made, it will still take many years for her to have a nuclear stockpile comparable to those of the United States and the Soviet Union. Second, even after she has had such a stockpile it will remain doubtful that,

[13] *The New York Times,* October 28, 1966.

barring insanity on the part of her leaders, she will ever be so reckless as to precipitate a nuclear holocaust that would be fatal to herself as well as to her intended victim. Thus the principal value of her nuclear capability appears to lie in its neutralizing effect on the same capabilities of her potential adversaries and in the prestige that it gives to her.

IX

Agricultural Policy Since 1949

中國共產運動簡史

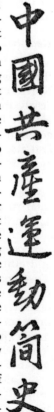

As has been noted, the formation of the CCP in 1921 represented an attempt to seek a quick and effective solution to modern China's multifarious problems. As a result of its Marxist-Leninist orientation, however, the party also undertook to remold man and society in accordance with the ideals of socialism and communism. The far-reaching economic, social, and cultural changes that it has brought about in China since 1949 can be fully understood only in light of this dual objective. Long before seizing power the CCP regarded collectivization as the only feasible and desirable way of developing agriculture and enabling it to make maximum contributions to industrialization, the economic well-being of the nation, and national defense. Upon its assumption of power, however, the party did not immediately proceed to collectivize agriculture at once for several reasons. First, the CCP had learned from the Soviet experience that collectivization would only alienate the peasants and dampen their enthusiasm for work, disrupting agricultural production rather than facilitating it, if the program was carried out in haste and before the peasants had been convinced of its superiority or at least before the government had firmly established its control. Second, the vastness of the Chinese countryside, the extreme fragmentation of the traditional Chinese system of land ownership and cultivation, and the high degree of rural illiteracy posed special technical problems for any attempt to collectivize agriculture at one stroke, especially in the wake of a devastating civil war on the heels of eight years of military resistance against the Japanese. To make collectivization initially less objectionable to the tradition-bound peasants, to enable them to appreciate the merits of collectivization at first hand through experimentation, and to lessen the managerial and other technical problems posed by the peculiarities of China's rural districts, the CCP could only carry out collectivization gradually by introducing a series of transitional forms of production and ownership. Third, there were political constraints: having won the peasants' support during the protracted civil war with a promise to reform the land-tenure system in the interest of the tillers, the party would have seriously undermined the peasants', if not the whole nation's, confidence in its good faith, if at the moment of its triumph it had chosen not to keep the promise and launched an immediate drive toward collectivization. The party, therefore, decided to carry out the promised program of land redistribution before initiating even the most preliminary phase of collectivization.

Redistribution of Land

The post-1949 land redistribution was confined essentially to the "newly liberated" areas in East China, Central-South China, Northwest China, and Southwest China; land redistribution in the "early liberated" areas in North China and Northeast China had already been carried out during the last phase of the civil war in accordance with the CCP Central Committee's May 4, 1946 directive and its "Outline of Agrarian Law" promulgated on October 10, 1947. Even in the newly liberated areas alone land redistribution was not a light task, however. The combined size of these areas was several times as large as that of the early liberated areas, with a total rural population of about 264 million as compared with only 145 million in the early liberated areas. The task in the newly liberated areas was further complicated by the recentness of the party's control and the relatively more complex social, economic, and ethnic problems existing in some of the territories concerned. Together with the need to avoid disruption of agricultural production in the wake of the civil war, these problems pointed to the necessity for careful preparations for implementing the agrarian program in the areas in question; therefore during the first years of the Peking regime only such transitional measures as reduction of rent and interest and "rational reassessment of tax burdens" were put into effect in these areas.

Land redistribution in the newly liberated areas did not begin until after the autumn harvest of 1950. In the next few months the program was carried out in the provinces in East China, Central-South China, and Northwest China, except for a few districts inhabited largely by certain national minorities, and a year later it was put into effect in Southwest China. By 1952 redistribution was largely completed throughout the country except for Tibet, which did not initiate agrarian reform until 1959. The nationwide land reform up to 1952 gave over 700 million *mou* (113 million acres) of free land to some 300 million peasants, together with large quantities of draft animals, implements, and dwellings. The redistribution was carried out in accordance with three much publicized documents.[1] The first, known as "the Agrarian Reform Law" and promulgated on June 30, 1950 by Mao Tse-tung in his capacity as chairman of the Central People's Government, was essentially an amplified version of "the Outline of Agrarian Law" mentioned earlier. The other two instruments, called "Decisions Concerning the Differentiation of Class Status in the Countryside" and "General Regulations Concerning the Organization of Peasants' Associations," had been put into effect by the CCP during the Kiangsi period and the final phase of the civil war and were made applicable to the newly liberated areas after the Government Administrative Council repromulgated them with slight revisions in the summer of 1950.

According to these regulations, rural residents were classified into five major categories: landlords, rich peasants, middle peasants, poor peasants, and farm hands. Space does not permit a full enumeration of the rather complex and often hair-splitting criteria governing the classifications. Generally speaking, a person was classified as a landlord if he owned land, either rented it to someone else or hired farm hands to cultivate it for him, and himself did not engage in labor. A rich peasant was a person who generally owned the land or part of it that he cultivated but was dependent on exploitation for a substantial part of his means of living—either by hiring farm hands to provide additional labor power or by letting out part of his land for rent. A middle peasant was one who owned all or part of the land he cultivated or who rented all his land from someone else but generally did not engage in exploitation by hiring others to work for him, and did not have to sell his labor power to supplement his income from the land; he usually had fairly adequate farm implements. A poor peasant, by contrast, had no adequate farm implements and owned only part of the land he cultivated or none at all. In general he had to rent land for cultivation and was exploited by others extracting from him rent, loan interest, or hired

[1] For their English texts, see *The Agrarian Reform Law of the People's Republic of China* (Peking: Foreign Languages Press, 1953).

labor in a limited degree. A farm hand usually had neither land nor farm implements and depended for his living wholly or mainly upon the sale of his labor power.

The differential treatment stipulated for these classes of people was succinctly expressed in the slogan "rely on the poor peasants and farm hands, ally with the middle peasants, neutralize the rich peasants, and struggle against the landlords." Specifically, the land, draft animals, farm implements, and surplus grain of the landlords and their surplus houses in the countryside were confiscated. Land owned by rich peasants was protected; only their "superabundant" land and part of their other properties were requisitioned, while land and other properties of the middle peasants were protected from infringement. All land and other means of production thus confiscated and requisitioned were distributed to the poor peasants and farm hands; politically acceptable landlords also received an equal share of land in the process of redistribution. Landlords who had been "rural despots," who had indulged in excessive exploitation of the poor, who had resisted the Communist takeover and the land reform or who had engaged in other "counterrevolutionary" activities, of course, were denied any land. Furthermore, "struggle meetings" and "people's tribunals" were organized to expose their past wrongdoings and to "settle accounts" with them. Before his case was finally disposed of, the landlord-culprit was usually subjected to humiliation and even torture. Formal penalties eventually imposed upon the culprits ranged from refunding excessive rent and interest collected in years past to sentences to hard labor at "reform-through-labor" camps and execution by firing squads. Several million landlords and "bad gentry" were reported to have been executed.

Land redistribution and the settling of accounts were all done by peasants' associations composed of farm hands, poor peasants, and middle peasants. Party cadres in the villages seldom took part in these undertakings openly; they merely directed matters from behind the scene. This way the rural poor themselves meted out punishment to the landlords, thereby making their commitment to the party's cause almost irreversible, for if the rural poor should fail to help uphold the new order, the former landlords might stage a comeback and seek reprisal against them.

Mutual Aid Teams

Land redistribution brought immediate relief to a vast number of impoverished peasants and heightened the peasants' enthusiasm for production, which in turn contributed greatly to the nation's economic rehabilitation. But its usefulness as a remedy to the ills of Chinese agriculture was very limited, just as the party had expected. First, redistribution did not completely deliver the majority of peasants from poverty. In the country as a whole, each peasant had after redistribution an average of only three *mou* of arable land, with each household possessing on the average no more than 14 *mou.* In some areas of South China, each peasant had only an average of one or less *mou* of arable land. At the same time each peasant household had on the average less than one draft animal, every two households a plow, and every ten a water-wheel.[2] The peasants thus were unable to make rational use of the land or use modern farm tools. Nor could they undertake large-scale irrigation, soil control, and other capital construction projects entailing greater manpower and more cash outlays.

Believing that only collectivization could provide a way out, the party began to promote a very rudimentary form of cooperative production in the countryside even before land redistribution had been completed. The widespread formation of "mutual aid teams" first occurred in 1949 and 1950 in the early liberated areas. In December 1951, the CCP Central Committee adopted the "Decisions on Mutual Aid and Cooperation in Agricultural Production" calling for the extension of the system of mutual aid teams to the newly liberated areas. By the fall of 1952, 40 per cent of the country's peasant households had joined such teams. As an elementary form of transition from individual peasant production to completely collectivized agriculture, the mutual aid team, composed of five to eight households, did not involve the pooling of land and other properties; members of a team merely engaged in collective labor on the basis of individual management and made common use of certain draft animals and farm tools. There were two types of mutual aid teams: the seasonal one, in which the peasants engaged in collective labor only during the busy seasons of the year; and the year-round team, whose members worked together all seasons of the year.

According to official reports, mutual aid teams proved to be very beneficial in that they overcame to a certain extent the problems of labor shortage and insufficient farm tools. Members of the year-round teams were able to carry out a limited measure of division of labor according to their skills, thus increasing labor productivity by more than 30 per cent over that of peasants who worked on their own. Yet the teams were regarded as inadequate to increase

[2] Hsueh Mu-chiao, *et al., The Socialist Transformation of the National Economy* (Peking: Foreign Languages Press, 1960), pp. 93–94.

production at a rate that would provide sufficient food for the people and adequate raw materials for industries. Furthermore, under individual management it was impossible to curb a tendency toward an increasingly pronounced differentiation in income among the peasants, as those members of a team who owned more land and other means of production could still "expropriate" a part of other members' labor in the very process of mutual aid.

Cooperative Farms

While mutual aid teams were being organized in the newly-liberated areas, the party already took measures to experiment with the formation of semi-socialist agricultural cooperatives in the early-liberated areas. Pilot cooperatives were also established in the newly liberated areas as soon as land reform was completed. Toward the end of 1952, when the nation's war-torn economy had been rehabilitated, the CCP put forward "The General Line for the Period of Transition," calling for a steady socialist industrialization of the country and transformation of agriculture, industry, handicrafts, and commerce. On December 16, 1953, the party adopted the "Decisions on the Development of Agricultural Producers' Cooperatives," the promulgation of which gave impetus to the formation of more experimental cooperative farms of the elementary type, characterized by unified management and the pooling of land, draft animals, and farm tools as shares. The peasants theoretically retained individual ownership of the properties turned over to such cooperatives. The aggregate agricultural and side-occupational products of the cooperative, after deductions had been made for capital depreciation, reserve and welfare funds, and taxes to the state, were distributed among the members in such basic forms as remuneration for work, dividends on land, and payments for other means of production. Together with the retention of the myth of private ownership, this semi-socialist form of income distribution was designed to minimize the reluctance of the relatively well-to-do peasants (mostly former middle peasants) to pool their resources for unified management. By October 1954 there were 100,000 such units in the country, each consisting of 30–40 households.

As the drive toward cooperative farming began to accelerate after the autumn harvest of 1954, a divergence of opinion developed within the party over its feasibility. Some cautious elements in the party believed that cooperative farming could never be successful in a country where the level of industrialization was still very low and where mechanization of agriculture could not yet be effected. For them, a hasty switch to cooperative farming would inevitably lower production, because the peasants were too poor to contribute funds to the cooperatives; they were illiterate and could not supply the cooperatives with qualified accountants; and they were psychologically unprepared to accept the new system. Additional misgivings about a rapid realization of cooperative farming were that it would create a large surplus of labor for which there were no new outlets, that there were not enough competent cadres to lead the cooperatives, and that it would intensify many peasants' dissatisfaction with the party that had been caused by the adoption in 1953 of the policy of unified purchase and marketing of grain, by which the peasants were obliged to sell their "surplus" grains exclusively to the state at officially fixed prices. But Mao Tse-tung insisted that the majority of the peasants would support the cooperative movement and only cooperative farming could prevent the revival of class cleavage in the countryside. He contended that agricultural mechanization could be carried out in China only through agricultural collectivization, not the other way around, believing that the rapid industrialization program under way in the country called for a corresponding rapid increase in agricultural output and that Chinese agricultural output could not be so increased without passing on to more advanced forms of collectivization. He expounded these points in a speech on July 31, 1955 at a Conference of Provincial and Local Party Secretaries.[3] The publication of this speech was immediately followed by an energetic drive to organize peasants into cooperative farms on a massive scale. In October, the sixth plenum of the CCP Seventh Central Committee adopted the "Decisions on Agricultural Cooperation," giving more impetus to the agricultural cooperative movement. By the end of 1956 more than 110 million peasant households, 96.3 per cent of the country's total, had organized themselves into some 750,000 cooperatives.[4]

At first, nearly all of these cooperatives were of the elementary type, but about three fifths of them were converted into "the advanced type" in the summer of 1956. Consisting of one to three hundred households, the advanced type cooperative was considerably larger than the elementary type and was based on common ownership of the means of production. Though land, draft animals, and farm tools were the common property of the collective, individual cooperative members continued to own other forms of property like

[3] Mao Tse-tung, "On the Question of Agricultural Cooperation," *People's Daily,** October 17, 1955.

[4] *People's Daily,** July 2, 1957.

household goods, small kitchen gardens, scattered trees, poultry, domestic animals, and small farm tools. The advanced type cooperative differed further from the elementary type in that income was no longer distributed among members on the basis of land, draft animals, farm tools and capital that they had contributed but solely according to the quantity and quality of their work. The advantages the CCP saw in cooperative farms of the advanced type were that their relatively large size would be more conducive to rational utilization of land and manpower, and the conversion of individual ownership of land and farm tools into collective ownership and the use of labor as the sole criterion for distributing income was more in keeping with the principles of socialism.

The party used both persuasion and coercion to promote cooperative farming. A massive propaganda campaign was conducted both before and during the upsurge of the movement in 1955–56 aimed at convincing the peasants of the merits of agricultural cooperation. Special efforts were made to persuade the poor and lower middle peasants to take the lead in the drive toward cooperation. Those who responded to the party's call were promptly rewarded with low-interest loans and other benefits provided by the government-sponsored credit and supply cooperatives. At the same time those (usually peasants with more and better land and other means of production) who were tardy in responding to the call were denied these benefits. For a while the party deliberately forbade well-to-do peasants to join cooperatives, even when they applied for membership, a policy of social ostracism apparently designed to make the poor and lower middle peasants believe that membership in a cooperative was actually a privilege rather than an obligation, thus inclining them to join it more willingly.

Thanks to generally favorable weather conditions, the amounts of grain production and the gross values of agricultural outputs alike registered sizeable gains in 1956 and 1957, when cooperative farming was in force. However, even the CCP itself admitted the existence of fairly widespread dissatisfaction with the system. Unwilling to hand over the fruits of their labor to the cooperatives and anticipating compulsory delivery of products to the government under the unified purchase and marketing program, peasants in many areas were said to be deliberately consuming their products wastefully.[5] Grains delivered by the cooperatives to the government often were of poor quality, and many cooperatives concealed part of their products in order to reduce their deliveries to the govern-

[5] *Ibid.*, November 26, 1955.

ment. Despite higher outputs, the government "purchased" less grains from the peasants in the winter of 1956–57 than it did in the previous year.[6]

People's Communes

Although the movement to organize people's communes in 1958 was, in a sense, a natural outgrowth of the CCP's policy of taking gradual but uninterrupted steps to collectivize agriculture, it seems to have stemmed directly from Mao Tse-tung's desire to further accelerate China's economic development on the heels of the Soviet Union's orbiting of the Sputnik in late 1957, which Mao seemed to regard as the beginning of a new era of international rivalry based on technological and economic innovations. This belief that the commune would be a more effective device for accelerating economic development might have been based on two major assumptions. First, with more land and manpower at its disposal, a commune could be expected to be better able to utilize human and material resources for agricultural production as well as other projects. Secondly, inasmuch as the communes were to be managed directly by rural cadres of the government instead of by the peasants as was the case under the cooperative farms, the party hoped to strengthen its control over both production and consumption in the vast countryside, especially if the plans for establishing communal kitchens could be put into effect.

Mao Tse-tung put forward the idea of combining cooperative farms into communes at an informal conference of party leaders held at Chengtu in March 1958.[7] Within a month the first people's commune, known as the Sputnik, made its appearance in Suiping County, Honan Province. In May the second session of the CCP Eighth National Congress proclaimed the "General Line for Socialist Construction," calling upon the Chinese people to overcome economic and cultural backwardness by exerting their utmost efforts and pressing ahead consistently to achieve greater, faster, better, and more economic results. This marked the beginning of the Great Leap Forward campaign in all fields. This new campaign spurred the party to press forward toward full-scale communization, and on August 29 the Politburo passed a resolution formally launching the commune movement on a nationwide basis. Believing that the communes were the best form of organization for the attainment of socialism as well as a possible short cut to communism, rural cadres

[6] *New China Semi-Monthly,** No. 108 (February 25, 1957), p. 108.
[7] *NCNA,* September 10, 1958.

immediately set out to carry out zealously the party's new policy. By the end of the year, the 120 million peasant households of the 752,113 cooperative farms had been reorganized into 24,000 people's communes.

The communes differed radically from the cooperative farms in the following ways: First, the smallest commune embraced more than ten times as much land and population as even the largest advanced type cooperative. Second, unlike the cooperative farms, which engaged in agricultural production alone, the communes combined agriculture, industry, trade, education, military affairs, social welfare, public health, public works, and village administration (i.e., communal membership meetings and communal management committees assumed the functions of the former village governments). Third, the peasants were to turn over to the communes the small private plots of land, their houses, scattered fruit trees, share-funds, and other belongings which they were permitted to possess in the cooperatives. Fourth, the communes were to establish public kitchens, public dormitories, and public nurseries so as to realize communal living, communal dining, and communal upbringing of children, whereas on the cooperative farms the peasants lived with their families in individually owned dwellings. In addition, the communes called for an early substitution of a regular wage system for the system of piece-rate and for a combination of a regular wage system with a system of supplying free food to the peasants through the planned communal kitchens.

Reorganization of the Communes

This colossal undertaking met immediate failure, and instead of bringing about a great leap in agricultural production, it severely disrupted the national economy as a whole. Instead of strengthening the regime's authority in the vast countryside, it almost ignited a flame of rural discontent to threaten the edifice of the Communist state. Contributing to the failure were the unwieldy size of the communes; the complexity of their functions; the inexperience of the cadres in charge; the absence of a modern technological base to support their operation; and the adverse effects on the peasants' work, enthusiasm, and health of the abolition of the private plots, the drastic reduction of other material incentives, the premature substitution of communal living and communal dining in many areas, and the unbearable work load required on the farms and various construction projects.

To avert a catastrophe, the party began to take remedial measures before the end of 1958. On December 10 the CCP Central Committee resolved to restore certain material incentives for commune members, to halt hasty attempts to enforce communal living, to allow communal members to engage in subsidiary occupations, to guarantee that all commune members would have 12 hours for meals, sleep, and recreation, and to effect a limited decentralization of the management of the communes. In the spring of 1959 it was decided to restore the small private plots of land to commune members (the combined size of the private plots were not to exceed 5 per cent of the land owned by each commune), to cease encouraging the communes to engage in industrial production, and to completely abandon the plans for establishing communal kitchens and dormitories.

Even these additional changes proved insufficient to arrest the deterioration in agricultural production aggravated in the spring, summer, and autumn of 1959 by widespread drought, typhoons, flood, and insect pests. In many instances floods were caused by the collapse of dams and dikes hastily built during the Great Leap Forward, while the unprecedented insect pests appeared to have been a result of the much-publicized campaign to eliminate sparrows, which had been important killers of insects. In any event, in August 1959 the eighth plenum of the CCP Central Committee decided to overhaul the communes anew by introducing the "three-level ownership system based on the production brigades." Under this system each commune was divided into production brigades which were independent accounting units and assumed the primary responsibility for organizing agricultural production, while their own subdivisions, called production teams, actually performed farm labor. The authority of the communal management committee was thereby reduced to little more than that of the former village governments. A production brigade generally corresponded in size to the former cooperative farm of the advanced type. This reorganization, together with the restoration of the small private plots, the revival of rural fairs at which commune members could sell the products of their private plots, and the institution of a more incentive-based remuneration system, virtually reestablished the agricultural production system that had existed in the period of advanced cooperative farming even though the production brigades, unlike the cooperative farms, also engaged in certain nonfarming production activities for the purpose of supplying their members with most of their daily necessities.

However, Chinese agriculture was to undergo at least two additional structural changes in the next few years. In 1961 the production teams replaced the production brigades as the basic accounting units with the primary responsibility for organizing production. Reducing the average size of farms still further, this reform made collectivized agriculture more manageable. The other apparently occurred sometime between 1961 and 1964,[8] and involved breaking up the original large communes into smaller ones, which increased the total number of communes from about 24,000 to more than 74,000. But this reorganization seemed to have had only an indirect bearing on farming, because by the time of its implementation the communal management committees had lost practically all their authority over agricultural production, although they still had the responsibility for developing water-control projects, running workshops and other enterprises, and coordinating the activities of the production brigades, which operated smaller workshops and enterprises jointly owned by the production teams. Within the small communes the production teams now remain as the basic accounting units.

Technical Transformation of Agriculture

Modernizing Chinese agriculture has always been as important a component of the CCP's farm policy as changing its structure. From 1949 to 1960, however, very little was done to implement this part of the envisioned reform though the party pressed forward relentlessly for a series of structural alterations. The low priority given to agricultural modernization in those years was dictated, first of all, by the fact that in the early 1950's the country simply did not have the necessary scientific, industrial, and financial resources for it. In the mid-1950's she did begin to make remarkable progress in industrial development and scientific training, but top priority in resource allocation was given to industry, especially heavy industry. The National Agricultural Development Program adopted by the CCP Politburo on January 23, 1956 did not envisage any serious efforts to effect a technical transformation of farming until after the fulfillment of the Second Five-Year Plan (1957–1962).[9]

The collapse of the Great Leap Forward, the failure of the commune movement, and the severe natural calamities that began in 1959 caused sharp drops in agricultural output for three consecutive years (1959–1961). This grave situation, accentuated by the loss of Soviet aid in the summer of 1960, prompted the party to reconsider the priorities in economic development. In November of that year it put forward the slogan, "Agriculture Is the Founda-

[8] Lin Kuo, "70,000 People's Communes in China," *SCMP*, No. 3307 (September 19, 1964), pp. 14–16.

[9] For the text of the program, see *People's Daily,** January 26, 1956.

tion and Industry the Leading Factor of the National Economy." Though somewhat ambiguous, this formulation nevertheless put an end, at least temporarily, to the one-sided emphasis on the development of heavy industry and ushered in an era in which the state was to seek a more balanced development of the various sectors of the national economy by allocating more material, scientific, and financial resources for the technical transformation of agriculture. Agricultural modernization received fresh impetus in the spring of 1962 when Premier Chou En-lai announced the CCP's 10-point economic readjustment program at the Third Session of the Second National People's Congress.[10] Among other things, this document unequivocally reset the priorities for economic development in the order of agriculture, light industry, and heavy industry. Ever since this radical shift in policy, the country has made considerable progress in the technical transformation of its agriculture, though much remains to be done to meet her staggering needs for farm products.

One of the most impressive achievements is the construction of irrigation and drainage projects. By 1964 more than 100 big reservoirs (each with the capacity of over 100 million cubic meters), 4000 medium-sized (each holding from 10 to 100 million cubic meters of water), and a still larger number of small reservoirs had been built all over the country.[11] Great achievements were also made in the construction of pumping stations: the aggregate capacity of mechanized rural pumping stations in 1965 was 30 times the 1957 figure.[12] Closely related to the construction of irrigation and drainage projects has been the development of rural electrification. In 1965 rural consumption of electricity was 25 times what it was in 1957. As a result, most of the villagers in over 1300 of the nation's 2126 counties in that year had electric services, whereas in 1949 electricity was available to only a few rural districts near some of the metropolitan cities. Facilitated by the electrification program, agricultural mechanization also has advanced. As of December 1964, more than 70 per cent of the nation's counties were served by 1500 farm machinery stations, which had more than 100,000 tractors (15 h. p. units), more than five times the 1957 figure. At the same time, the farm machine building industry had developed more than a hundred types of semimechanized farm implements. Over 30 million such implements were being used in plowing, irrigation, plant protection, harvesting, threshing, transport, livestock breeding, and processing farm products.

[10] Peking Radio domestic service, April 16, 1962.
[11] *Ta-kung Pao** (Hong Kong), September 17, 1964.
[12] *SCMM*, No. 449 (December 28, 1960), pp. 24–28.

In recent years there has been a rapid increase in the production of chemical fertilizers. In 1971 the country produced about 14 million tons of liquid fertilizer, or more than one-third of what she needed.[13] As late as 1961 the output of chemical fertilizers was only 2.5 million tons. There has also been a marked increase in the supply of improved seeds, and insecticide spraying and dusting equipment. In 1964 over one hundred good strains of rice, wheat, cotton, and other crops used on a wide scale generally increased crop yields from 10 to 20 per cent. These seeds were chosen from more than 1000 crop strains, all bred after 1949 from crossing and selection. Breeding and propagating good crop strains is now systematized: as of November 1964, there were some 1700 state seed breeding demonstration farms, state seed supply centers in 90 per cent of the counties, and seed-breeding plots in the communes.[14]

A central aim of the campaign to modernize agriculture has been the large-scale training of agrotechnicians and accountants. In addition to the many full-time colleges of agriculture and full-time agrotechnical secondary schools, more and more half-farming, half-study institutions on the college and secondary school levels have been established. Meanwhile, the party has been making a great effort to persuade educated youths, who in the past invariably shunned farm labor, to return or go to rural areas to work. As of August 1964, some 40 million educated youths, mostly senior grade school graduates, had responded to this call. According to an official report, among those who had gone to the countryside were children of ministers, provincial governors, generals, mayors, professors, writers, engineers, painters, musicians, and doctors.[15] Obviously, the party is aware of the fact that without a mass infusion of educated youths into the rural districts, it would be very difficult to carry out the technical transformation of agriculture. Yet the role of the several hundreds of millions of illiterate peasants in this vast undertaking has not been neglected. In 1962, the CCP called upon them, along with the industrial workers, to conduct scientific experimentations on a mass scale. Since then mass communication media all over the country have been urging the peasants to break down superstitions, to liberate their minds, and to give free rein to their imagination for making technical innovations. This has been accompanied by a nationwide campaign "to learn from the advanced and help the less advanced." Meetings are held, exhibitions are put on, and short-

[13] Edgar Snow, "Talks with Chou En-lai," *The New Republic*, Vol. 164, No. 13 (March 27, 1971), p. 20.

[14] *NCNA*, November 3, 1964.

[15] *Ta-kung Pao** (Hong Kong), August 28, 1964.

term visits are arranged. Other important features of the CCP's agricultural program in the last 20-odd years include the establishment of over 2500 state farms with a total of 5 million hectares of land (mostly situated in outlying regions), the reclamation of some 10 million hectares of wasteland (offset, however, by land lost to construction activities), the extension of rural banking and credit institutions, the development of forestry and afforestation, the expansion of marine and fresh-water fishery and animal husbandry, the gradual reduction of rural illiteracy, the promotion of cultural activities, and the formation in 1963 of poor and lower-middle peasants' associations to conduct the socialist education movement and to wage class struggles in defense of collective farming. Among the measures that have been implemented in greater earnest since the GPCR are the policy of taking grain as the key link and insuring an all-round development, the reduction of prices of some major agricultural means of production (like chemical fertilizers, insecticides, and diesel engine oil), the payment by the state of higher prices for farm produce and subsidiary products, the establishment of a low-cost cooperative medical insurance system, the training of tens of thousands of commune members to be "barefoot doctors" who can render first aid and other elementary medical services to the vast rural population without disengaging themselves completely from farming, and the movement to emulate Tachai. As alluded to in Chapter VII, the Tachai Brigade of a rural commune in Shansi Province caught Mao Tse-tung's attention in 1964 with its incredible success in turning a poor mountain gully into a prosperous village by firmly keeping to the socialist orientation and by displaying the spirit of self-reliance and hard work in undertaking such gigantic projects as terracing twisting gullies and canyons; building reservoirs, dams, and irrigation canals; and constructing stone houses to replace the caves in which the villagers had lived. Although Mao's call, "In Agriculture, Learn from Tachai," was reportedly sabotaged by the Liu Shao-ch'i faction prior to the GPCR, since then Tachai's spirit and experience have played a great role in transforming the countryside.

The technical transformation, it was estimated, accounted for about a 10 per cent increase in food crops in the early 1960's, which, though small, might have contributed appreciably to the agricultural recovery that began in 1962 as a result of more favorable weather conditions and of the drastic reorganization of the communes from 1959 to 1961. In 1957, on the eve of the Great Leap Forward, the country produced 185 million tons of grain. Both bad weather and the Great Leap Forward policies reduced the figure for 1961 to about 162 million tons, and necessitated the importation of approximately 5 million tons of grain annually in the years that immediately followed. Food crop production began to improve in 1962. In 1964 the output was somewhere in the range of 190 to 195 million tons, surpassing the 1957 figure for the first time since the failure of the Great Leap Forward. Crop weather in 1965 and 1966 was not as good as 1964; but grain output in those two years did not decline appreciably from the 1964 level, apparently because of the increasing technical innovations and other measures referred to earlier. Although in December 1966 some ultra-leftists attempted to extend the GPCR to the countryside on a large scale, which could have seriously disrupted agricultural production, the Maoist leadership blocked the effort when it reaffirmed in February 1967 the correctness of the majority of the rural cadres. Thus, the scope and intensity of the tasks of "struggle-criticism-transformation" in the rural districts were greatly restricted.

The relative tranquility that continued to prevail on the farms, coupled with more wholehearted implementation of Mao's policy of taking agriculture as the foundation, enabled the country to reap "record harvests" in 1967. As production continued to increase in ensuing years, Premier Chou En-lai was able to tell the American writer Edgar Snow late in 1970 that China had not only achieved self-sufficiency in grain, but had accumulated state grain reserves of about 40 million tons.[16] China's continued importation of limited amounts of wheat from abroad, the Premier explained, was due to the fact that imported wheat was cheaper in China than rice; that China could keep the cheap wheat for domestic consumption or reserves and export rice, in balance, to Cuba, Ceylon, and some African countries in exchange for sugar, rubber, and other commodities; and that China also sent millions of tons of rice to help Vietnam and other friendly countries. The reported grain output in the last few years was 240 million tons in 1970, 246 million tons in 1971, and 240 million tons in 1972.[17] The slight drop in 1972 was due to prolonged drought in the north and widespread floods in the south. Much headway has also been made in making each of the traditionally grain-deficient provinces in northern China self-sufficient, thus eliminating the cost of shipping grain in from the south. Self-sufficiency in grain for each province also helps strengthen each region's ability to wage a people's war against foreign invaders with its local resources.

[16] Edgar Snow, "Talks with Chou En-lai."

[17] Premier Chou En-lai gave these figures to a delegation of the American Society of Newspaper Editors. See *The Wall Street Journal,* October 11, 1972.

Together with the determination to take the socialist road, the steady growth in grain production, forestry, animal husbandry, side occupations, fishery, and industrial crops has created the material basis for the communes to put into effect the "five guarantee" program, under which everyone in the collective is assured sufficient food, clothing, and fuel, an honorable funeral, and education for his children. The improved lot of the rural population is also evidenced by the fact that the total rural savings deposits in 1971 reportedly increased 101-fold compared with 1952.[18] Rural residents have not been the only beneficiaries, however. The agricultural sector of the economy now provides the state with an ever-increasing quantity of marketable grain to meet the requirements of the urban population. Meanwhile, thanks to the considerable progress made in forestry, animal husbandry, side occupations, and fishery, the quantity of nonstaples such as meat, eggs and egg products, fish, poultry, vegetables, and fruit supplied to the market is over a dozen times larger than that before 1949.[19] Furthermore, because of the expanding farm production, light and heavy industries, too, have developed substantially. For example, in 1971 the output of cotton yarn, cotton cloth, paper, sugar, salt, cigarettes, leather, and other main consumer goods that were made of rurally produced raw materials was very much larger than that of 1949.[20]

[18] Hung Chiao, "Why Prices Are Stable in China," *Peking Review*, No. 40 (October 6, 1972), p. 21.

[19] *Ibid.*, p. 22.

[20] *Ibid.*

X

Industry, Commerce, and the Five-Year Plans

中國共產運動簡史

Socialist Transformation of Industry, Commerce, and Handicrafts

Upon its seizure of power in 1949, the CCP did not immediately nationalize China's privately owned industrial plants, commercial establishments, and handicraft shops, although the People's Government did promptly seize all the business enterprises left behind by the Kuomintang government and individual Kuomintang leaders. Both ideological and practical considerations dictated this line of action. Ideologically, the continued existence of private capitalism and the individual economy of handicrafts and small traders at the initial stage of its rule was necessary if the CCP was not to openly repudiate the concept of "People's Democracy" based on a mixed economy. Chief among the practical considerations for temporarily preserving capitalist enterprises and individually owned stores and workshops was the realization that before the newly founded regime had made proper and necessary preparations for directly managing all the industrial and commercial establishments in the country, any move to nationalize privately owned enterprises would only aggravate the war-torn national economy and plunge the country into the same chaotic state as the policy of "war communism" had in Russia on the heels of the October Revolution.

To bring about a speedy economic rehabilitation while endeavoring to pave the way for the attainment of socialism, the party adopted a policy of using, restricting, and transforming capitalist industry, commerce, and the handicraft trades, with the emphasis first placed on using, then on restricting, and finally on transforming. The policy of "using" capitalist industry and commerce was given its legal expression in a section of the Common Program of the CPPCC, which among other things enjoined the People's Government to rehabilitate and develop the national economy in accordance with the principles of "taking into account both public and private interests and of profiting both labor and capital." To implement this policy, the regime supplied private industries with raw materials, placed orders with them for processing and manufacturing goods, and let the state enterprises purchase and market all or part of their products. With regard to privately owned commercial establishments, they were used as retail distributors or commission agents for the state enterprises. Thanks to this policy, from 1949 to 1952 the privately owned industries increased their gross output value by approximately 54 per cent, while the retail sales of privately owned commercial firms rose by about 20 per cent. The upsurge of private industry and commerce played an important role in the recovery of the national economy, which, together with the Chinese People's Volunteers' military exploits in Korea, gave the CCP higher prestige both at home and abroad than any previous Chinese ruling elite in modern times.

The policy of restricting private industry and commerce was aimed at curbing those aspects of their operations that the regime regarded as inconsistent with the national welfare and the long-range objectives of the CCP's economic development policy. To enforce this policy, the government set limits to the profit margins of private enterprise by enacting regulations on labor protection and remuneration and through price policy and taxation. It also checked speculation, hoarding, and excessive competition by controlling the supply of credits, raw materials, and goods in stock and markets, by defining the scope of the operations of the privately owned enterprises, and by a host of other measures.

The policy of transformation was to gradually place privately owned enterprises under joint state-private management, a subtle variant of outright seizure by the state. This was accomplished in two steps: joint state-private operation of individual enterprises and joint operation by whole trades. During the first stage the assets of the private firms were turned into private shares and the investment made by the state became state shares. However, in many cases, the investment made by the state actually did not come from the state treasury but from the former owners of the firms concerned in the form of fines, delinquent tax assessments, or "returned stolen assets." In any event, once a privately owned concern had been converted into a joint state-private enterprise, the state would run it through its cadres. Those former owners or their agents who had held management positions in the past were usually retained as employees of the state. The profit of a joint enterprise was distributed according to the principle of "dividing profit into four parts": income tax, reserve funds for the enterprise, workers' welfare funds, and profit for the former owners (including dividends and bonus). The portion allotted the former owners constituted only a quarter of the total net earnings.[1] The conversion of individual business firms into joint state-private enterprises began as early as 1949 but did not gather momentum until 1954, when the first five-year plan had been in operation for a year. By the end of 1955, the number of jointly operated industrial establishments exceeded 3000, with an output value equivalent to 49.7 per cent of the total produced by the private and jointly owned industrial enterprises. In the latter half of 1955, following the upsurge of cooperative farming, the socialist transformation of capitalist industry and commerce entered its second stage of development: joint operation by whole trades. In the first quarter of 1956, the high tide of this development swept the whole country, and by the end of that year, practically all the nation's private enterprises had changed over to joint state-private operation. In the same year some 400,000 private commercial establishments were placed under joint operation and more than 1,440,000 smaller ones were converted into cooperatives.

In accordance with the regime's "buying off" policy, all the former owners of the converted enterprises were to be paid interest on their shares at a fixed rate by the state (generally 5 per cent per annum) for seven years. Payment of such interest, in most cases, started from January 1956. The total payment amounted to 120 million *yuan* a year, and the recipients numbered about 1,140,000. The seven-year period ended in 1962. But in the spring of that year the government announced an extension of payments of fixed interest rates for the capitalists for another three years beginning 1963 and that at the end of that period it would consider anew the problem of further extending the payments. The CCP's adoption of the "buying off" policy rather than one of confiscation as in Russia some 30 years earlier was designed to induce the capitalists, many of whom possessed sorely needed managerial and scientific skills, to actively place their knowledge and experience at the service of "socialism." For the same reason, the party also gave political recognition to the more cooperative and more prestigious elements of the national bourgeoisie and the petty bourgeoisie, although, like those leaders

[1] Article 17 of the Provisional Regulations for the Joint State-Private Industrial Enterprises. For its text, see *People's Daily,** September 6, 1954.

of the minor parties who were in the government, none of the businessmen serving in the organs of the state were allowed to exercise any authority in contradiction to the policies of the CCP. Accompanying the socialist transformation of industry and commerce was a political and ideological remolding of the capitalists. Accomplished largely through persuasion and re-education, this remolding was designed to change the capitalists' political views and way of life so that they would gradually become full-fledged members of the working class. Its immediate objective was to reduce the capitalists' resistance to the socialist transformation of their enterprises.

Although the ideological remolding and the buying off policy apparently did play a part in inclining the businessmen to accept in a voluntary and peaceful way the socialist transformation of industry and commerce by whole trades in 1955–56, the latter's compliance with the new policy seems to have already been ensured by their helpless situation starting from the days of Communist terror during the "Five-Anti" campaign in 1951–52. Preceded by the "Three-Anti" campaign (anti-corruption, anti-waste, and anti-bureaucratism) against the rank and file of officialdom, the Five-Anti campaign was launched by the regime to combat five alleged evils of business: bribery, tax-evasion, fraud, theft of state property, and theft of state economic information. Countless businessmen were fined, imprisoned, executed, or driven to suicide. This campaign so terrified the businessmen that they soon lost the courage to show any defiance at all. Unable to meet the demand for fines and repayment of taxes and stolen assets and anxious to remove the bourgeois stigma, quite a few merchants and industrialists may have even welcomed the change-over to joint operation as a convenient way to get out of their predicament. At any rate, during the high tide of the conversion, hundreds of thousands of businessmen in the country held festivals and celebrations ostensibly to honor the occasion. The change-over was immediately followed by the merging of some of the small-sized joint enterprises. In the meantime, within the enterprises changes were made in management and business methods. During the Great Leap Forward, more small trades under joint operation merged with larger ones or with enterprises owned and operated exclusively by the state, although the fixed interest and positions of the capitalists were kept intact.

As for the small traders and peddlers, who were not officially classified as capitalists but individual working people engaged in commercial transactions, the socialist transformation of commerce in 1956 resulted in the absorption of about 78 per cent of them into cooperatives. Others were taken into joint state-private enterprises, and still others (about half a million units) continued to operate on an individual basis as they were too widely scattered to be collectivized.

The operations of individual handicraftsmen also underwent a series of transformations. Shortly after the Communist takeover, they were urged to organize supply and marketing cooperatives. With their activity confined to exchange, these cooperatives were used mainly for enabling the handicraftsmen to shake off their dependence on commercial capital and to acquaint themselves with the ideas of collectivism. At the beginning of 1956, spurred by the socialist transformation of industry, commerce, and agriculture, a nationwide campaign was launched to persuade the handicraftsmen to extend their cooperation from the realm of exchange to the field of production by organizing themselves into handicraft producers' cooperatives. By June of that year, 90 per cent of the handicraftsmen in the country had complied with the new policy of the government, but the hasty manner in which the cooperatives were formed caused insurmountable managerial problems, which in turn brought about a reduction in the variety of products, a lowering of their quality, and imbalance of supply and demand. Under these circumstances the customers experienced great inconveniences while the handicraftsmen suffered a sharp decline in income. To correct the situation, the regime shortly disbanded the producers' cooperatives in those trades that could serve their customers better uncollectivized. In 1958, during the Great Leap Forward, a number of those handicraft producers' cooperatives were converted into state factories under a Federation of Handicraft Cooperatives. Theoretically, all the establishments so affected underwent a transition from collective ownership to ownership by the whole people. But the real significance of this latest change lay in the complete integration of those handicraft trades with the rest of the state-run economic enterprises.

Industrialization and the Five-Year Plans

The great importance that the CCP has attached to industrialization since 1949 was foretold by Mao Tse-tung in April 1945, when he stated in his report to the Seventh National Congress of the party: "Without industry there can be no solid national defense, no well-being for the people, and no prosperity or strength for the nation." [2] Reflecting the party's determination to industrialize the country at the highest possible speed was the subordination of many

[2] Mao Tse-tung, *Selected Works* (Peking: 1965), III, 302.

of its social, economic, and cultural policies to that end. Even the socialist transformation of agriculture, industry, commerce, and handicraft trades was consciously used to facilitate industrialization, although it also served to realize a much-cherished Communist ideal —the abolition of private ownership of the means of production, which it regarded as the source-spring of virtually all social evils including the exploitation of man by man and the resultant social cleavages or class struggles. As the CCP saw it, the utility of the socialist transformation of the economy to industrialization lay in the fact that it would make it possible for the state to utilize most fully and rationally the nation's manpower and material and financial resources in the interest of the society as a whole and to guide the operations of all enterprises on the basis of a unified plan. In particular, the party believed that the socialist transformation would enable the state to control more effectively the rate of capital accumulation and to use the accumulated funds for industrial development in a planned manner as well as for meeting the other needs of the country, such as national defense and cultural and educational developments.

The CCP's large-scale drive to develop industry began in 1953. By then the war-torn economy of the nation had recovered and even surpassed the pre-1949 peak level of production. The transportation system had been rehabilitated and improved by the restoration of the railroads destroyed during the civil war and the construction of several new rail lines. The People's Government had consolidated its power on the mainland, the Korean War had subsided in intensity, and the Soviet Union's own economic recovery had reached the point where she could begin fulfilling her promises to provide China with machinery, equipment, and technical advice for achieving industrialization. The initial Chinese approach to industrial development bore much resemblance to that of the Soviet Union under Stalin: both countries sought to obtain capital funds from forced savings, both gave top priority to heavy industry, and both attempted to achieve their goals through a series of five-year plans.

China's first five-year plan was inaugurated in 1953, although official information on the plan (1953–57) was not made public until mid-1955.[3] As announced, the plan allocated capital construction investments as follows: 58.2 per cent to industry (of this total 88.8 per cent to heavy industry and 11.2 per cent to light industry); 19.2 per cent to transportation and communications; 7.6 per cent to

[3] For the text of the plan, see *People's Daily,** August 13, 1955.

agriculture, forestry, and water conservation; and 15 per cent to education, health, culture, municipal utilities, banking, trade, stockpiling, and other purposes. The plan called for roughly doubling the value of gross industrial output (98.3 per cent), increasing gross agricultural output by close to one quarter (23.3 per cent), and increasing by about one half the gross commodity output of agriculture and industry combined (51.5 per cent). To achieve these goals, the plan demanded average annual increases in production as follows: 14.7 per cent in industry; 4.7 per cent in agriculture; and 8.6 per cent in gross commodity output.

When the plan was fulfilled in 1957, a total of 20 billion dollars instead of 18 billion had been invested in capital construction. The value of gross industrial output had increased by close to 120 per cent, gross agricultural output by 25 per cent, and gross commodity output by 60 per cent. The output of major products in 1957 is shown in Table I. The progress made in industrial production during the first five-year plan period can be fully appreciated only if one recalls that prior to 1949 China could not manufacture even a bicycle, let alone heavy machinery and equipment. By 1957, however, the newly-established machine-building industry was able to produce among other things whole sets of 12,000-kilowatt steam turbine power-generating equipment and 15,000-kilowatt hydraulic turbine power-generating equipment, 1000-cubic-meter blast furnace equipment, over 200 types of modern machine tools, electric tubes, whole sets of textile, paper-making, rubber-processing, and sugar-refining equipment, jet planes, lorries, and locomotives of modern designs. The total number of industrial and mining projects under

TABLE I. OUTPUT OF MAJOR INDUSTRIAL PRODUCTS IN 1957 AND THEIR PERCENTAGE INCREASES OVER 1952 *

Item	*Output in 1957*	*Percentage Increase Over 1952*
Steel	5,350,000 tons	296
Pig Iron	5,940,000 tons	208
Coal	130,000,000 tons	96
Electricity	19,300,000,000 kwh	166
Cement	6,860,000 tons	140
Cotton Yarn	4,650,000 tons	28

* Source: Hsueh Mu-chiao, *et al., The Socialist Transformation of the National Economy in China* (Peking: Foreign Languages Press, 1960), p. 83.

construction in the 1953–57 period exceeded 10,000. In 1957, 537 of the large-sized industrial projects had gone into full or partial operation. Considerable progress was made also in the development of transportation and communication services. The total length of newly built or restored trunk lines, branch lines, and special lines serving certain factories and mining fields, and the double-tracking of some existing lines was more than 6200 miles. From the latter part of the nineteenth century to 1948 the nation built only about 12,000 miles of railroads, but by the end of 1957 the combined mileage of highways in operation exceeded 155,300 miles, compared with about 82,000 miles in 1952. Considerable progress was also made in inland shipping and civil aviation, postal service, and telecommunications. The Soviet Union and other Eastern European countries played an important role in this impressive industrial development in China, especially in the construction of heavy industries. They provided complete equipment and essential raw and processed materials for many of the newly launched projects. Their engineers, technicians, and scientists rendered technical assistance all the way from the collection of technical data on factory construction, surveying, selection of premises, planning, guidance of construction, installation, transport, training of technical personnel, the preparing of blueprints, etc., to the initial output of products from the factories.[4] It should be noted however that China paid for all this technical and material assistance with agricultural products, minerals, textile goods, and cash. Although far from meeting China's needs, these construction projects laid at least a preliminary foundation for her industrialization, a feat that none of the antecedent regimes in modern times was able to accomplish.

The second five-year plan was launched in 1958. As originally announced, upon the fulfillment of this plan in 1962 China's national income would increase by about 50 per cent over 1957. Industrial output was to be doubled while the increase in agricultural output was to be 35 per cent. Industries to be given special emphasis were the expanding ones like metal processing, machine-making, electric power, coal, and building materials, along with weaker ones like petroleum and radio, and the yet-to-be-created ones including synthetic chemicals and nuclear power. The regime could have successfully fulfilled the second five-year plan on time and thus strengthened the foundation for further industrial growth but for the following: (1) the launch of the Great Leap Forward and the Commune Movement in the summer of 1958, (2) severe

[4] Lin Hai-yun, "China's Trade with the Soviet Union and Other Socialist Countries in the Past Ten Years," *ECMM,* No. 206 (March 28, 1960), pp. 35–39.

natural calamities for three consecutive years from 1959 to 1961, and (3) Moscow's withdrawal of technical and material assistance in the summer of 1960.

Based on "the general line of going all out and aiming high to achieve greater, quicker, better, and more economical results in building socialism" and aimed at surpassing Britain in major industrial output in 15 years, the Great Leap Forward campaign led the regime to throw out all caution about the speed and scope of economic development and unrealistically increased investments for the development of heavy industry in 1958, 1959, and 1960. It obliged local governments and communes to establish medium-sized and small enterprises of all kinds using both modern and indigenous methods of production (i.e., the "walking on two legs" policy) and called upon citizens in cities and towns to make steel in backyard furnaces—this combined with efforts to make a great leap forward in all other fields of work. In spite of the fact that the nation apparently did respond to the regime's call with great enthusiasm and by the end of 1959 the quotas for 1962, as originally set forth in the Second Five-Year Plan, had been fulfilled in many cases, the Great Leap Forward caused serious imbalances or bottlenecks in the national economy, which soon resulted in production stoppages in the over-extended enterprises. In their desperate attempts to fulfill the high production quotas the Great Leap Forward required, cadres and workers alike often sacrificed quality for quantity and turned out shoddy and even completely useless products. The Great Leap Forward also rendered economic planning itself a nearly impossible task inasmuch as the central authorities responsible for compiling targets for monthly and yearly plans could not keep up with swift changes in practical conditions that required almost constant revision of the targets. This difficulty was compounded by the fact that at the height of the campaign statistics were reported by the cadres in the field according to their "enthusiasm in socialist revolution" rather than on the basis of fact.

The Commune Movement and natural calamities adversely affected industrial growth in various ways. First, they caused a sharp decline in the output of industrial crops, which paralyzed many light industries, especially the textile industry. Second, they drastically reduced the amount of funds that the government could derive from agriculture and invest in industry. Third, the resultant decline in the output of food crops forced the government to import over 5 million tons of grain from abroad annually. Thus, sizeable sums of foreign exchange, which otherwise could have been used for buying equipment and machinery needed for restoring balances in industrial development, were spent for importing supplementary foodstuffs.

The sudden withdrawal of Soviet aid in the summer of 1960 crippled many industrial plants that had relied upon the Soviet Union for technical advice and for the supply of machinery, equipment, spare parts, and materials. This of course seriously upset China's original overall plan for economic development and added greatly to her difficulties.

Toward the end of 1960, the CCP began to re-examine its economic policies in the light of the mounting crises in industry and agriculture. This reappraisal brought an immediate end to the Great Leap Forward and gradually changed the order of priority in economic development from one of heavy industry, light industry, and agriculture to one of agriculture, light industry, and heavy industry. By 1961 Chinese industry had entered a period of "readjustment, consolidation, filling out, and raising standards." Meanwhile, an "Adjusted Plan for the Last Two Years of the Second Five-Year Plan" was drafted, approved, and put into effect. Instead of allowing itself to be demoralized by the loss of Soviet aid, the CCP now set forth a policy of self-reliance to overcome the difficulties the country was facing and to seek a new upsurge in industrial and agricultural production. Great efforts were made to bring into full play the ingenuity and talents of the administrative and managerial personnel, technical experts, and ordinary workers. The virtues of diligence, thrift, plain living, and hard work were exhorted, although care was taken to avoid an egalitarian wage policy and to ensure that labor would be alternated with rest.

These and other measures, along with the benefits of the gradual rehabilitation of agriculture, helped industrial production begin its recovery in 1962. In general, recovery and adjustment first occurred in the electrical equipment, farm machine, chemical fertilizer, and petroleum industries. Late in 1964 the government stepped up efforts to adjust and improve the industries of iron and steel, coal mining, and individual branches of machine-making. From 1961 to 1964, there were about 24,000 new varieties of leading industrial products, trebling the figure of 1958–60,[5] with a general rise in the quality of products and in labor productivity, while the costs of production were greatly reduced. With the discovery of new oil fields, the petroleum industry took a great stride forward, and by 1966 the nation had achieved self-sufficiency both in quantity and variety of petroleum products for economic and military needs.

[5] Premier Chou En-lai's report to the First Session of the Third National People's Congress on December 21–22, 1964, *NCNA,* December 30, 1964.

Although the estimated 13 million tons of steel produced in 1964 was substantially below the level of 1960, when more than 18 million tons of steel were produced, there were marked improvements in both the quality and variety of steel products.[6] Gains also were made in coal production. In 1965 the coal-mining capacity was estimated at 300 million tons, compared with only about 130 million tons in 1957.

The period of readjustment also saw a big development in light industry. In 1964 the production of machine-made paper, aluminum utensils, enamel ware, bicycles, radios, and other goods increased by more than 50 per cent over the 1963 level. Thanks to the recovery in cotton production, increases in cotton imports, and expansion of mill capacity, an 18 per cent increase in cotton yarn production was claimed in 1966. A great expansion of mill capacity apparently took place in 1964 when 1.4 million spindles and a corresponding number of looms were installed.[7]

The regime also made progress in its effort to achieve "self-reliance in technology." From 1961 to 1965 Chinese engineers independently completed 113 industrial plants, many of which had been planned initially under the supervision of Soviet advisors. As part of the effort to achieve self-reliance in technology, a very large number of institutes of industrial design have been established in recent years. Their principal functions are to copy and adapt to Chinese conditions model plants and individual equipment. Indicative of China's achievements in theoretical research were her successful manufacture of synthetic benzene and her success in totally synthesizing crystalline insulin.[8]

Coupled with the recovery and increases in agricultural output, these favorable developments in the industrial field led to a marked improvement in supplies of commodities and a considerable expansion of foreign trade. For example, supplies of pork, mutton, vegetables, and other non-staple foodstuffs in 1964 were said to be more than 30 per cent greater than in 1957. At the same time, prices were stable and the government budgets remained balanced despite the repayment to the Soviet Union of 1.4 billion new rubles of debts and the furnishing of a far larger total in money and products in assistance to various countries.

Given this promising development, Premier Chou En-lai was able to announce in December 1964 at the First Session of the Third

[6] Anna Louise Strong's interview with Po I-po on economic development, *Ta-kung Pao** (Hong Kong), January 15, 1964.

[7] *Peking Review*, No. 8 (February 18, 1966), pp. 22–25.

[8] *Ibid.*, No. 1 (January 1, 1967), pp. 15–17.

National People's Congress that the work of readjustment in the national economy was about completed and preparations would be made for the third five-year plan beginning in 1966. In the beginning of 1967, the regime reported that it had fulfilled ahead of schedule all tasks for the first year of the newest economic development plan. It claimed, among other things, that in 1966 industry achieved an overall increase in output. Iron and steel, machine-building, coal, petroleum, electric power, chemicals, building materials, timber, textiles, and other light industries all topped their plans ahead of time. The nation's grain output was more than 20 per cent above that of 1965.[9] However, there have never been any official data on the contents of the third five-year plan as a whole. The official report cited above merely suggested that among the industries to be developed during the remaining four years of the plan would be large integrated iron and steel works, coal mines, oil fields, oil refineries, chemical works, cement plants, power stations, aircraft and tractor plants, and machine-building plants.

As the third five-year plan entered its second year on January 1, 1967, the surging torrent of the GPCR was rapidly engulfing economic enterprises throughout the nation. Red Guards were dispatched to factories, mines, and commercial establishments to help workers and staff members organize themselves into "revolutionary rebel" committees. The latter were to seize power from "those handfuls of persons in authority who had taken the road of capitalism." Although the official policy was to "take firm hold of the revolution and stimulate production," the attempt to dislodge wayward officeholders from leadership positions quickly led to serious interruptions of production. This stemmed from the fact that "those in authority who were taking the capitalist road," instead of yielding to the Red Guards and the "revolutionary rebels," set out to seek support from the workers by resorting to offering such incentives as increased wages and welfare benefits. Some officeholders "hoodwinked" large numbers of workers to engage in sit-down strikes or to make trips to Peking to file complaints. Violent clashes also occurred in several cities between "revolutionary rebels" and Red Guards on the one hand and "hoodwinked" workers on the other. Although the "revolutionary rebels" in some cities soon "dealt a smashing blow to the counterattack of the bourgeois reactionary line" and many "hoodwinked" workers quickly returned to their production posts, disruptions of industrial production and the transportation system remained widespread throughout 1967 and the first few months of 1968 largely as a result of factional strife

[9] *Ibid.*, No. 2 (January 6, 1967), pp. 15–17.

among the rebels themselves. Thus, early in February 1968, Premier Chou En-lai was quoted as having admitted that industrial output failed to meet the 1967 targets and that the output of many products was lower than in 1966. Chou, however, minimized the loss by saying that "the price paid for the Cultural Revolution is far smaller than that paid for the War of Liberation and the Korean campaign." [10] The Maoist leadership also contended that the impact of the GPCR did not disrupt to any important degree the most important projects such as the guided missile and hydrogen bomb tests, the development of an all-purpose transistor computer, and the construction of the Yangtze River bridge at Nanking, which foreign engineers in the past had thought could not be built. In any event, by the spring of 1968 order had been restored on the industrial and transportation fronts, and industrial output began to go up in various areas. The upward trend apparently accelerated in July and August. Thus on the eve of the nineteenth anniversary of the Peking regime, the official news agency was able to claim that workers all over the country had pushed production to "new levels of quantity, quality, and variety." [11]

More important, by removing those party leaders who had been obstructing his policies, the GPCR cleared the way for Mao to put into effect his "revolutionary line" for economic development, which has since proved to be a more realistic approach to China's modernization problems, even though it was once severely discredited during the Great Leap Forward because of overzealousness and inexperience in execution. One of Mao's basic tenets that seems to have contributed greatly (after it was more rationally applied) to China's resurgent industrial growth since the summer of 1968 is the principle of "walking on two legs"—that is, as noted earlier, the simultaneous development of industries under the central and local authorities and the development of large, small, and medium-sized enterprises, with emphasis on the small and medium-sized. With determined efforts to implement this policy, numerous small and medium-sized industrial enterprises have been set up in all parts of the country. Utilizing mainly local resources, sometimes assisted technically by larger state-run enterprises, and operated by provinces, administrative districts, counties, rural communes, or production brigades, they produce a great variety of products, including iron, steel, machinery, chemical fertilizers, cement, and consumer goods. The significance of these enterprises to China's economic

[10] "Chou En-lai's Speech of February 2, 1968," *SCMP*, No. 4154 (April 8, 1968), p. 3.

[11] *NCNA*, September 24, 1968.

well-being can be seen from the fact that in 1971 small local iron and steel works turned out several million tons of pig iron and steel, and that the output of cement and chemical fertilizers from small factories in the same year made up 44 and 60 per cent respectively of the nation's total.[12] The growth of local industry is also expected to play an increasingly larger role in improving industrial distribution, supporting agriculture, alleviating pressure on the nation's expanding but still inadequate transportation system, and strengthening China's preparedness against foreign attack.

The resurgence of industrial growth, which in 1970 was estimated at 18 per cent, including the production of 21 million tons of steel, made it possible for the country to commence its fourth five-year plan in January 1971. As in the case of the third five-year plan, Peking has not yet published any data on the contents of the new blueprint; but fragmented reports indicate that among the industries to be developed with great energy under the latest plan are steel, mining, metallurgy, machine-building, farm implements, fertilizers, chemicals, cement, mining equipment, electronics, electrical equipment, military aircraft, ship-building, plastics, machine tools, and textile machinery. Annual industrial growth under this plan has been estimated at 12 per cent for 1971 and somewhat higher for 1972. Although much remains to be done before China can achieve a really advanced level of industrialization and per capita output of such vital products as steel and electric power, the resumption of industrial expansion in recent years appears to have laid a solid foundation for further development. Even today the steady development of industrial and farm production has already provided the market with an abundant supply of basic consumer goods at stable prices. The resultant increases in personal income and the improvement in the basic living standard are indicated in part by the fact that in 1971 the volume of retail sales was more than six times that of 1949.[13]

[12] Chi Wei, "We Are Advancing," *Peking Review*, No. 39 (September 29, 1972), p. 12.

[13] *Ibid.*, p. 19.

XI

Social, Cultural, and Educational Policies Since 1949

中國共產運動簡史

Reforming the Family System

For millenniums before the Communist takeover the Chinese family had been the basic social and economic unit of the land. It assumed the primary responsibility for providing shelter, food, and love for its members, rearing the young, and caring for the old. It was the molder of personal conduct, the transmitter of technical skills and everyday wisdom, the custodian of traditional values, beliefs, customs, and habits, and the strongest magnet of loyalty. Although many of the functions that it performed and most of the personal traits that it fostered contributed much to the moral and material well-being of the society, the Chinese family system was not an unmixed blessing. Its stress on familial loyalty and self-sufficiency often hindered collective endeavors outside a single blood-related group. The veneration for ancestry which it prized augmented the conservative strain of the Chinese mentality, discouraging innovations in all fields. Politically, the individual's strong attachment to his family usually weakened his commitment to the state. As an ordinary citizen, he tended to be indifferent to public affairs and to circumvent state laws and regulations. As an official of the state, he was tempted to indulge in nepotism, favoritism, and financial irregularities, thus undermining the elaborately developed civil service merit system and the much extolled virtues of impartiality, propriety, and incorruptibility.

These and other ill effects of the traditional family system played a large part in the periodic dynastic decay of the imperial era and in the ineffectiveness and corruption of the warlord and the Kuomintang regimes of the republican period. Determined to free the "new" China from the same dilapidating influences, the CCP set out to reform the family system shortly after its seizure of power.[1] It began with the promulgation of the Marriage Law on April 30, 1950.[2] The new legislation banned arranged and child marriage, sale of children, concubinage, polygamy, discrimination against illegitimacy, and interference with the right of a widow to remarry. It gave women equal rights with men to work, in status in and outside the home, in property rights, in divorce, and allowed them to retain their maiden names.

To be sure, many of these principles had been incorporated into the Civil Code of the Kuomintang regime about 20 years earlier, but that code had little impact on the traditional family system, inasmuch as it was largely unenforced. The Communist regime, by contrast, made the enforcement of the Marriage Law one of its most important tasks; no sooner had the law been promulgated than a nationwide campaign to publicize and enforce it got under way. In addition to using all available mass communications media, the regime sent vast numbers of cadres to the nation's cities, towns, and villages to acquaint the public with the provisions of the instrument and to urge the "victims" of the traditional family system to seek redress under the new enactment. The official agitation soon prompted mistreated wives, daughters-in-law, and child brides to hold "speak-bitterness" meetings; parents who still insisted on arranging marriages for their children were made targets of "mass struggles." The main thrust of the campaign was directed at the concepts of familial solidarity, male supremacy, and parental authority, and perhaps the deadliest blow of all was dealt to parental authority when children were instigated to expose and denounce their parents for "counterrevolutionary" or "reactionary" thought and action. Probably most effective in undermining familial solidarity and male supremacy was the effort to encourage divorce, especially by the wife—an act that traditional China strongly frowned upon, and the regime's policy quickly triggered a mass rush to the divorce courts. According to official statistics, the numbers of matrimonial cases adjudicated by the people's courts in the nation were 186,167 in 1950, 409,500 in 1951, and 398,243 in the first six months of 1952.[3] Some zealous cadres even urged married couples without serious matrimonial complaints to seek

[1] For a detailed discussion of the family reform, see C. K. Yang, *The Chinese Family in the Communist Revolution* (Cambridge, Mass.: Massachusetts Institute of Technology Press, 1959).

[2] For its text, see *New China Monthly*,* No. 7 (May 1950), pp. 33–34.

[3] See Liu Ching-fan's report in *ibid.*, No. 42 (April 1953), p. 67.

divorce. Unwilling to follow the cadres' advice but unable to withstand the pressure, many women committed suicide. From May 1950 to July 1951 more than 10,000 such cases were reported.[4]

Wishing only to correct abuses and to weaken the family as a competing center of personal loyalty, the party soon took steps to curb the excesses of the campaign, for fear they might lead to a complete destruction of the family, which in its opinion not only still retained its customary usefulness to the individual and the society, but might play important roles in the socialist construction under party control. By 1956 the party had clearly defined the role of the family in the construction of a new nation. First, the family must be harmonious and democratic with the husband and wife equal and happy, because a good home life, said the party, increases the productive enthusiasm of both the husband and the wife. While women should take active part in industrial production and other tasks of construction, they must also make a success of their housekeeping and various side occupations and manage their homes with thrift and diligence. The new family must also assist the state in training children to be hardworking, hardy socialists. The husband and wife, too, must engage in ideological study regularly, with the objective of correcting their own feudal or bourgeois view of life and developing the right attitudes toward work and the collective. Young people and adults must support and respect their parents so that the aged who are incapable of working will receive reasonable care late in their life and enjoy mental ease—the last function doubtless assigned to the family mainly because the state was not yet ready to feed and keep the elderly.

Mobilizing Women for Nation-Building Tasks Outside the Home

The new emphasis on the family, however, did not prevent the regime from continuing its efforts to broaden women's opportunities to serve the state outside the family. Thus in recent years China's women have been playing an increasingly important role in the work of government, in building the country's economy, in science and technology, in education, culture, art, and sports.

As of March 1966,[5] there were 542 elected women deputies in the Third National People's Congress. This was 17.87 per cent of the total. Nineteen had seats on the Standing Committee of the Congress. No fewer than 1.43 million women were serving as deputies at local people's congresses at various levels in the country,

[4] *People's Handbook: 1952** (Tientsin: Ta-kung Pao, 1952), p. 216.
[5] *NCNA,* March 6, 1966.

constituting 22 per cent of the total membership of these congresses.

The country had more than 300 women heads or deputy heads of provincial, city, county and *ch'ü* governments. According to an earlier report, women also accounted for more than 80 per cent of the cadres of the urban inhabitants' committees and for an equal percentage of the heads and deputy heads of the village governments.[6]

At one time there were as many as four women ministers and four women vice ministers in the State Council.[7] Today, one of the two vice chairmen of the state is a woman (Madame Sun Yat-sen).

The number of women in industry in 1966 was more than double what it was in 1957 at the end of the first five-year plan. With the exception of certain kinds of work unsuitable for women for health reasons, every branch of industry is now open to them.

All working women draw equal pay with men for the same work. All women workers have 56 days of maternity leave with full pay, with medical expenses borne by the enterprises. Factories provide regular facilities for nursery mothers, have a special staff for maternity and child welfare, and run their own nurseries and kindergartens.[8]

Women constitute 30 to 40 per cent of the agricultural labor force. In cotton cultivation, women usually do about 70 per cent of the field work. Women are also playing a big part in water conservancy, soil transformation and afforestation, and especially in scientific experiments. Women may work in every branch of science and technology, and in education, industry, atomic energy, and medical science.[9] There are also women air pilots, women militia, and women locomotive operators. Many women have had outstanding performances in all fields. In 1957, for example, more than 270,000 women were elected "advanced workers." [10] In June 1960, of the 6000 participants at the National Conference of Outstanding Groups and Workers in Education, Culture, Public Health, and Physical Culture and Journalism, more than 1300 were women.[11]

Expanding and Improving Medical and Public Health Services

Developing the nation's medical and public health services is another important task to which the CCP has addressed itself since

[6] *People's Daily,** March 8, 1957.
[7] *China Daily News** (New York), March 23, 1957.
[8] *NCNA,* November 27, 1957.
[9] *People's Daily,** September 10, 1957.
[10] *Ibid.,* March 8, 1957.
[11] *NCNA,* June 1, 1960.

1949. The party regards this work as an integral part of its over-all program for modernizing China. The CCP seems to have felt a special urgency for making energetic efforts to develop medical and public health services because of the pitiful negligence of the task by the antecedent regimes in modern times.

As a result of several years of hard work, there now exists a nationwide public health service that parallels the general administrative structure of the country, reaching down from Peking and the provincial capitals to the lowest level of the communes—the production teams. According to the latest available official report,[12] by the end of 1961 there were about 700,000 hospital beds in the nation or nine times as many as in 1949. There were also 210,000 health centers and clinics, 270 times the 1949 figure.

Special attention has been paid to the health of industrial workers. Workers and staff members now reportedly enjoy free medical care and hospitalization and their dependents pay only half the medical charges.[13] Also enjoying free medical care are government employees, teachers at all levels, and college students.

Health and medical services have also been expanded in the rural districts, including the sparsely-populated outlying areas and national minority regions. In addition to regular hospitals in county seats, clinics and health centers in production brigade centers, and part-time medical workers, midwives, and nurses in production teams, doctors in urban centers often leave their posts for a time to stay in rural areas to make investigations and give treatment or popularize knowledge of hygiene. During the busy farm season, mobile teams are organized to tour the countryside to give on the spot treatment.[14]

Apart from the general hospitals, there are also specialized ones for pediatrics, obstetrics, chest diseases, tumors and cancer, and neurosurgery. Compared with 1949, the beds in the maternity and children's hospitals in 1961 were said to have increased more than five and three times respectively.[15] As a result of the popularization of modern midwifery, infantile tetanus and puerperal fever have been greatly reduced. Common children's diseases and infantile mortality have declined sharply.[16] In metropolitan cities children are now given periodic check-ups and treatment for eye trouble, tooth decay, and intestinal disorders.[17]

[12] *Ibid.*, September 21, 1962.
[13] *Ibid.*, October 22, 1963.
[14] *Ibid.*, September 28, 1965.
[15] *Ibid.*, September 21, 1962.
[16] *Ibid.*, June 23, 1964.
[17] *Ibid.*, March 3, 1962.

Infectious diseases and epidemics ravaged the Chinese people in the past. Emphasizing "prevention first," by 1962 the regime had established more than 1700 anti-epidemic stations in the country. Cholera, scarlet fever, smallpox, typhoid, typhus, and venereal diseases have been almost eliminated. Schistosomiasis, a parasitic infection seen chiefly in South China, has been brought under control. So has been Trachoma, a disease of the eyes causing a good deal of blindness among older people in China.

Contributing to the successful attack on infectious diseases and epidemics has been the intensive radio and group talks to enlighten and direct the entire population in a mass program of health and sanitation consciousness. The massive campaign to eliminate flies, mosquitoes, and rats that attracted world attention in the 1950's also played a significant role in the war on communicable diseases.

Peking has also made considerable progress in training medical and public health personnel. In 1949 China had only about 20,000 doctors trained in Western medicine. From 1949 to 1964, however, some 450,000 doctors, surgeons, dentists, nurses, and other medical personnel were trained.[18] As of November 1964, every province and autonomous region except Tibet had one or more medical colleges. There were altogether 80 such colleges as compared with only eight in 1949.

The colleges give five- or six-year training. Each is attached to one or more hospitals where students go for clinical training. According to Dr. G. Leslie Wilcox, a Canadian surgeon, at least in those medical colleges and hospitals which he visited in the fall of 1964, the facilities for research and surgical operations were "excellent." [19]

As of 1964, some 90,000 students were enrolled in the medical colleges, eight times as many as there were in all the medical colleges in 1949. Cognizant of the continuing usefulness of traditional Chinese medicine, which had been belittled for some time prior to 1949, Mao Tse-tung took steps to restore it immediately after his party's victory in 1949. Today, all medical graduates spend some of their time learning traditional Chinese medicine, including acupuncture and moxibustion (burning of the dried herb moxa), which have often been particularly useful in treatment of functional disorders. In addition, 20 medical colleges and schools train doctors in traditional Chinese medicine. The regime has also shown much interest in putting traditional Chinese medicine on a more scientific basis and in integrating it with Western medicine.

[18] *Ibid.*, November 23, 1964.

[19] G. Leslie Wilcox, "Observations on Medical Practices," *Bulletin of the Atomic Scientists,* XXII (June 1966), 51–56.

Not only has the Peking regime made great progress in training medical and health personnel, but it has registered considerable gains in building up a pharmaceutical industry. Early in 1963 it claimed that it was already "approaching self-sufficiency in most of the widely used medicines." [20] Every province and autonomous region had its own pharmaceutical plant, the regime asserted. In the first quarter of that year, these plants, continued the official report, turned out as much in five days as the output for the whole year of 1949. The drugs produced in 1963 numbered several hundred as against a dozen in 1949. About a dozen plants were producing antibiotics, including penicillin, streptomycin, sintomycin, aureomycin, tetracycin, chloromycin, illotycin, terramycin, and neomycin. This meant that henceforth the country could fight many infectious diseases with domestically-made medicines.

Controlling Population Growth

As noted in Chapter I, population pressure was one of the basic causes of modern China's poverty and political instability. According to census figures of 1953, the total population on mainland China was 590,194,715. In 1957 the regime estimated that the number had increased to about 654 million. The latest official estimate, which was reported in July 1966, put the population at 700 million. Although the per-thousand annual growth rate in these past years was relatively modest in comparison with those in some other countries, the increment in absolute terms often exceeded 10 million per year. Realizing that with this vast number of additional mouths to feed each year it would be exceedingly difficult for the country to achieve a substantial gain in living standards, the CCP decided to seek a reduction of birthrates soon after its assumption of the reins of the state. Conscious of the apparent inconsistency between its action and the Marxian doctrine that there can be no population pressure under socialism, the CCP justified its policy with the ingenious theory that although population growth will no longer pose any problem to a country that has already built socialism, a nation that has long anguished under feudalism, imperialism, and bureaucratic capitalism, one that is only in the process of building socialism, can be greatly hampered for a time by a large, rapidly growing population.

The party's efforts to reduce the rate of population growth began with the issuance in August 1953 by the Government Administrative Council of a directive to the Ministry of Public Health, giving its approval to the latter's proposed regulations on birth

[20] *NCNA*, April 27, 1963.

control and induced abortions and instructing the latter to make promotion of birth control one of its most important tasks. On December 29, 1954, Liu Shao-ch'i presided over an officially sponsored symposium on birth control. This was followed by the formation of an ad hoc committee to study birth control methods. In September 1956, while reporting on the proposed second five-year plan to the Eighth National Congress of the CCP, Premier Chou En-lai reiterated the party's conviction that birth control must be practiced. But during the Great Leap Forward the CCP abandoned the policy of promoting birth control, and many of its top leaders, including Liu Shao-ch'i, now asserted that the high population was not a liability, but an asset. "By relying on this great force," Liu stated on May 5, 1958, "we can or soon can do anything within the realms of human possibility." [21] Yet the collapse of the Great Leap Forward caused the party to revert to the policy of promoting birth control. The revived campaign gathered momentum in 1962 when the press and other mass communications media made a concerted effort to publicize contraceptive knowledge, to expound the merits of planned childbirths, and to urge young people to postpone marriage until 25 years of age for women and 28 years of age for men. This was accompanied by an increase in the supply of contraceptive devices. As in the 1950's, sterilization now could be obtained by a male or female at any time, with no questions asked. The most promising aspect of the birth control campaign at present lies in the availability of the intrauterine device, which is effective, easy to use, and inexpensive. When the supply of this and other contraceptive devices becomes readily available, birth control in China is likely to yield noticeable results, because unlike many other countries in the world, fertility reduction practices in China are not hindered by religious taboos.

Policy Toward the National Minorities

China has more than 50 national minorities with a total population of nearly 40 million. Although they constitute only 6 per cent of the country's population, these minority groups occupy as much as 50 to 60 per cent of the country's total area. Many of the national minority areas are rich in resources and are of strategic importance. For more than a century prior to 1949, foreign powers, playing the game of divide and rule, repeatedly sought to detach from China such pivotal national minority regions as Tibet, Sinkiang, and Mongolia by exploiting traditional misunderstanding, suspicions, and hatred between the Han Chinese and the national minorities

[21] *New China Semi-Monthly,** No. 133 (June 10, 1958), p. 11.

in those areas. Although Sun Yat-sen attempted to correct the situation by advocating a policy of complete equality for all the ethnic groups in the country, when it was in power the Kuomintang did little to alleviate the tensions that existed among the various nationalities.

Since 1949 the CCP's policy toward the national minorities has been aimed at achieving national solidarity and territorial integrity, ensuring the successful development of the socialist revolution and socialist construction throughout the nation, ending the economic and cultural backwardness of the minority groups, and promoting equality, unity, mutual support, and cooperation and common growth of all the nationalities in the land. One of the major measures that the party has taken to attain these goals is the effort to overcome "great-Han chauvinism." Although it had never taken such extreme forms as enforced segregation of minority groups and attribution of innate inferiority to the latter, great-Han chauvinism had often been manifested in the Han people's propensity to deride the national minorities for their peculiar costumes, habits, customs, and other aspects of cultural backwardness. Great-Han chauvinism had also been at the roots of some Han officials' patronizing attitude toward the non-Han groups and their lack of serious concern for the aspirations and grievances of the national minorities. To combat great-Han chauvinism, the party made the principle of equality a basic national policy and had it incorporated first into the Common Program of the CPPCC and then into the state Constitution. These basic laws stipulated the prohibition of all acts of discrimination, oppression, and splitting of the unity of the various nationalities. Supplementary to this constitutional interdiction have been many administrative orders and regulations issued over the past years by the party, government, and army. In 1949, for example, PLA units entering the northwestern provinces were instructed to respect Moslem beliefs and customs, protect mosques and priests, and avoid disturbing religious services.[22] On May 16, 1951, the Government Administrative Council issued a directive banning all derogatory references to the national minorities.[23] Meanwhile, the Han cadres in the national minority areas were told to learn the local languages. When new school texts were prepared, extreme care was taken to emphasize the theme that the new China is a big fraternal family of all nationalities, to condemn all past instances of the oppression of one nation by another, especially the oppression of the national minorities by the "ruling class" of the Han nationality, and to

[22] *NCNA*, October 24, 1950.
[23] *New China Monthly*,* No. 20 (June 15, 1951), p. 288.

publicize the accomplishments and fine attributes of all the ethnic groups of the country.

Another important component of the CCP's policy toward the national minorities is the principle that all the minority groups living in compact communities may organize various kinds of autonomous organs according to population and extent of the territory concerned.[24] At present national autonomous governments exist at regional (equivalent to provinces), prefectural, and county levels. There are now five autonomous regions: the Inner Mongolia Autonomous Region (established in May 1947); the Sinkiang Uighur Autonomous Region (September 1955); the Kwangsi Chuang Autonomous Region (March 1958); the Ninghsia Hui Autonomous Region (October 1958); and the Tibet Autonomous Region (September 1965). Small groupings are represented by 29 autonomous prefectures (comprising several counties each) and 65 autonomous counties. In addition to exercising the functions assigned to the local organs of state power in general, these bodies have certain special rights by virtue of their autonomous status. They may adopt special regulations or by-laws in the light of the special conditions of the local nationalities. They may establish and maintain local public security forces. They have a greater share of the state revenues. All nationalities under their jurisdictions are guaranteed the use of their own languages and dialects in transacting governmental business. Perhaps the most significant feature of the CCP's policy of national regional autonomy is the principle that members of the national minorities should be the main force to run local affairs, even though in some autonomous areas, including the Inner Mongolia Autonomous Region, the Ninghsia Hui Autonomous Region, and the Kwangsi Chuang Autonomous Region, the various non-Han nationalities are actually outnumbered by local inhabitants of the Han stock. As of 1966, the chairmen of the autonomous regions, the heads and vice heads of all the autonomous prefectures, and the heads of all the autonomous counties were of minority nationality. In provinces where there are scattered non-Han inhabitants, some of the provincial vice governors and heads of provincial departments are members of the national minorities.

When the CCP first came into power, however, there were among the national minorities few men and women qualified to hold responsible positions in the organs of the party and the state. This

[24] "Regulations on the Implementation of National Regional Autonomy" (issued on August 9, 1952 by the Government Administrative Council), *People's Daily*,* August 13, 1952. See also Articles 67–71 of the Constitution of the People's Republic of China.

situation greatly hampered its effort to implement the policy of making members of the national minorities the main force to run the affairs of the minority regions. To overcome this problem the CCP set out to train large numbers of cadres from among the national minorities. Since then the number of cadres of minority origin has increased steadily. As of August 1963, there were more than half a million of them in the country, or more than 50 times their number in 1949.[25]

Closely related to the policy of national regional autonomy has been the effort to increase opportunities for members of the national minorities to take part in state affairs on the national level. They are now found in the CCP Central Committee (even in the Politburo prior to the GPCR), the State Council, the National Defense Council, and the Standing Committee of the National People's Congress. In the National People's Congress itself, national minorities have always had a disproportionate representation. For example, out of the 1226 delegates to the Second National People's Congress (1959–64), 179 or 14.6 per cent were of minority nationality, although the combined population of the national minorities accounted for only about 6 per cent of the nation's total population.

Considerable progress has been made in developing general educational facilities in the national minority areas. As compared with 1951, the 1964 school enrollments in such regions had increased by four times at primary school level, by eight times in the middle schools, and by more than 12 times in higher education.[26] Before 1949 Tibet had not a single elementary school. By 1964 it had more than 1400 elementary schools with 40,000 pupils or 95 per cent of the school-age children in the region.[27]

As part of the effort to promote education, national minorities have been helped to create and reform their own written languages. Large numbers of books, newspapers, and magazines have been published in the national minority languages.

To mobilize the rich resources of the national minority areas for national construction and for improving the living standards of the national minorities with a view to contributing to their well-being as well as to strengthening their centripetal tendencies, the CCP has sought to develop the economy of the national minority regions. In allocating investment funds, special consideration is given to the needs of the national minority areas, and sizeable subsidies have been allocated to such areas, along with various kinds of

[25] *NCNA*, August 29, 1963.
[26] *Ibid.*, December 20, 1965.
[27] *Ibid.*, March 25 and July 27, 1964.

loans, relief funds, and free gifts of farm implements.[28] For example, from 1959 to 1963, 700,000 iron farm tools were supplied by the government to peasants in Tibet, who until then had only wooden implements.[29] In pasture areas and certain agricultural areas where the development of production is backward, the ethnic minorities are now charged less taxes, and in some areas are exempt from taxes altogether.

To increase agricultural production, the acreage of land under cultivation in many minority areas has been expanded greatly. The amount of farmland opened up in Sinkiang from 1950 to 1965 was more than the total acreage under cultivation up to 1949.[30] At the same time, the irrigated area in the region had been doubled. Much of the reclaimed land in that desert area is now protected by shelter belts. In 1965, Sinkiang produced three times as much grain and 11 times more cotton than in 1949.[31]

Livestock breeding in the national minority areas has received equal attention from the government. In 1964, the number of livestock in Inner Mongolia was nearly five times that of 1947.[32] Similarly, the number of livestock in Sinkiang has also increased considerably. In 1965 the region had two and a half times the number in 1949.[33]

Prior to 1949, the national minority regions had few or no modern industries, and some areas were devoid of even handicraft shops. Since 1949, the regime has made special efforts to build industrial plants in many of these territories. Sinkiang, for example, in 1949 had only a dozen small factories producing only 11 products. In 1965 it had over 500 modern industrial plants producing more than 2000 products including cotton yarn and silk fabrics, refined sugar, electrical machines, petroleum, tanned leather, chemicals, and rolled steel.[34]

To facilitate economic development, to bring about a greater integration of the country, and to strengthen national defense, the Peking regime has endeavored to construct railroads, highways, and air transport services in the national minority areas. In 1964, the total mileage of railroads in such areas was ten times greater than in 1949.[35] The first railroad linking Sinkiang with China proper

[28] *New China Semi-Monthly,** No. 162 (August 27, 1959), pp. 109–112.
[29] *NCNA,* March 27, 1964.
[30] *Ibid.,* September 21, 1965.
[31] *SCMM,* No. 512 (February 21, 1966), pp. 25–29.
[32] *NCNA,* November 10, 1964.
[33] *SCMM,* No. 512 (February 21, 1966), pp. 25–29.
[34] *NCNA,* September 21, 1965.
[35] *SCMM,* No. 450 (June 4, 1965), p. 12.

(the Lanchow-Sinkiang Railroad) was built in the early 1960's. Meanwhile, the construction of the Szechwan-Tibet, Chinghai-Tibet, and Sinkiang-Tibet highways has ended Tibet's age-old geographical, economical, and political isolation. In Sinkiang and Inner Mongolia, vehicles are now gradually superseding camels, donkeys, and mules. As of 1964, all the counties and rural peoples' communes in Sinkiang had been linked with highways and postal and telephone services.[36] In the same year, the total mileage of highways in Inner Mongolia was more than 12 times that in 1949.[37]

Thanks to the economic growth and the abolition of the privileges of feudal lords and slave-owners, there has been a noticeable improvement in the living standard of the national minorities. For example, Tibetan peasants and herdsmen bought 25 per cent more commodities in the first half of 1964 than in the same period of 1963. In a number of mountainous counties of southeastern Tibet the total sales in local supply and marketing cooperatives went up to 86 per cent compared with the first half of 1963.[38] Tibetans in the Ali area in western Tibet bought four times as many commodities in 1964 as in 1959, when the traditional serfdom was abolished, and former slaves were given the land of their former masters. In the same period the annual per capita consumption of tea in the area increased six times.[39] In Sinkiang, personal income in 1965 was nearly three times that of 1949.[40]

The higher living standard, coupled with a tremendous expansion of medical and public health services, has led to great increases in the population of the national minorities. The Mongolian population of Inner Mongolia, for example, increased by 60 per cent from 1947 to 1964.[41] The increases in the population of the national minorities in Sinkiang in the period of 1949–65 ranged from 20 to 50 per cent.[42] In Tibet the population increased by 10.4 per cent from 1960 to 1965.[43]

Although the CCP has taken many constructive steps to win the loyalty of the national minorities, its efforts to achieve greater national unity have not always met with complete success. For one thing, the limited scope of national regional autonomy has caused some members of the national minorities to question its real sig-

[36] *NCNA*, September 21, 1965.
[37] *Ibid.*, May 1, 1964.
[38] *Ibid.*, July 16, 1964.
[39] *Ibid.*, February 25, 1964.
[40] *Ibid.*, September 21, 1965.
[41] *Ibid.*, May 1, 1964.
[42] *Ibid.*, September 21, 1965.
[43] *Ibid.*, August 20, 1965.

nificance, and they have demanded an expansion of its scope. Certain elements in Sinkiang and elsewhere once even wanted to change the autonomous regions into "independent" or "federal" republics. In the early 1950's the CCP relied heavily on Han cadres to run the organs of the party and the state in the national minority areas because of the lack of qualified cadres of minority nationality. This prompted the charge that even the limited autonomy was a farce, because few members of the national minorities were actually put in charge of the autonomous governments. Cadres of the Han nationality were particularly resented when they manifested great-Han chauvinism toward the local population in general and minority nationality cadres in particular. The migration of Han people into Sinkiang, Inner Mongolia, and Tibet has been another source of tension in the areas concerned. Some members of the national minorities fear that the influx of the Han people into their regions will eventually lead to the disappearance of their own groups. In the 1950's objections were expressed about the CCP's land reform program, the campaign to suppress counterrevolutionaries, and the socialist transformation of agriculture, industry, and commerce. Some members of the national minorities contended that those measures were not needed in their areas where, in their opinion, the social-economic conditions were vastly different from the regions inhabited by the Han people.

Regarding most of these signs of dissatisfaction as manifestations of "local nationalism," which serves the interests of feudal lords and bourgeois rightists and opposes the unity of nationalities, socialism, and the hegemony of the party, the CCP has from time to time taken stern measures against its advocates. One of the major campaigns to criticize local nationalism was launched in conjunction with the nationwide anti-rightists campaign in 1957–58. The strongest actions were taken in March 1959 and the summer of 1962, when force was used to quell armed rebellions in Tibet and Sinkiang. It would appear, however, that in both cases the CCP skillfully exploited the seditious acts of the local elites to effectively uproot their political influence, thus making it possible for the party to install more cooperative local cadres in positions of authority. In particular, the revolt in Tibet led by the Dalai Lama gave the CCP an excuse to terminate its policy of postponing "democratic" and socialist reforms in Tibet—a course of action that the party had taken only two years earlier in exchange for the Dalai Lama's pledges of loyalty. As alluded to earlier, the social, economic, and political reforms carried out in Tibet since 1959 have led to a noticeable betterment of the average lot of the Tibetan people. Meanwhile, the party has demonstrated its determination to go to any length to remove obstacles to the implementation of its policies in Tibet. This can be seen from its dismissal in late 1964 of the Panchen Lama from his posts of vice-chairman and acting chairman of the preparatory committee for the Tibetan autonomous region, after his being accused of engaging in "organized activities against the people, the motherland, and socialism." [44] When the Tibet Autonomous Region was formally inaugurated in September 1965, however, the Panchen Lama was given a minor place as a member of the standing committee of the CPPCC Tibetan Autonomous Region Committee. This was done, said the CCP, "in order to give him a last opportunity to turn over a new leaf." The same policy of forgiveness has been extended to those self-exiled Tibetans, presumably including the Dalai Lama, who is now in India, "if they go back voluntarily to China and admit their wrongdoings to the people, regardless of what crimes they committed and what their positions were in the past." [45]

Thought Reform of Intellectuals

Reforming the thought of intellectuals has been an important component of the CCP's cultural policy. As early as 1945 Mao Tse-tung focused upon the need for such a reform when he said:

> . . . To sweep away foreign and feudal oppression and build a new democratic China, we need large numbers of educators and teachers for the people, and also people's scientists, engineers, technicians, doctors, journalists, writers, men of letters, artists and rank-and-file cultural workers. They must be imbued with the spirit of serving the people and must work hard . . . The old type of cultural educational workers and doctors should be given suitable re-education so that they can acquire a new outlook and new methods to serve the people.[46]

Following their nationwide victory in 1949, the Communists promptly put this program into effect. The first group of non-Communist intellectuals to go through the thought-reform process were college students, teachers of elementary and high schools, and Kuomintang officials who had failed to flee the mainland when the CCP overran it. Most of the college professors were not affected until the summer of 1951.

Thought reform is a phenomenon unique to China, used pri-

[44] See Premier Chou En-lai's report to the first session of the Third National People's Congress, *ibid.*, December 30, 1964.

[45] See Vice Premier Hsieh Fu-chih's speech at a mass rally in Lhasa on September 9, 1965, *ibid.*, September 10, 1965.

[46] Mao Tse-tung, *Selected Works*, III (Peking: 1965), 304–305.

marily to establish social conformity among groups normally resistant to the regime—the intellectuals and the bourgeoisie. It is predicated on the belief that individuals can and should be politically and socially re-educated and that they must constantly pursue, through self-examination, a sort of political and doctrinal purification.[47] Robert J. Lifton, in his article, "Thought Reform of Chinese Intellectuals. A Psychiatric Evaluation," [48] described the classical model of the process, the method used in the "revolutionary colleges" set up by the Communists after they came to power. Individuals take part in the thought-reform program either voluntarily or under various degrees of external coercion. In the revolutionary colleges students are assigned to small groups, usually of six to ten persons; each group stays together throughout the process. Lifton divides the process into three phases: (1) "The Great Togetherness—group identification." During this phase lectures and discussions are held, designed to produce *esprit de corps* within the group and identification of the members with the national Communist movement—a feeling of working together toward a common goal. (2) "The Closing-in of the Milieu—The Period of Emotional Conflict," in which there is a shift of emphasis from the intellectual and ideological to the personal and emotional. There develops a pattern of criticism, self-criticism, and confession, by which the individual is detached from the former social and political loyalties and learns to adhere to Communist patterns, and a break is made away from traditional family and cultural ties. (3) "Submission and 'Rebirth.'" In this final phase, the culmination of the entire process, the individual must produce an overall thought summary, a final confession which includes a detailed analysis of his class origin; this usually has as its central feature a denunciation of his father, both as symbol and as individual. When the process has been effective, the result of this final phase is a great emotional relief. It is a symbolic submission to the new order and an expression of rebirth as a member of the Chinese Communist community.

For college professors, thought reform proved a greater ordeal than for any other group. Their confessions were evaluated not only by their colleagues but by their students as well. Moreover, since many of their confessions were published in newspapers and magazines, they also had to satisfy the general public as to the sincerity of their convictions. It often happened that even after a professor

[47] For an exposition of this view, see John Wilson Lewis, *Leadership in Communist China* (Ithaca, N. Y.: Cornell University Press, 1963), pp. 35–69.

[48] For Lifton's article, see *Journal of Asian Studies,* XVI (November 1956), 76–86.

had been approved by his colleagues and students, further self-scrutiny was necessary whenever a newspaper or magazine reader found any fault with his published confession. If he showed "uncooperative attitudes" at any stage of the process, he was usually sent to witness some "revolutionary struggles," such as "mass trials of counterrevolutionaries" or "mass liquidation of 'oppressive' landlords." The party claims that such experiences enable the professor to see the social realities more clearly and thus become more conscious of mistaken ideology, but it is likely that they are also designed to inculcate fear and thus undermine his resistance.

In the early 1950's, thoughts and attitudes to be confessed and cleansed from the minds of the intellectuals included the following major varieties:

1. political—distrust of the CCP, antagonism to the Soviet Union, subservience to the Kuomintang, worship of America, indifference to the people's revolutionary struggle, reformism, conservatism, and bureaucratism.
2. social—opportunism, lack of sense of duty, purely technical viewpoint, employee's viewpoint, contempt of labor, and desire to exploit fellow human beings.
3. academic—intellectual sectarianism, subjective dogmatism, formalism, liberalism, pragmatism, and pure professional interest.
4. personal—egotism, selfishness, arrogance, extravagance, and emotionalism.

In addition to requiring large groups of non-Communist intellectuals to go through the process of thought reform *en masse,* the party from time to time singled out one or two individuals for attack and used them as object lessons.[49] Among such victims were Professors Yü P'ing-po, Hu Shih (attacked in absentia), Liang Sou-ming, and Feng Yu-lan.

The difficulty in reforming the thought of senior intellectuals was revealed by Premier Chou En-lai early in 1956, when he said that at least 60 per cent of mainland China's "high-level" intellectuals still did not believe in Communism.[50] Not only did the thought-reform program fail to give the Chinese intellectuals a unified political outlook, but it caused considerable ill feeling and in some instances hatred of the party. On January 14, 1956, Chou En-lai made a special report on the problems of intellectuals to the

[49] For more information, see Theodore H. E. Chen, *Thought Reform of Chinese Intellectuals* (Hong Kong: Hong Kong University Press, 1960).

[50] Chou En-lai, "A Report on the Problems of Intellectuals," *People's Daily,** January 30, 1956.

Central Committee of the party.[51] He showed concern over the "passive attitude" of the bourgeois intellectuals, which he felt resulted from the "crude" method of ideological remolding which they had undergone, and promised remedial measures. The non-Communist intellectuals were told that henceforth the thought reformers would be more patient and gentle in criticizing their unproletarian thought as long as nothing was said or done against the interests of the people.

Meanwhile, the slogan "Let One Hundred Schools of Thought Contend and One Hundred Flowers Bloom" was proclaimed by Mao Tse-tung in a speech on May 2, 1956 before the Supreme State Conference. It has never been entirely clear what Mao meant by the slogan, though many non-Communist scholars interpreted it as implying toleration of freedom of intellectual and political expression. According to Lu Ting-i, then Director of the party's Propaganda Department, Mao intended to foster a kind of socialist competition in the educational, literary, and artistic fields.[52] Scientists, philosophers, novelists, playwrights, artists, and other intellectuals were encouraged to be active and explicit in rectifying one another's non-Marxist views and in raising their professional standards, thereby to increase their effectiveness in building a socialist society. On February 27, 1957, Mao Tse-tung, in his famous speech "on the correct handling of contradictions among the people," reiterated this policy and the slogan and extended an open invitation for public criticism of the regime's shortcomings.[53] As noted in Chapters VII and VIII, this apparent display of liberalism led many non-Communist intellectuals and politicians and even some Communists to voice their dissatisfaction, and the fierceness of the attacks soon alarmed the party. By June 18, Mao had revised his statement to permit of a less liberal interpretation,[54] the outspoken critics had been labeled poisonous weeds rather than flowers, and the way was clear for the start of an anti-rightist campaign, which culminated in the "Dedication of Hearts Campaign" in March 1958, during which non-Communist intellectuals, particularly those in the minor parties, pledged that they would henceforth completely "surrender their hearts" to the CCP and socialism.

By 1961, however, the party had once again eased its pressure on the intellectuals in an effort to gain their cooperation in coping

[51] *Ibid.*

[52] *Ibid.*, May 26, 1956.

[53] For its text, see *ibid.*, June 19, 1957.

[54] Franklin W. Houn, *To Change a Nation: Propaganda and Indoctrination in Communist China* (New York: The Free Press, 1961), pp. 33–34.

with the aftermath of the collapse of the Great Leap Forward, the withdrawal of Soviet scientists and technicians, and the three consecutive years of natural calamities. From the summer of 1961 to September 1962, there were even faint echoes of the Hundred Flowers period. Although the revived overtures of liberalism were less dramatic and more restrictive, intellectuals were encouraged to air their views on academic subjects so long as their discussions did not touch on political questions and abided by the six criteria governing actions and words that Mao had prescribed in the published text of his speech on the correct handling of contradictions among the people.[55] With regard to ideological remolding, the party now devised a new technique known as "meetings of immortals." Intellectuals attending such meetings discussed the incorrectness of their views in an atmosphere of "gentle breeze and mild drizzle" so that they would have an ethereal feeling and henceforth heartily love and support socialism and the leadership of the party.[56] In the meantime, some spokesmen of the party made pronouncements indicating that the regime at the time was more interested in the intellectuals' professional contributions than in their ideological remolding. "You cannot say," declared Deputy Propaganda Director Chou Yang, "that one must transform his world viewpoint properly before he can serve socialism." [57] Going a step further, Vice Premier Ch'en I asserted that intellectuals could best demonstrate their political loyalty not by constantly professing their devotion to socialism, but by contributing to the development of modern industry, agriculture, science, and culture.[58] Despite explicit admonitions against making impermissible criticisms, the limited relaxation of intellectual control tempted some intellectuals to write articles and books containing veiled criticisms of the regime's policies and advocating new lines of action in various fields. Unlike the critics during the Hundred Flowers campaign, the intellectuals who expressed their dissatisfaction in the early 1960's were mostly veteran Communists who appear to have been disenchanted with the party over a wide range of issues including the Great Leap Forward, the

[55] The six criteria were that words and actions must: (1) help to unite the various nationalities of China and not divide them; (2) be beneficial to the socialist transformation and the socialist construction; (3) help to consolidate the democratic dictatorship; (4) help to consolidate democratic centralism; (5) help to strengthen the leadership of the CCP; and (6) be beneficial to the international socialist solidarity and the solidarity of the peace-loving peoples of the world.

[56] Dennis Doolin, "The Revival of the 'Hundred Flowers' Campaign: 1961," *China Quarterly*, No. 8 (October–December 1961, pp. 34–41.

[57] *People's Daily*,* July 22, 1966.

[58] *Kuang-ming Daily*,* September 3, 1961.

Commune Movement, the Sino-Soviet dispute, the dismissal of P'eng Teh-huai as Defense Minister, business management, and literary policies. As will be examined more fully in Chapter XIII, some critics even mocked Mao Tse-tung personally by using historical analogies.

Mao viewed the dissident intellectuals as antiparty and antisocialist representatives of the reactionary bourgeois line who had wormed their way into the party and were plotting to prepare public opinion for the restoration of capitalism. Exasperated by many party bureaucrats' failure to wage a resolute struggle against the "class enemy" and "revisionists" within the party, he eventually mounted the GPCR, during which the entire nation was to "struggle against and smash those persons in authority who are taking the capitalist road, to criticize and repudiate the reactionary bourgeois academic 'authorities' and the ideology of the bourgeoisie and all other exploiting classes, and to transform education, literature and art and other parts of the superstructure that do not correspond to the socialist economic base." [59] Unwilling to jeopardize the country's scientific and technical developments, the party declared at the very outset of the cultural revolution, however, that resolute struggles would not be waged against "scientists, technicians, and ordinary members of working staffs, as long as they are patriotic, work energetically, are not against the party and socialism, and maintain no illicit relations with any foreign country." [60] Moreover, the party stated that "special care should be taken of those scientists and scientific and technical personnel who have made contributions," and that "special efforts should be made to help them gradually transform their world outlook and their style of work."

Educational Policy

Inasmuch as the problem of the CCP is not merely to transform a traditional society into a socialist one, but also to change from an agricultural to an industrial society, its educational policy since 1949 has been designed to facilitate the attainment of these twin objectives. Officially, the goals have been: to combat illiteracy; to train personnel for various tasks of nation-building; to eradicate the "feudal, compradore and fascist" ideology; to foster the concept of dedicated service to the people; to develop a new public spirit stressing love of the fatherland, love of the people, love of labor, love

[59] "Decisions of the Central Committee of the CCP Concerning the Great Proletarian Cultural Revolution," *Peking Review*, No. 33 (August 12, 1966), p. 6.

[60] *Ibid.*, p. 10.

of science, and care of public property; and to promote the application of "a scientific-historical viewpoint to the study and interpretation of history, economics, culture, and international affairs." [61]

The substitution of a new ideology and a new philosophy of life for the old ones has been deemed essential to the socialist transformation and the socialist industrialization, if they are to be accomplished with maximum dispatch and minimum obstruction. For one thing, the idea of centralized planning and centrally-controlled administration is predicated upon the existence of a highly disciplined citizenry, ever ready to accept orders and willing to subordinate personal, family, group, and local interests to those of the state as defined by the top leadership of the party. To bring such a citizenry into being, old traditions like excessive family solidarity, provincialism, contempt of manual labor, indifference to politics, personal fame and profit, and private ownership of property, as well as some recently acquired concepts like civil liberty and democracy, must be expunged.

The importance of combating illiteracy to the attainment of the twin objectives lies in the fact that while it is difficult to inculcate socialist principles and aims in the people without the written word, it is impossible to operate an industrial society without a reasonable level of literacy. In 1949 only about 20 per cent of the Chinese population was literate. The fight against illiteracy has made considerable progress, as can be seen by the fact that between 1949 and 1960, some 100 million more people became literate.[62] A major handicap in this endeavor is the nonphonetic system of writing Chinese, which takes years to master. The simplification of ideographs is not a new phenomenon in China, but it has always been slow and sporadic. After its seizure of power the CCP set out to simplify the Han characters systematically, to popularize the standard spoken language, and to promote the use of a phonetic alphabet in school textbooks as an aid to pronunciation. Since then it has simplified a total of 2,252 most commonly used characters,[63] making the fight against illiteracy relatively easier.

The need for a massive effort to train personnel for national construction work can be best appreciated if one recalls that in 1949 China had only about 75,000 "high-level" intellectuals in the

[61] Articles 41, 42 & 44 of the Common Program of the CPPCC.

[62] *People's Daily,** June 1, 1960.

[63] See Chou En-lai's report on "The Current Tasks of the Language Reform," *ibid.,* January 13, 1958. *See also* Constantin Milsky, "New Developments in Language Reform," *China Quarterly,* no. 53 (January–March 1973, pp. 98–133).

humanities, arts, letters, sciences, engineering, medical and other allied fields.[64] The scarcity of competent personnel for nation-building was accentuated by the fact that only a very small percentage of the educated Chinese at all levels were trained in natural sciences and engineering. For centuries Chinese intellectuals had always preferred humanistic studies over scientific pursuits.

The CCP has developed a variety of institutions to educate the Chinese people. Besides the regular elementary and middle schools and universities and colleges, there are *inter alia* spare-time schools, half-study and half-work schools, half-study and half-farming schools, winter schools for adult peasants, and various kinds of literacy classes. Nearly all the irregular educational institutions are novel devices used by the Communist regime to extend the benefit of education to the largest possible number of youths and adults who cannot attend the regular educational institutions for one reason or another. The half-study and half-farming schools, for example, were organized in 1958 during the Great Leap Forward to provide education for rural youngsters who must work on the farms part of the time. Providing education from the elementary to the college level, the part-time and spare-time schools have been playing a significant role in the fight against illiteracy, in imparting technical knowledge to industrial workers and farmers, and in facilitating their vocational advancement.[65] As of January, 1964, over 10 million persons were participating in part-time study.[66] In April of that year four out of every ten Chinese workers in the spare-time schools had reached the level of a middle school or college education, whereas in 1949 more than 70 per cent of the Chinese workers could not read or write.[67] In the 1960's several thousand workers in the spare-time schools completed the equivalent of a college education annually. Many such workers have been promoted to be engineers and technicians. In 1964, one-sixth of the engineers and technicians in the famous Anshan steel plant were said to be graduates of spare-time engineering colleges.[68]

The CCP has also endeavored to increase regular school facilities.

[64] This figure is computed from the statistics given by Kuo Mo-jo in his report on "The Tasks of Intellectuals in the High Tide of the Socialist Revolution," *CB*, No. 377 (February 15, 1956), p. 8.

[65] See Robert D. Barendsen, *Half-Work and Half-Study Schools in Communist China* (Washington, D. C.: U. S. Government Printing Office, 1964); and Paul Harper, *Spare-Time Education for Workers in Communist China* (Washington, D. C.: U. S. Government Printing Office, 1964).

[66] *People's Daily,** January 6, 1964.

[67] *NCNA*, April 25, 1964.

[68] *Ibid.*

Table I shows the increase in enrollment in schools and colleges from 1949 to 1963. Although exact figures on school enrollment in recent years are lacking, it was officially reported in 1964 that as of then all elementary school-age children in the large and medium-sized cities were attending school and that in the rural districts about 80–90 per cent of the elementary school-age children were in school.[69] The enrollment in colleges was the highest in the 1960–61 school year. The subsequent reduction appears to have stemmed mainly from a desire to improve the quality of higher education after a decade of rapid expansion.

TABLE I. ENROLLMENT IN SCHOOLS AND COLLEGES IN COMMUNIST CHINA. 1949–1963 *

School Year	*Elementary Schools*	*Middle Schools*	*Colleges and Universities*
1949–50	24,391,033	1,267,089	111,133
1950–51	28,928,988	1,566,540	138,731
1951–52	43,154,440	1,964,071	155,570
1952–53	49,766,114	3,145,866	194,378
1953–54	51,504,312	3,628,264	216,768
1954–55	51,190,000	4,246,000	258,000
1955–56	53,100,000	4,437,000	290,000
1956–57	57,000,000	5,000,000	400,000
1957–58	63,000,000	5,160,000	447,000
1958–59	86,000,000	12,000,000	660,000
1959–60	90,000,000	not available	810,000
1960–61	not available	not available	855,000
1961–62	not available	not available	815,000
1962–63	not available	not available	820,000

* Sources: official Peking press reports.

Despite the new emphasis on quality, the expansion of higher education since 1949 has been nonetheless impressive. A few comparisons will illustrate this point. First, the enrollment in colleges in 1963 was five times that of 1947, the year in which pre-Communist China had its largest number of college students. Second, in the 50 years that preceded the Communist takeover, the country's institutions of higher learning graduated only 214,001 students, whereas in 1963 alone that many college students finished their undergraduate studies.[70] Third, the total number of teaching personnel in the colleges and universities in 1963 was eight times that

[69] *Ibid.*, May 26, 1964.

[70] *Kuang-ming Daily,** October 1, 1957, and *NCNA,* August 11, 1963.

of 1947.[71] Fourth, new buildings covering 20 million square meters of floor space were built from 1949 to 1963—six times the total erected before 1949.[72] What is more, all universities and colleges not only do not charge tuition, they also provide free living accommodations and medical services for all students.

Quantitative expansion represents only one aspect of the CCP's policy regarding higher education. Other salient features include structural reform of the colleges and universities; curricular revisions; party control of college instruction and administration; the fostering of the study of natural sciences, engineering, and medicine; promotion of combining education with labor; revision of admission policy, and compulsory assignment of jobs for college graduates.

With regard to structural reform, in 1951 and 1952, the Peking regime reorganized existing universities and colleges. Prior to 1949 some of the famous Chinese universities, such as the National Peking University and the National Tsing-hua University, had strong traditions of their own. As champions of liberalism and academic freedom, they had functioned almost independently of the government, and in many cases actively promoted academic disputes between diverse schools of thought. In reorganizing the universities, the CCP had two objectives: specialization and political control. The former was achieved by a thoroughgoing regrouping of departments and units of the existing universities and independent colleges. For example, the college of engineering at the National Peking University was transferred to the National Tsing-hua University, which is now a polytechnical institution, while the latter's colleges of humanities and sciences were amalgamated with the corresponding units of the National Peking University, which is now classified as a university of comprehensive education (i.e., one specializing in humanities and sciences). There are now 11 different kinds of institutions of higher education: comprehensive education, polytechnic, teacher-training, agriculture and forestry, medicine, finance and economics, political science and law, languages, arts, physical culture, and institutions for minority nationalities.

Politically, this regrouping gave the CCP the chance to break up liberal and prestigious institutions as strongholds of intellectual resistance. To eradicate the influence of "foreign imperialism," the CCP took the opportunity of regrouping to dissolve altogether all the institutions sponsored by foreign missionaries. In addition, the reorganization facilitated the CCP's effort to place party members or

[71] *Ibid.*, August 14, 1963.
[72] *Ibid.*

trusted collaborators in strategic administrative positions in the universities and colleges. Although reputable and nonpartisan scholars were in some cases retained as presidents, deans, or departmental chairmen, it soon became clear that they had no authority. All decisions, academic or administrative, were made in their names by the party committees within the institutions.

The curricular reform was most drastic in the fields of the humanities and social sciences. Texts and subject matter for these disciplines were completely revised in accordance with the principles of dialectical and historical materialism and for the promotion of patriotism and social consciousness. Teachers were encouraged to emphasize the present rather than the past in order to discount the old traditions and clear the way for collectivist ideals.[73] Meanwhile, the government instructed the colleges to offer new courses designed to teach Communist theories and politics. Curricular changes in elementary and middle schools followed a similar pattern. Accompanying the party's assertion of its authority in educational institutions was its effort to reduce the authority traditionally wielded by Chinese teachers. The party realized that its control of the educational process could never be complete unless its own authority had fully replaced that of the teacher in the classroom.

The policy of fostering the study of natural sciences, engineering, and medicine is closely related to the party's ambitious program for modernizing the country, and the CCP has been very successful in this endeavor. For example, in 1949 only 17.8 per cent of college students were majors in engineering, whereas in 1958 those studying engineering accounted for 37 per cent of the total college student body.[74] The impact of the same policy can be seen also from the fact that among the 1.1 million persons who graduated from universities and colleges from 1949 to 1963 there were 370,000 engineers, 325,000 teachers, 110,000 physicians and pharmaceutists, 100,000 agronomists and foresters, 70,000 natural scientists, and 125,000 specialists in the fields of economics, law, literature, physical culture, and the arts.[75]

Another significant change in education has been the presence in colleges of a growing number of students from peasant and work-

[73] See Ch'en Po-ta's statement on the subject in *People's Daily,** March 11, 1958; and Kuo Mo-jo, "On the Problem of Stressing the Past and Slighting the Present," *ibid.,* June 11, 1958.

[74] *Ibid.,* October 8, 1959.

[75] *NCNA,* August 14, 1963. See also Chu-yuan Cheng, *Scientific and Engineering Education in Communist China* (Washington, D. C.: National Science Foundation, 1965).

ing-class families, due to the tremendous expansion of facilities for higher education, the availability of free living accommodations, and an admission policy that gives priority to applicants with the proper political orientation and social origin. In 1952 students from peasant and working class families accounted for only 22 per cent of the total college enrollment; the percentage rose to 34.1 per cent in 1957, 45 per cent in 1958, and 58 per cent in 1963.[76] Since a person's educational attainment usually affects his or her social and economic status upon graduation, the steady broadening of opportunities for young men and women to get a college education will facilitate social mobility, which, in turn, is likely to have a profound bearing on the party's ability to retain popular support.

The policy of combining education with labor is a reflection of the basic Communist view of society: the intellectual is simply a specialized member of the proletariat and he must never forget his basic role and function; his specialty alone can never justify his existence. Whereas the educated Chinese in the past considered manual labor beneath his dignity, the Communist intellectual must share in the work of his fellow members of the proletariat. This is not only a matter of principle but also of necessity. Unless large numbers of educated people are willing to work on the farms and in the factories, the nation can hardly achieve modernization. When the policy was first put into effect on a systematic basis in 1957, teachers and students were required to spend one-third to one-half of their time taking part in manual labor. The official view was expressed by Lu Ting-i, then the party's propaganda director, in an article contributed to the *Red Flag*.[77] After giving extensive quotations from Communist classics, Lu said that in the future education and material production were to be combined; only through such a combination could the distinction between manual labor and mental labor be obliterated—a prerequisite for the emergence of a Communist society. He saw in such a combination a way to cultivate Communist affection, manner, and the temper of collective heroism. Citing Mao's theory of knowledge, Lu also contended that only the combination of labor and study can produce relatively perfect knowledge, as knowledge obtained solely from books or the senses is apt to be imperfect.

Although the CCP's achievements in the educational field are substantial, its work has not been without difficulties. For one thing,

[76] *People's Daily,** May 29, 1954 and October 8, 1959; *Kuang-ming Daily,** October 1, 1957; and *NCNA,* August 11, 1963.

[77] Lu Ting-i, "Education Must Be Combined with Productive Labor," *Red Flag,** No. 7 (September 1, 1958), pp. 1–12.

the rapid expansion of school facilities in the 1950's necessitated the hiring of many inadequately trained teachers. The insistence on political orthodoxy inhibited many scholars' intellectual creativity, thus resulting in a scarcity of textbooks and scholarly treatises. The demand that teachers must engage in political and other extracurricular activities, the relegation of the teaching profession from its traditional lofty position to a lowly status under the absolute control of the party, and, of course, the humiliating process of thought reform all have served to demoralize large numbers of teachers at all levels and adversely affect their effectiveness in the classroom. The heavy load of extracurricular activities also interfered with the students' scholastic pursuit. The most vexing problem appears to have been how to achieve an optimum balance between "redness" (political orthodoxy) and "expertness" (professional proficiency). Despite the party's repeated emphasis on the equal importance of both qualities, it is clear that during the first decade of its rule "redness" actually received more attention. By 1961, however, some leaders in the party began to advocate a policy stressing "expertness" in education. Having no apparent intention of abandoning the demand for "redness," these leaders sought to give more weight to academic excellence by advancing the thesis that while participation in extracurricular activities was essential, studying books was equally important.[78] Believing that quality education could not be achieved if the school administration and students alike continued to undermine the position of the teacher, these leaders now set out to advise the students to show proper respect for their teachers in academic matters, even if the latter had not yet completely divested themselves of their nonproletarian ideologies.[79] They expressed concern for the possible ill effects of the heavy extracurricular activities on the students' health as well as on their academic work. In the name of rectifying serious deviations, they soon had these activities greatly reduced. For example, college students were now required to do only one month's physical labor a year in factories or fields. The same leaders also seemed to have questioned the effectiveness of the spare-time and part-time schools. There were indications in Premier Chou En-lai's report to the first session of the Third National People's Congress on December 21 and 22, 1964 that on the insistence of Liu Shao-ch'i the Peking regime was putting greater emphasis on improving the full-time

[78] See Fu Chen-sheng, "Relationship Between 'Redness' and 'Expertness': Concerning the Question of Study," *Kuang-ming Daily,** October 17, 1961.

[79] See K'uang Ya-ming, "A Brief Discussion of the Teacher-Student Relations," *Red Flag,** No. 17 (September 1, 1961), pp. 25–29.

school system while treating the spare-time and part-time schools merely as experimental projects.[80]

Many of the changes made in the early 1960's as well as some other features of the educational system came under strong attack shortly after the outbreak of the GPCR on the ground that "by placing not proletarian but bourgeois politics in command," they had made the educational system "a breeding ground in which intellectual aristocratic and high-salaried strata are nurtured." [81] The attack began with the announcement on June 13, 1966 of a notice by the CCP Central Committee and the State Council, calling for a complete transformation of the "old educational system" and postponing the college enrollment for the 1966–67 academic year by six months.[82] In particular, the official document indicated that there would be a thorough overhauling of the system of examinations and enrollment for the institutions of higher education, which was said to have "shut out many outstanding children of workers and former poor and lower-middle peasants while opening the gate wide to the bourgeoisie to cultivate its own successors." Apparently in an attempt to lend popular support to the attack, on July 13 the *People's Daily* gave front-page prominence to a letter written by seven students at the Chinese People's University to the CCP Central Committee and Chairman Mao. The letter stated that "under the existing system, education lasts too long and has many defects." It complained that "17 years of hard academic study [six years for primary school, six years for middle school, and five years for college] really wastes one's youth and leads the young generation astray." It charged that the existing system runs counter to Chairman Mao's theory of knowledge, for it treasures book knowledge as all-important, despises practical work, isolates the students from contact with the workers and peasants, and trains the young people to become bourgeois specialists whose main concern is personal fame, wealth, and position. The letter asserted that the present system puts too much stress on so-called systematic knowledge and that in reality it encourages dogmatism, metaphysics, and scholasticism.

The changes sought by the students touched many bases. In regard to teaching methods, they insisted that the stress should be put on self-study and discussion. The teachers, they said, should tutor in a subject at length and "resolutely abolish the cramming method of teaching." To speed up learning, the students urged the faculties of arts to reduce the time for their subjects to one, two, or

[80] *NCNA*, December 30, 1964.
[81] *People's Daily*,* June 18, 1966.
[82] *Ibid.*

three years, depending on the details involved. They also recommended that graduation be moved up by at least two years. With regard to putting proletarian politics in command, the students proposed that the arts faculties must use Mao Tse-tung's works as teaching material and make class struggle the subject of profound study. A certain amount of time each year should be devoted to taking part in factory or farm work, military drill, and class struggle in society. In addition, it was suggested that "from now on the colleges should enroll new students from among young people who have tempered themselves in the great revolutionary movements, whose ideology is progressive, and who have reached a certain educational level and not necessarily just from those who have been through senior middle school."

The voice of the students at the Chinese People's University was echoed by youths in some middle schools. The clamor for reforming the educational system received more impetus when the eleventh plenum of the CCP Central Committee adopted on August 8, 1966 a "Decision Concerning the Great Proletarian Cultural Revolution." Article 10 of this document made it perfectly clear that a thorough reform of the educational system along the lines "suggested" by the students was to be carried out as an integral part of the cultural revolution itself. In the meantime, all schools and colleges in the country suspended regular classes to enable students and "revolutionary teachers" to take part in the GPCR. In January 1967, as power had been seized back from "those top party persons in authority taking the capitalist road," Peking instructed all elementary and secondary schools to resume instruction by the following March despite the fact that no concrete plans for overhauling them had been formulated. Elementary schools generally did resume classes in compliance with the order, but many secondary schools could not do so until July 1968, because continued factional struggles among the "young revolutionaries" had delayed the formation in secondary schools of the "revolutionary committees" that were to run them. Each of these committees was to consist of representatives of the student body, the faculty, the military, and workers (in urban areas) or peasants (in rural districts). Colleges and universities, though kept open throughout the GPCR for revolutionary activities, did not resume academic operations until 1970. As of December 1972 the process of reforming the entire educational system was still far from completed, as most of the changes that had thus far been made remained largely experimental in nature.

Among the more important tentative innovations are the shortening of college education to from two to three years and elementary and secondary schooling to a combined total of nine years; the assumption of leadership in education by workers and peasants; reforming curricula at all levels of the educational system in accordance with the principle of "less quantity and better quality"; greater emphasis on practical knowledge and the linking of theory with practice in instruction; greater integration of book learning with productive labor; promotion of on-the-spot teaching; making experienced workers and peasants part-time teachers at elementary and secondary schools; flexible hours and school terms for peasant children; close cooperation between colleges and industry; more attention to political education and the inculcation of the idea that one studies not for the sake of seeking personal gains or fame but for preparing oneself to serve the people; and selection of students for colleges from among: (1) workers, peasants, and young cadre members of about twenty years of age who have come to the fore in revolutionary struggles and whose educational level corresponds to that of junior or senior middle school; (2) educated young people who have been sent from cities to settle in the countryside and who have good records; and (3) veteran workers and poor and lower-middle-class peasants who have abundant practical experience despite age and educational level.[83] Although the nationwide enrollment in elementary and secondary schools in recent years has reportedly registered a significant increase over that in the years immediately prior to the GPCR, enrollment in most of the colleges and universities in the fall of 1972 was apparently no more than one-fourth to one-third the enrollment on the eve of that campaign. This decline seems to have been in part the result of a deliberate official policy of keeping college population in line with current needs for college-trained personnel. Another contributing factor appears to have been the greater complexity of educational reform at the college level as compared with those at the elementary- and secondary-school levels. Until the many drastic experimental changes in higher learning have produced satisfactory results, the regime apparently deems it wise to keep college enrollment at a relatively low level. Some of the tentative innovations, it would seem, that

[83] "Some Tentative Programmes for Revolutionizing Education," *People's Daily*,* November 3, 1967; "A New-Type School Where Theory Accords With Practice," *Peking Review*, No. 44 (November 1, 1968), pp. 4–7; "Draft Program for Primary and Middle Schools in Chinese Countrysides," *NCNA*, May 13, 1969; "Chairman Mao Tse-tung on Revolution in Education," *CB*, No. 888 (August 22, 1969), pp. 1–20; "Peking University Establishes Revolutionary Committee," *NCNA*, October 6, 1969; and "Strive to Build a Socialist University of Science and Engineering," *Peking Review*, No. 31 (July 31, 1970), pp. 5–15.

must be first tested on a limited scale in order to avoid any possible adverse effect of intolerable proportions are the college admission procedures and standards. Regardless of its potential merits, the admission to colleges of students with vastly divergent academic achievements and of similarly diverse age groups could conceivably pose insurmountable instructional and learning problems. It may also lead to a decline in the quality of higher education in general. If so, the avowed goal of training college graduates to be both "red" and "expert" would be impossible to attain. While the efficacy of the college admission policy remains to be tested, there have been strong indications since the middle of 1972 that colleges and universities in China are developing a new system of examination for students in residence. According to one report, the purpose of this endeavor is not to revive the "revisionist" policy of putting "marks in command" that would once again make institutions of higher learning a breeding ground for bourgeois intellectuals; rather, it is to "serve the purpose of training successors to the revolutionary cause of the proletariat." Specifically, its aim is "to help the students consolidate and deepen through examination the theoretical knowledge and technical skills they have learned." It is also "to help examine the result of learning so as to facilitate study and improvement of instruction." "Grading in examination," asserted the report, "is like quality specifications for products manufactured in a factory where quality must be inspected." Some of the suggested guidelines for a new system of examination are that questions must be practical, comprehensive, and flexible; that grading must be combined with the summing up and exchange of study experience; that both open-book and closed-book methods may be used, depending on the characteristics of the subjects and requirements in study; and that examinations must be part of the effort "to strengthen the student's consciousness in learning for the sake of revolution." [84]

[84] Department of Chemistry, Kirin University, "Establish a New System of Examination Through Practice," *People's Daily,** June 24, 1972.

XII

Foreign Policy

中國共產運動簡史

One of the party's major goals is to safeguard the territorial integrity and political independence of the Chinese nation. This is certainly not a unique objective; all sovereign nations regard their territorial integrity and political independence as sacred and inviolable. Nor are the Communists the only political group among the Chinese people who insist on this goal. Long before the emergence of the CCP, the Kuomintang and practically all the other revolutionary and reformist groups that appeared on the Chinese scene in response to foreign encroachments and internal disorder had made the preservation of China's territorial integrity and political independence one of their principal objectives. The only major difference between the Communists and the non-Communists in their pursuit of this goal is that the Communists have been more effective and are far more determined than the non-Communist groups, even though thus far the Communists' effectiveness in this regard also has its limits as evidenced by their inability to "liberate" Taiwan.

The CCP's determination to protect China's territorial integrity and political independence, it should be noted, has not prevented it from making compromises or even practising self-abnegation if the stake is relatively small, in order to better serve China's long-run national interest—if it is done of her own volition. The 700 square miles of territories that Peking handed over to Pakistan under the border agreement of March 2, 1963 and the exchange of land with Burma in 1960 are notable cases in point.

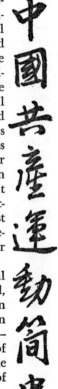

However, the CCP now appears to be determined to preserve China's sovereignty in all the outlying regions including Sinkiang, Tibet, and Taiwan. For historical, legal, and practical reasons Communist Chinese and non-Communist Chinese alike (including Chiang Kai-shek and his followers on Taiwan) regard these territories as integral parts of China. Since these territories have been among the major targets of foreign encroachment in modern times (Russia had designs on Sinkiang, England brought Tibet under her influence, and Japan occupied Taiwan), their retention has taken on a symbolic significance to the Chinese. Thus the reported Russian attempts to sow dissension among the national minorities in Sinkiang, the Indian and Western desire to create an "independent" Tibet, and the "plots" to create "two Chinas" or "one China and one Taiwan" and the assertion that "the status of Taiwan has not yet been settled" have been looked upon by the Chinese not only as a menace to their country's territorial integrity but as a continuing insult to their national pride, as well as a disturbing reminder that their mission of national salvation and rejuvenation remains to be completely fulfilled.

There is little likelihood that the Chinese will ever be moved by the argument that the attempt to make Tibet and Taiwan independent states is aimed primarily at preserving the freedom of the residents of those territories. Apart from the reasons mentioned above, the Chinese regard the argument as spurious, recalling the fact that those who have lately expressed an interest in the freedom or the right to self-government of the residents in Tibet and Taiwan maintained for a long time an indifferent attitude toward those very people when they were under indirect British control in the case of Tibet and direct Japanese occupation in the case of Taiwan. Considering full sovereignty in both cases a question of "great right and great wrong," the Chinese, instead of inclining to compromise on the matter, are apt to become all the more infuriated by attempts to detach any of these territories from their country. If so, they are likely to rally more closely behind the elite that can give them effective leadership in resisting foreign attempts at China's dismemberment. In other words, foreign designs to strip China of either Taiwan or Tibet or both, even if forcibly implemented, are bound to add fuel to an already raging fire of Chinese nationalism, which according to many observers has contributed much to the rise of the CCP and is certain to provide it with a convenient tool for exhorting the Chinese to make more sacrifices and efforts required for internal development as well as for preserving the nation's territorial integrity and political independence. It goes without saying that any such foreign designs would dash the much cherished hope that with the passage of time and particularly with the replacement of the present leaders in Peking by men of a younger generation, mainland China might gradually lose its revolutionary militancy in general and its hostility to "imperialist powers" in particular.

The determination to safeguard territorial integrity and political independence does not mean that Peking will always take drastic measures against foreign trespassers without regard to consequences. Patience, prudence, and shrewd alternation of tactics have been as characteristic of its approach to their problems as determination. Perhaps this was most clearly demonstrated by Peking's decision in March 1969 to meet Soviet armed "intrusion" into the area of Chenpao Island with armed resistance and by its readiness, following Premier Kosygin's talks with Premier Chou En-lai in Peking on September 11 of that year, to hold negotiations with Moscow on border problems. In the case of Taiwan, Peking's patient but steadfast stand, coupled with changing power relations in the world at large, has already yielded some significant initial dividends. One was the U. S. declaration in the Chou-Nixon Joint Communique of February 27, 1972, that "the U. S. Government does not challenge the position held by all Chinese on either side of the Taiwan Strait that 'there is but one China and that Taiwan is part of China.'" In the same joint communique, President Nixon also, in effect, pledged the U. S. not to interfere with Chinese attempts at a peaceful reunion between Peking and Taipei, while explicitly "affirming the ultimate objective of the withdrawal of all U. S. forces and military installations from Taiwan." Another encouraging development was the statement in the Chou-Tanaka Joint Communique of September 29, 1972, that "the Government of Japan recognizes the Government of the People's Republic of China as the sole legal government of China" and that "the Government of Japan fully understands and respects" the Chinese stand that "Taiwan is an inalienable part of the territory of the People's Republic of China." Even before these recent shifts in U. S. and Japanese positions on Taiwan, the leaders in Peking, while obviously realizing that Washington's and Tokyo's surreptitious efforts to detach the island permanently from the mainland, if unchecked, could complicate matters, seemed to have been quite confident all along that time was on their side and that sooner or later any one of the following developments or a combination of them would help bring Taiwan under their control: (1) their own military strength would become sufficiently strong to challenge the American military umbrella over Taiwan; (2) the mainland would take such giant strides toward industrialization and general economic prosperity that its magnetism would be too strong for the political dissidents on Taiwan to resist any longer; (3) the authorities on Taiwan would become totally disenchanted with Washington and Tokyo and would believe their best recourse to be to reach an understanding with Peking; (4) Washington would reach the conclusion that after all Taiwan's strategic importance to the U. S. does not justify the assumption of risks attendant to the defense of the island; and (5) Washington would come to the point of view, as President Nixon seems to have, that for global strategical considerations it is more desirable to seek a detente with Peking than to infuriate it continuously over Taiwan, whose detachment from the mainland, even if attainable against Peking's wishes, would not significantly reduce China's potential as an increasingly weighty factor in world affairs.

Peking's determination to safeguard China's territorial integrity and political independence has not involved any territorial expansion at the expense of her small neighbors, contrary to a widely-held popular assumption. Militant practitioners of Marxism-Leninism, the Communist Chinese appear to be genuinely sincere when they time and again reiterate the well-known Marxist admonition, "No nation can be free if it oppresses other nations." In a widely-read essay written long before his recent disgrace, Liu Shao-ch'i elucidated this point most succinctly:

> . . . Communists will be betraying the proletariat and communism and playing the game of the imperialists all over the world and will make themselves pawns of the imperialists, if, after their own nation has been freed from imperialist oppression, they descend to the position of bourgeois nationalism, carrying out a policy of national selfishness and sacrificing the common international interests of the working people and the proletarian masses of all the nations throughout the world for the interests of the upper stratum of their own nation; or if they not only fail to oppose imperialism but on the contrary rely on imperialist aid to carry out aggression or oppression against other nations; or if they adopt the policy of national seclusion and chauvinism to oppose proletarian internationalism. . . .[1]

The Sino-Indian military conflict in October 1962 has often been treated in the Western world as a Chinese act of aggression. The incident, however, was due mainly to conflicting claims over long sections of disputed territory along the Himalayan border between the two countries. The immediate cause of the conflict seemed to be China's determination to assert her right to maintain a recently constructed highway in the Aksai Chin area (in the western sector

[1] Liu Shao-ch'i, *Internationalism and Nationalism* (Peking: Foreign Languages Press, 1952), p. 9.

of the disputed territory), to expel the Indian troops which from 1959 on had penetrated into areas north of the controversial MacMahon Line in the eastern sector of the disputed territory, and to forestall a much-publicized Indian general offensive to clear Chinese troops from the disputed territory. In any event, as soon as the Indian army along the border had been routed, the Chinese side promptly announced three proposals to end the military conflict, reopen negotiations, and settle the boundary question peacefully. This was followed up by the unilateral declaration of a cease-fire, the voluntary withdrawal of troops from the areas into which the Chinese forces had newly advanced, the voluntary release of captured Indian personnel, and the return to India of large stores of military equipment. These measures effectively brought the armed conflict to a speedy conclusion and indicated that Peking probably had only a limited objective in launching the attack: to "teach India a decisive lesson" in the border dispute and punish her alleged complicity with the Dalai Lama and other Tibetan rebels during the uprisings in March 1959 and after.

Nor is it feasible for the Communist Chinese to encroach upon their small neighbors; any such attempt would probably prompt the intended victim to seek help from the United States or the Soviet Union or both, whose influence in Asia Peking has sought to reduce. If any intended victim is led by a revolutionary elite such as in Hanoi, then any adventurist Chinese leader would have to ask himself whether even in the absence of direct intervention by any of the superpowers his country could fare better in attempting to subdue a smaller country than the far more powerful and far more affluent America has been able to do in Indochina in recent years. Expansion beyond the traditional territorial limits also has few roots in Chinese history. Since the Ch'in (221–207 B.C.) and Han (206 B.C.–220 A.D.) Dynasties the Chinese have seldom given any serious thought to the idea of pushing their frontiers beyond the Gobi desert in the north, Sinkiang and Tibet in the west, Kwangtung and Kwangsi Provinces in the south, and the sea coast and Taiwan in the east. To be sure, from time to time China established tributary relations with such countries as Korea, Vietnam, and Nepal, but her authority over those nations was more symbolic than real. In the absence of economic exploitation and political oppression, the tributary relations mainly served to guarantee peace between China on the one hand and the tributary states on the other. Occasionally, some Chinese rulers did indulge in expansionist designs. Their efforts, however, were often abortive and never became a sustained national drive. Throughout the centuries China remained a self-sufficient and self-sustained nation with an essentially defensive mentality, which was epitomized in the construction and periodical repairing of the Great Wall as well as in her unwillingness in the fifteenth century to use her then unrivaled naval power to seize territories in Southeast Asia and on the east African coast to which her mighty fleets made seven expeditions from 1405 to 1433. Needless to say, this conduct was in sharp contrast to the subsequent European expansion, which, among other things, was rooted in the European people's quest for trade opportunities, their missionary zeal, and their interest in geographical explorations, all of which were alien to the Chinese.

The absence of territorial designs, however, does not preclude the desire to see that her small neighbors are not used by her principal antagonists for carrying on sabotage, espionage, and warlike activities against herself. Peking's policy of resolutely supporting Hanoi and the Viet Cong apparently has been partly prompted by this desire. So must have been the decision to send "volunteers" to Korea in late 1950. For many years Peking has made the elimination of American influence (and, since the late 1950's, Soviet influence as well) over her immediate neighbors one of her most important diplomatic tasks. In order to accomplish this task, Peking has endeavored to assure many of these countries of its reasonableness and good-neighborly intent. In April 1954 it proclaimed "the five principles of peaceful co-existence" as the basic policy governing its relations with countries having different social systems: (1) mutual respect for each other's territorial integrity and sovereignty; (2) nonaggression; (3) noninterference in each other's internal affairs; (4) equality and mutual benefit; and (5) peaceful co-existence. At the Bandung Conference in April 1955 Premier Chou En-lai successfully convinced many of the assembled Afro-Asian leaders of his government's sincerity in pursuing this policy. Since the late 1950's Peking has supplemented its declarations of good-neighborly intent by signing treaties of friendship, nonaggression and/or boundary demarcation with such immediate neighbors as Afghanistan, Pakistan, Nepal, Burma, Cambodia, and Outer Mongolia. Although one can only speculate on the further evolution of this good-neighbor policy it is clear that faithful adherence to the five principles of peaceful co-existence is in line with Peking's major goal of eliminating U. S. influence in the area and that so far this policy has been effective in making some of the neighboring countries less fearful of Peking and in persuading them to refuse to permit the United States to use their military bases for "encircling" China. Peking, however, has not felt obliged to observe the five principles of peaceful co-existence in its dealings with some neighboring countries whose ruling elites are hostile to China and collaborate with major "imperialist" powers, especially "U. S. imperialism." Thailand is a notable case in point. Nor has Peking ever shown a want of resolution in chastising an erstwhile friendly neighbor that has begun to develop potentially threatening relations with China's principal adversaries. Peking's hostility toward Rangoon from the summer of 1967 to the summer of 1971 typified this behavior. What Rangoon actually did that drew Chinese verbal attacks on the Ne Win regime in 1967 and thereafter and, in the meantime, caused Peking to make open declarations of support for the White Flag guerrillas in Burma were Ne Win's attempts to move away from Burma's earlier "neutral" position to a policy of strengthening ties with Washington, Moscow, and New Delhi, particularly his visit to Washington in September 1966, during which he held talks with President Johnson on "matters of mutual concern," including resumption of American military aid to Burma. That it was indeed these Burmese actions, not any Chinese premeditation, that turned Peking against Rangoon after years of *paukpaw* (kinfolk) relationship has been made unmistakably clear by the newly achieved detente between the two capitals, which came on the heels of the virtual termination of the U. S. aid program in Burma and the departure from that country on June 30, 1971, of the last contingent of the American Military Equipment Delivery Team.

In the case of Japan, until Tanaka's replacement of Sato as Prime Minister in July 1972, which led to a dramatic reversal of Japanese policy toward China, not only had Tokyo aroused Peking's ire by closely allying itself with Washington since the early 1950's but its own ambitions and capabilities had caused Peking's apprehension that, if the hands of "the Japanese reactionaries" were not stayed in time, Tokyo, even without American encouragement and support, would pose an increasingly grave threat to her neighbors in Asia, including China. In addition to Tokyo's "designs with regard to Taiwan," other ambitions and activities of "the Japanese reactionaries" that had been disquieting to Peking were their assiduous efforts to revive the *bushido* spirit of the Japanese people, their ever-expanding programs of rearmament, their growing capability and desire to manufacture nuclear weapons, their diplomatic flirtations with Moscow, their economic penetration into South Korea and many Southeastern Asian countries, and, above all, their "dream" of recreating "the Greater Asia Co-Prosperity Sphere." However, Peking's enmity toward "the Japanese reactionaries" even then did not imply a hatred of the Japanese people in general. As in the case of all the other countries whose governments have not been friendly to the new China, Peking has always made a distinction between the people of a country and their government. Moreover, Peking's profound distrust of Prime Minister Tanaka's various predecessors in the Japanese government had kept it from being tempted to promote a Communist revolution in Japan, which it did not deem realistic. Rather, Peking sought recourse in the raging of a joint struggle with all the Japanese political parties and groups that were opposed to the revival of Japanese militarism and aggression. Meanwhile, it did its best to arouse general international vigilance against Tokyo's "dangerous ambitions." That Peking had indeed been sincere in professing since the early 1950's a preference for developing neighborly relations with Tokyo if the latter would only forsake its design on Taiwan and abandon its hostile posture toward China has been made unmistakenly clear by its prompt and positive response to Prime Minister Tanaka's friendly overtures, which were made shortly after the latter's assumption of office in July 1972. A new chapter in Sino-Japanese relations formally began on September 29 of that year with the issuance of the above-mentioned Chou-Tanaka Joint Communique toward the end of the new Japanese Prime Minister's visit to China. In addition to what has been noted earlier, that historical document also contained several other policy pronouncements of great importance not only to the two countries concerned but also to peace and security in the Asian-Pacific region in general. Among such pronouncements were the establishment of diplomatic ties between Peking and Tokyo; the promise to hold further negotiations aimed at the conclusion of a treaty of peace and friendship as well as the signing of agreements on trade, navigation, aviation, fishery, etc.; mutual renunciation of the ambition to gain hegemony in the Asian-Pacific region and mutual opposition to efforts by any other country or group of countries to establish such hegemony. As an integral part of the new Sino-Japanese relationship, Tokyo severed its diplomatic links with Taipei a few hours before the issuance of the joint communique. On the same day, Foreign Minister Ohira of Japan told a news conference in Peking that the 1952 "peace treaty" between Japan and the Chinese Nationalist authorities in Taipei was "considered to have expired."

Although the CCP has not pursued a policy of self-aggrandizement at the expense of other countries, it does want to restore China to a respectable place in the family of nations. Conscious of the country's past greatness and incensed by the humiliation that she has suffered in modern times at the hands of Western powers and

Japan, Mao Tse-tung and his associates have taken this task most seriously. On September 21, 1949, Mao declared at the first plenum of the CPPCC: "Our nation will never be insulted again. We have stood up." In keeping with the spirit of this statement, the Peking regime let it be known at its inception that the new China would establish diplomatic relations with only those countries that would treat her on the basis of equality and friendliness[2] and had severed relations with "the Kuomintang reactionaries"; rather than automatically abide by the treaties and agreements concluded between the Kuomintang and foreign governments, she would "recognize, abrogate, revise, or renegotiate them according to their respective contents." [3] Not a few of the treaties and agreements signed by the Kuomintang and foreign governments, including those concluded after the abrogation in 1943 of the "unequal treaties," contained provisions injurious to Chinese interests and undermining Chinese pride.

Indicative of the Peking regime's early determination to rid China of all lingering legacies of foreign domination and exploitation were the expropriation of Western business firms in China, the seizure of Western military barracks in the former legation headquarters in Peking, the closing down of foreign-owned newspapers and other publications, the termination of the control by foreign missionaries of Catholic and Protestant churches, the efforts to "deflate the arrogance" of those Western diplomats, businessmen, and missionaries who had been accustomed to "riding roughshod" over China, and the shelling of the British gunboat *Amethyst* on the Yangtze River on April 20–21, 1949—a step that not only quickly forced England to give up its residual right to sail naval vessels on Chinese inland waterways but also dramatized the new China's boldness in defending her national interest and dignity. With the possible exception of the Manchu government's support of the Boxer Rebellion against foreign imperialism in China at the turn of the century, no Chinese regime since the Opium War had dared to act so fearlessly in dealing with a major Western power.

In the meantime, Peking's quest for a respectable place in the family of nations manifested itself in the assertion that the Chinese revolution is "the classical type of revolution in colonial and semicolonial countries," [4] in its repeated vows not to tolerate any foreign

[2] Article 56 of the Common Program of the CPPCC.

[3] Article 55 of *ibid.*

[4] Lu Ting-i, "The World Significance of the Chinese Revolution," *People's Daily,** July 1, 1951, and Liu Shao-ch'i's speech at the Conference of Asian and Australian Trade Unions, *NCNA,* November 23, 1949.

interference with Chinese affairs, and in its determination to develop nuclear weapons. That Peking's primary objective in developing atomic and nuclear weapons is to enhance her international prestige and to neutralize the same weapons possessed by her potential adversaries has been attested to by Foreign Minister Ch'en I in 1962 when he was quoted as having said: ". . . We are likewise working to develop an atomic bomb of our own for the sole reason that the capitalists consider us underdeveloped and defenseless as long as we lack the ultimate weapon." [5] In addition, since she began testing nuclear weapons in October 1964, China has repeatedly reaffirmed the essentially defensive nature of her nuclear policy by emphasizing that her nuclear program is designed to ward off nuclear blackmail by her opponents and that she will never be the first to use nuclear weapons in a war.

In the late 1950's the quest for major nation status, coupled with other issues, prompted Peking to refuse to "crawl to the baton of the Soviet leaders," to espouse "complete equality" for the "socialist states" and the Communist and workers' parties, and to emphasize the policy of self-reliance for economic development and national defense, lest reliance on foreign assistance lead to foreign domination or at least foreign derision as Peking had experienced in its relations with Moscow. Peking's determination to establish itself as a major power in the world is reflected in the policy of refusing to abide by any international agreement that has been concluded without her consent. For about a century prior to 1949 China was forced to accede to many international agreements against her wishes and much to her detriment. While admission to the United Nations was deemed likely to enhance her prestige, the Peking government did not regard membership in that body as an indispensable symbol of international respectability if it was to be attained at the risk of prejudicing its claim over Taiwan. Thus it insisted on the expulsion of the Nationalist delegation from that body and the absence, in the United Nations resolution admitting Peking's delegation, of any reference to the effect that "the status of Taiwan remains to be determined." The General Assembly's adoption of the Albanian Resolution on October 25, 1971, reflected the international community's realization that Peking indeed would not join the United Nations under any other circumstances. In an apparent effort to woo small and medium-sized countries while castigating Washington and other big powers, then Foreign Minister Ch'en I, speaking at a press conference in Peking on Septem-

[5] *Frankfurher Rundschau,* August 6, 1962.

ber 29, 1965, raised even more conditions to be met before his government would consider membership in the world organization. They included: (1) cancellation by the United Nations of its resolution condemning China and the Democratic People's Republic of Korea as aggressors and adoption of a resolution condemning the United States as the aggressor; (2) review and revision of the United Nations Charter by all countries, big and small, with the objective of freeing the United Nations from the control of the United States and other major powers; (3) admission of all independent states to the United Nations; and (4) expulsion of all imperialist puppets from it.[6] Peking's subsequent willingness to drop these conditions, which do not directly affect China's vital interests, no doubt indicated its conviction that its entrance into the United Nations would help demoralize the Nationalist regime and thus make the latter more susceptible to pressure and/or overtures from the mainland.

Another diplomatic goal that Peking seeks is to develop diplomatic, economic, and cultural relations with other countries that will facilitate the economic construction of China. While believing that "China can never win genuine independence and equality by relying upon foreign aid,"[7] Mao Tse-tung and his party do not reject international cooperation and trade.[8] Indeed, Mao once categorically stated that it is impossible for a genuine people's revolution to win victory and to consolidate it in any country without international help.[9] Up until the late 1950's the Peking regime attached the greatest importance to the development of close relations in various fields with the Soviet Union and the other socialist countries while maintaining little or no contact with the "imperialist" powers. This "lean to one side" policy was justified on the ground that only from "the anti-imperialist front headed by the Soviet Union" could China secure "genuine and friendly help,"[10] whereas the British and U. S. governments "would give aid only conditionally" and/or only to their "fifth column in China."[11] Mao's faith in the socialist states apparently sprang from ideological, historical, and political factors. Ideologically, it was Mao's assumption that the socialist states, using the "proletarian internalist approach" to the national question, were opposed to any kind of national oppression

[6] See Ch'en I's press conference statement on September 29, 1965, *Peking Review,* No. 41 (October 8, 1965), p. 12.

[7] Mao Tse-tung, *Selected Works,* III, 307.

[8] Articles 54–57 of the Common Program of the CPPCC and Mao Tse-tung, *Selected Works,* IV, 416.

[9] *Ibid.*

[10] *Ibid.,* IV, 417.

[11] *Ibid.,* IV, 417, 437.

and felt duty-bound to give unconditional aid to a fraternal state like the People's Republic of China. Capitalist countries, by contrast, were believed to be inherently predatory, aggressive, and exploitative in their mutual relations as well as in relations with colonies, semicolonies, or the emerging nations. Whatever aid the capitalist states gave, they did so in order to use as a lever for exacting privileges from the recipient countries or as a remedial measure to "benumb the revolutionary consciousness of the peoples in oppressed and exploited nations."

Historically, Mao's preference for the socialist states stemmed from the past association of the CCP with Soviet Russia. First of all, the Chinese party was founded in 1921 under Soviet inspiration and guidance. For the next decades the CCP continued to receive Soviet encouragement and occasional assistance. Although at times Soviet guidance was ruinous to the Chinese Communist movement, until the late 1950's few Communist Chinese ever questioned the intentions of the Soviets on those occasions. Instead, they time and again publicly reaffirmed their belief that in those years the Soviet Union rendered great assistance to their cause and "the struggles of other peoples." The Communist Chinese desire to forge close links with the socialist states was also based on internal political considerations. Mao and his associates apparently believed that modern China's multifarious problems could be solved only under a government emphasizing discipline, dedication, and hard work, monopolizing all the instruments of mass control, and relying upon such means as centralized planning, collectivization, and political indoctrination for mobilizing human and material resources. They thought that only by closely associating with the socialist states subscribing to the same principles could they hope to insulate their system from the "evil" influences of "liberalism," "individualism," and other "decadent" ideologies and systems prevalent in the capitalist states.

Since 1956 the once very close alliance between Peking and Moscow has been replaced by mutual accusations and animosity. This, however, does not appear to mean that Peking has repudiated the belief that states truly dedicated to socialism are more prone to be genuine and helpful friends to a country like China than states of other political persuasions. The Sino-Soviet "dispute" seems to have sprung, to a great extent, from Peking's attempt to check Moscow's adulteration of revolutionary socialism which, in the opinion of Peking, has led Khrushchev and the present Soviet leaders to forsake proletarian internationalism and to commit the crime of adopting the policy of "four alignments with and four against." This policy advocates "alignment with imperialism against socialism; alignment with the United States against China and the other revolutionary countries; alignment with the reactionaries everywhere against the national liberation movements and the people's revolutions; and alignment with the Tito clique and renegades of all descriptions against all the fraternal Marxist-Leninist parties and all revolutionaries fighting imperialism."[12] Mao Tse-tung is strongly of the opinion that only by waging an "ideological struggle" against the revisionist Soviet leaders will it be possible to restore socialism to Russia and thus make that country once again a true friend of China. Another major factor underlying Peking's denunciation of Khrushchev and his successors in the Kremlin may have been its apprehension that their policy of relaxing control in various fields of Soviet life might inspire the Chinese people to demand the adoption of the same measures for their own country and thus disrupt the discipline and order that the CCP under Mao's leadership has painstakingly developed.

As has been noted above, the ideological dispute led to the withdrawal of Soviet aid from China in the summer of 1960. This spurred China to expand trade with the non-Communist world, especially Japan and Western Europe, so that she could buy from them machinery, industrial equipment, and other goods previously supplied by the Soviet bloc. Since then non-Communist countries have displaced the Soviet bloc as China's most important trading partners, even though until recently such trade had been conducted mostly in the absence of diplomatic ties between Peking and the non-Communist countries concerned.

Meanwhile, Peking has not allowed its trade with non-Communist countries to interfere with its own priorities in, and approaches to, the nation's economic development. Remembering past foreign economic domination and exploitation and determined to build the country mainly with indigenous resources and efforts, the Maoist leadership has stated time and again in recent years, amid expanding contacts with the outside world, that, while China's foreign trade would steadily increase in volume in the years to come, she would never again permit herself to be a dumping ground for foreign-made consumer goods, that she would jealously guard herself against any foreign attempt to exploit and plunder her natural resources, and that she would seek neither foreign investment nor the opportunity to invest in foreign lands.

[12] P'eng Chen's speech at the Aliarcham Academy of Social Sciences on May 25, 1965, *NCNA*, May 27, 1965.

Still another external goal is to change the status quo in the world. This is aimed not only at "assisting the oppressed and exploited peoples to deliver themselves from the yoke of imperialism, colonialism, neo-colonialism, and social-imperialism (Soviet expansionism and hegemonic designs)," but also at reducing the strength of the two superpowers which have been colluding with each other for world domination while contending over certain issues and in certain regions. Insofar as the United States is concerned, until the recent thaw in Sino-American relations resulting from President Nixon's overtures to Peking, the CCP leaders' intense hostility toward "U. S. imperialism" had sprung from the following major causes: it once assisted the Kuomintang during the last phase of the Chinese civil war on the mainland; was hostile to the new China; occupied Taiwan, Quemoy, and Matsu by means of supporting the Chiang Kai-shek regime in Taipei; asserted that the status of Taiwan had not yet been settled; plotted to detach Taiwan permanently from the mainland; thwarted Peking's efforts to assert China's legitimate claims as a major power; attempted to strangulate the new China economically by pressuring its allies to enforce "the China Differential" (a longer list of embargoed goods than that applied to trade with most other Communist countries) in their trade with China; encircled China with a cordon of military bases; intruded into Chinese air space and territorial waters with airplanes and warships; threatened China's southern frontier with its invasion of the Indochinese states; colluded with the Soviet "revisionists" and the "reactionaries" in New Delhi, Tokyo, and elsewhere for an anti-China holy alliance; and stood in the way of the world Communist movement. One of Peking's major strategies for effecting a total alteration of the status quo in the world is to organize an international united front against imperialism, colonialism, and neo-colonialism. Such a united front is deemed feasible because Peking perceives "an inexorably anti-imperialist current in the Afro-Asian countries as well as in Latin America." While admitting that victories of great historic significance have already been won by the national liberation movements in Asia, Africa, and Latin America, the Communist Chinese do not share the view held by many in the West and by the "leaders of the CPSU [Communist Party of the Soviet Union]" that colonialism has disappeared or is disappearing from the present-day world and that combating colonialism and imperialism therefore is no longer an important issue facing the peoples in Asia, Africa, and Latin America. On the contrary, Peking contends that imperialism, colonialism, and neo-colonialism remain "the most ferocious enemies" of the peoples in those regions and that the struggles against these "enemies" will continue to surge ahead rather than recede. *Red Flag* has stated the official view as follows:

. . . Most countries in Asia, Africa, and Latin America are still victims of imperialist aggression and oppression and of old and new colonialist enslavement. Although a number of countries have won their independence in recent years, their economies are still under the control of foreign monopoly capital. In some countries, the old colonialists have been driven out, but even more powerful and dangerous colonialists of a new type have forced their way in, gravely threatening the existence of many nations in these areas. . . . To struggle against imperialism and new and old colonialism remains the cardinal and most urgent task of the oppressed nations and peoples in the vast regions of Asia, Africa, and Latin America.[13]

Forming a united front with the peoples in Asia, Africa, and Latin America, the Communist Chinese believe, not only would be an effective way of fighting imperialism, colonialism, and neocolonialism as it may force their enemies, especially "U. S. imperialism," to disperse their strength and thus lessen pressure on China, but it may also facilitate the overthrow of capitalism in North America and Western Europe and hasten the victory of the world Communist movement. This belief is based on the Leninist theory that the colonies and semicolonies in Asia, Africa, and Latin America constitute the rear of the capitalist world (as the latter's sources of raw materials and outlets for manufactured goods and surplus capital) and that if the capitalist world has been stripped of its rear, then it can be easily toppled. Employing Maoist terminology, Lin Piao, in his famous article entitled "Long Live the Victory of People's War,"[14] described this Leninist strategy as one of encircling the cities from the countryside. Considering the entire globe, Lin calls North America and Western Europe the cities of the world and Asia, Africa, and Latin America its rural areas. Proceeding from the premise that the revolutionary movement in the rural areas of the world must be a two-stage operation with anti-imperialist struggles preceding a socialist revolution, Peking in recent years has made the struggle against imperialism and social-imperialism the *immediate* objective of its effort to organize an international united front, and in fact has generally pursued a policy of refraining from giving active support to local Communists in neutralist countries where the governments are genuinely anti-imperialist, and maintain friendly relations with China. There is no contradiction between

[13] "More on the Differences Between Comrade Togliatti and Us," *Red Flag,** Nos. 3–4 (March 4, 1963), p. 16. An English version of the article can be found in *CB,* No. 706 (March 7, 1963), pp. 1–99.

[14] For an English text of the article, see *NCNA,* September 2, 1965.

this behavior and the avowed policy of hastening the victory of the international proletarian revolution by the formation of a united front with the neutralist countries in Asia, Africa, and Latin America. The restraint that Peking has imposed upon itself in dealing with the neutralist countries is aimed at minimizing obstacles to the formation and maintenance of the anti-imperialist international united front that it seeks to organize. To the Communist Chinese, only after such a front has come into existence and has successfully carried out the more urgent and crucial task of defeating colonialism, neo-colonialism, and imperialism can it fulfill the mission of hastening the victory of the international proletarian revolution. Thus, withholding active support from local Communists in the neutralist countries for the formation and preservation of that front is deemed essential to the eventual triumph of communism in those countries as well as in North America and Western Europe—"the motherlands of capitalism and imperialism." On the other hand, active support to local Communists in the neutralist countries, if given at this stage of the struggle, is thought likely to hinder the formation and maintenance of the proposed united front, for it will alarm and alienate the nationalist governments of the neutralist countries at a time when the local Communists are still too weak to take over the reins of their respective states. Peking's support for the Nimeri regime in Sudan during the abortive Communist-dominated coup in July 1971 was a dramatic application of this policy. A better understanding of this Chinese objective apparently was one of the factors that recently prompted the conservative or "moderate" governments of Burundi, Ghana, and Tunisia to resume diplomatic ties with Peking—which they had suspended for a number of years because of an earlier fear of Chinese attempts to foment Communist revolutions in their countries. As for Peking's alleged involvement in the massacre of six anti-Communist generals in Djakarta on October 1, 1965, all available evidence indicates that the bloody duel between the Indonesian Communist Party and the army was in part a result of the former's own folly in resorting to putschism, in which Peking apparently played no part. In fact, Peking has since openly criticized the then leadership of the Indonesian Communist Party for its "opportunism."

Although the policy of organizing an international united front thus far remains more a vision than a reality, Peking's flexibility and patience in dealing with the emerging nations and its self-projected image as the champion against the injustices and inequities of the status quo have enabled it to develop friendly or at least polite relations with more than 50 non-Communist countries in Asia, Africa, and Latin America. More significantly, many of these countries played important roles in Peking's admission to the United Nations and have publicly endorsed Peking's position on some international problems of utmost importance to China. Among such problems are the future of Taiwan and the war in Indochina. The official statements made by many Afro-Asian countries that Taiwan must be returned to China might have helped convince President Nixon and Prime Minister Tanaka of the untenability of their respective predecessors' "two Chinas" policy, "one China and one Taiwan" policy, or "one China and two governments" policy.

Recognizing the wisdom of uniting with all that can be united for struggling against the principal enemy and aware of the developing schisms in NATO and other U. S.-led alliances, Peking since 1964 has broadened the scope of the proposed united front by advancing the concept of "two intermediate zones" and by stressing the urgency of "opposing the U. S. imperialist venture to dominate the world." [15] According to the concept of two intermediate zones, there is a vast intermediate area between the United States and the Soviet Union "whose leaders are now colluding with U. S. imperialism for world domination." The intermediate zone is composed of two parts. One part consists of the independent countries and those striving for independence in Asia, Africa, and Latin America; it is called the first intermediate zone. The second part consists of the whole of Western Europe, Oceania, Canada, and other capitalist countries and is called the second intermediate zone. Countries in this second intermediate zone are said to have a dual character. "While their ruling classes are exploiters and oppressors, these countries themselves are subjected to U. S. control, interference, and bullying. They therefore try their best to free themselves from U. S. control. In this regard, they have something in common with the socialist countries and the peoples of various countries." [16]

One of the preliminary steps taken by Peking to bring about the envisaged grand alliance of the two intermediate zones was its establishment of diplomatic relations with France in January 1964. Peking's recent expression of approval of the admission of Britain and two other countries into the Common Market was also in line with this policy, for as the Chinese saw it, an enlarged and deepened economic community in Western Europe would "constitute a serious obstacle to the United States and the Soviet Union in pushing their

[15] "All the World's Forces Opposing U. S. Imperialism Unite!", editorial in *People's Daily,** January 21, 1964. An English text of the editorial appears in *Peking Review,* No. 4 (January 24, 1964), pp. 6–8.

[16] *Ibid.,* p. 7.

policies for hegemony in Europe."[17] Another development of the same policy was Peking's diplomatic initiative toward Eastern Europe. Since the Soviet invasion of Czechoslovakia in 1968 and the subsequent "fabrication" of the Brezhnev Doctrine which asserts that Moscow has the right to take military action against any socialist country in the interest of the security of the socialist community as a whole, Peking has seen both a need and an opportunity to seek the cooperation of as many Eastern European countries as possible in thwarting "the Soviet socio-imperialists' rapacious expansionist ambitions." Such cooperation is deemed necessary because it would have the direct effect of disrupting the Soviet Union's western flank and the indirect effect of limiting its freedom of action vis-à-vis China. As for the opportunity to secure such cooperation, Peking finds it in the Eastern European people's covert and overt resistance to Soviet "domination," "plunder," and "intimidations." Out of these considerations Peking now has strengthened its influence in the Balkans, first of all, by supplementing its long-standing alliance with Tirana with the development of increasingly close ties with Bucharest. Since 1969 there also has been a slow but significant improvement in relations with Belgrade, which for the preceding ten years had been a target of bitter Chinese attacks for its "revisionism" and its "traitorous" ties with the West. Among other Chinese attempts to undermine Moscow's hold on Eastern Europe are Peking's expressions of sympathy and respect for the Czechoslovakian people's "heroic struggle" to regain independence, its leveling of charges at the Soviet Union for alleged betrayal of East German interests in achieving a Moscow-Bonn detente, and its pledging of support for all the eastern European peoples in their defiance of Soviet "dictate" and "exploitation." Among other major manifestations of the policy of working with countries in the intermediate zones for the purpose of thwarting the two superpowers' attempts to dominate the world have been the development since 1970 of cordial relations with Canada, Italy, West Germany, Iran, Turkey, and a host of other nations; the support of Pakistan's efforts to ward off the secession of East Pakistan, which Moscow, in cooperation with New Delhi, had been "plotting" to bring about as part of its grand plan to make South Asia one of its spheres of influence; the endorsement of the contention that the Mediterranean Sea must cease to be a scene for superpower rivalry and that the superpowers must leave the Mediterranean Sea to the Mediterranean countries; the condemnation of the Soviet and Japanese call that the Straits

[17] "Unite to Oppose the Superpowers: Agreement on Britain's Entry Into the Common Market Reached," *Peking Review*, No. 27 (July 2, 1971), p. 36.

of Malacca be "internationalized"; and the approval of some Latin governments' proposal that Latin America be made a nuclear-free zone. While the normalization of relations with Japan in September 1972 was made possible primarily by Prime Minister Tanaka's willingness to accept Peking's "Three Conditions," [18] there can be no doubt that it was also prompted by a desire to encourage Tokyo to pursue a more independent policy vis-à-vis Washington and to dissuade it from "flirting" with Moscow. The statement in the Chou-Tanaka Joint Communique that both China and Japan are opposed to efforts by any other country or group of countries to establish hegemony in the Asian-Pacific region must be read in this light insofar as Peking is concerned.[19] Although there is little reason for Peking to be overly optimistic about the real chances of forming a worldwide united front against "U. S. imperialism" and "Soviet social-imperialism," the substitution of the concept of two intermediate zones for the theory that there is no third road between the socialist and capitalist camps and the new emphasis on encouraging international resistance to "social-imperialism" rather than restoring ideological orthodoxy in the world Communist movement are nonetheless significant in that the new formulations are likely to give Peking more maneuverability in the international arena.

It has been widely suggested that Peking's willingness to reach a detente with Washington first by inviting a group of American ping-pong players to visit China in April 1971 and then by receiving President Nixon in February 1972 stemmed mainly from the desire to obtain American help in checking Moscow and Tokyo. Actually, the Chinese have taken these and some other steps in the last two years or so largely in response to President Nixon's own conciliatory overtures, especially his prior assurance to Peking that he would not do anything to undermine its claim to Taiwan.[20] As Edgar Snow has pointed out,[21] Mao took the position on the eve of the "ping-pong diplomacy" that since the Nixon overtures afforded a chance to re-

[18] The "Three Conditions" were as follows: (1) Japan must recognize the Government of the People's Republic of China as the sole legal government of China; (2) Taiwan is an integral part of the People's Republic of China; and (3) the Japan-"the Republic of China" peace treaty of 1952 was illegal and must be abrogated.

[19] For an English text of the joint communique, see *The New York Times*, September 30, 1972.

[20] Max Frankel, "Nixon's China Goal: Genuine Diplomatic Turning Point," *The New York Times*, July 23, 1971.

[21] Edgar Snow, "A Conversation with Mao Tse-tung," *Life*, April 30, 1971, p. 47; Edgar Snow, "China Will Talk from a Position of Strength," *Life*, July 30, 1971, pp. 22–26.

cover Taiwan—his only remaining major goal of national reunification—there was no reason for his government to refuse to look at them. If the thaw had indeed sprung from Peking's desire to enlist American assistance in curbing Moscow and Tokyo, how can one explain the fact that President Nixon saw fit to visit Peking himself instead of waiting for the Chinese to call on him in Washington. Moreover, while any American cooperation in restraining Soviet "ambitions" and Japanese militarism would be helpful, the Maoist leadership, which had been profoundly disillusioned by their erstwhile Soviet ally, certainly would not abandon self-reliance as the principal way of achieving national security (as well as economic development) in favor of a new foreign promise of aid. Furthermore, the U. S. Government's statements concerning Taiwan in the above-mentioned Chou-Nixon Joint Communique and the Chinese Government's reaffirmation in the same document of its support of the Indochinese peoples' struggle for national liberation made it abundantly clear that Peking never had the intention of "softening" basic positions such as those regarding Taiwan and the American military presence in Indochina in exchange for some form of American aid or even sheer American neutrality in Sino-Soviet and Sino-Japanese relations—especially when a large-scale military confrontation with Moscow and Tokyo was neither imminent nor inevitable. As for President Nixon's momentous new approach to Peking, it seems to have been based on a number of considerations. One of them was the recognition of the futility of the long-standing policy of all-around confrontation with the new China. Another factor was the desire to use the new China to balance the growing power of the Soviet Union and Japan. The President probably also hoped to minimize the likelihood of a new Soviet-Chinese alliance after Mao's departure from the Chinese scene. Enlisting Peking's help in finding a solution to the war in Indochina obviously was another objective. A more long-term aim of the President was to develop a "multipolar diplomacy" in the world that would give Washington, Peking, and other major powers more options in safeguarding their national security and economic interests in the years to come. Although China, as already noted, will continue to pursue a policy of self-reliance, she may very well look upon such a diplomacy with considerable interest provided her participation in it is not predicated on her forsaking any of her vital interests or her national dignity. Finally, the dramatic change in American policy toward China, if proved to be not just a stunt for tactical advantages, would not have occurred had there not been a basic alteration in President Nixon's assessment of Peking's intentions and conduct in the international arena. Instead of perceiving the leaders in Peking as "irrational, bellicose, and expansionist, posing a mortal danger not only to her neighbors in Asia but also to the whole world," President Nixon and some of the principal advisers on foreign policy now reportedly regard Mao and Premier Chou as "extremely serious and far-sighted men, working at their own long-range purposes and not for narrow tactical gains, eager to extend their influence in Asia and the rest of the world, but not by territorial expansion." [22]

[22] Max Frankel, "Nixon's China Goal." © 1971 by The New York Times Company. Reprinted by permission.

XIII

The Great Proletarian Cultural Revolution

中國共產運動簡史

The Great Proletarian Cultural Revolution was the most far-reaching rectification campaign ever conducted by the CCP. A continuation and further development of all the rectification campaigns since the late 1950's, the GPCR was rooted partly in the failure of the Great Leap Forward and the Commune Movement of 1958–59, and partly in Mao Tse-tung's quest for a solution to "the theoretical and practical questions of carrying on the revolution and preventing a restoration of capitalism under the dictatorship of the proletariat." Mao's search began in earnest after the rise of "Khrushchev revisionism" in Russia. Having assumed the responsibility of upholding "revolutionary socialism" throughout the world, Mao strongly desired to immunize the CCP from the viruses of Khrushchev revisionism and other kinds.

Mao made a number of theoretical formulations to forestall revisionism. First, he believed that classes and the class struggle continue to exist during the historical period of the dictatorship of the proletariat; the question of who will win in the revolution has yet to be finally settled. In other words, if the questions of classes and class struggle are not handled properly, there is the possibility of a bourgeois counterrevolution. The bourgeoisie, Mao said, has a variety of sugar-coated bullets, among the most potent of which are literature and art. Making use of "the old ideas, culture, customs, and habits, the bourgeoisie seeks to conquer people's minds and thus weaken the dictatorship of the proletariat and pave the way for a counterrevolutionary restoration." Those plotting to prepare public opinion for the seizure of power from the proletariat, Mao believed, are apt to be the "representatives of the bourgeoisie who have sneaked into the party, the government, the army, and various cultural circles." "Once conditions are ripe," Mao pointed out, "these elements will seize power and turn the dictatorship of the proletariat into a dictatorship of the bourgeoisie."

To cope with and overcome this "reactionary threat," Mao prescribed a series of proletarian cultural revolutions over a long period of time, during which the masses—the workers, peasants, soldiers, revolutionary intellectuals, youth, and cadres—are to use "the new ideas, culture, customs, and habits of the proletariat" to change the mental outlook of the whole society and thoroughly criticize and repudiate "the open and hidden representatives of the bourgeoisie" in all walks of life. Mao insisted that "those bourgeoisie representatives who do the greatest harm to the dictatorship of the proletariat are the ones who have sneaked into the leading organs of the party and the government" where they wave "red flags" to oppose *the* red flag; these people naturally constitute the main target for a proletarian cultural revolution.

The Struggle Between Mao and Liu

Agricultural policies. There is no doubt that Mao's desire to halt "revisionism" in China was immeasurably sharpened by Liu Shao-ch'i and his faction's efforts to adulterate Mao's "revolutionary line." They had strongly disagreed with Mao on a host of policies after the unsuccessful Great Leap Forward and the Commune Movement. One of the irreconcilable differences that has not been correctly understood in the West concerns agriculture during the later stage of the economic readjustment period in the early 1960's.[1] It has been generally assumed by Western scholars that the agricultural dispute sprang mainly from Mao's attempt to revive some "radical features" of the original communes by nullifying many of the sensible and necessary changes introduced in late 1959 and the ensuing three years. These changes included the restoration of small private plots of land; the revival of carefully controlled rural fairs, where commune members could dispose of the products from their private plots; and the establishment of the "three-level ownership" system, which greatly reduced the authority of the communal management committee and ultimately charged the commune's lowest subdivisions (the "production teams") with the primary responsi-

[1] The Editorial Departments of *People's Daily,** and *Red Flag,** and *Liberation Army,** "Struggle Between the Two Roads in China's Countryside," *Peking Review,* No. 49 (December 1, 1967), pp. 11–19.

bility for organizing agricultural production and distributing income to commune members.

However, there is every reason to believe that shortly after the initial communization program ran into problems, which were compounded by three consecutive years of droughts and floods and by the abrupt withdrawal of Soviet economic aid and technicians, Mao either personally initiated these changes or gave his blessing to whoever had proposed them—none of which, it should be noted, could have seriously undermined the socialist foundation of the commune's production and distribution systems. Mao never intended to rescind those changes in launching the GPCR; the GPCR's famous Sixteen-Point Program neither attacked them as being revisionist nor tried to nullify them; and during the GPCR there was no official statement to the contrary. There is unmistakable evidence that Mao accepted these changes in the fact that the reported draft of a new national constitution included a provision that gave explicit sanction to them.

The real agricultural policy difference centered on Liu's advocacy of "three extensions and one contractual obligation"—the extension of plots for private use; the extension of free markets, or rural fairs; the increase in the number of small rural enterprises with sole responsibility for their own profits or losses; and the virtual revival of individual farming, with output quotas fixed on the basis of individual households. Clearly, the Liu Shao-ch'i faction made these proposals because they had been profoundly disillusioned with the socialist transformation of agriculture. They apparently had concluded that, in order to fully revitalize the country's rural economy, those changes which had been implemented up to 1961 were insufficient and must be supplemented. More concerned about increasing production than preserving socialism, Liu Shao-ch'i is quoted as having said: "Don't be afraid of capitalism running amok," and "we must fall back as far as necessary both in industry and in agriculture, even to the extent of fixing output quotas based on the individual households and allowing individual farming." Teng Hsiao-p'ing, then General Secretary of the CCP and Liu's most important collaborator against Mao's policies, reportedly elaborated this in a more figurative way: "So long as it raises output, 'going it alone' is permissible. Whether cats are white or black, so long as they can catch mice, they are good cats."

Mao, on the other hand, viewed this scheme with great alarm. He was convinced that it would disintegrate agricultural collectivization and restore capitalism in the countryside, which, in turn, would give rise to ever-widening economic, social, and political cleavages—a plague that had brought untold miseries to the Chinese time and again in the past and that Mao had worked so long to prevent. Mao had an additional reason to block the Liuist scheme with all the power at his command. That was his belief that because of the extreme smallness of per capita farm land in China agricultural collectivization must precede agricultural mechanization and rural electrification, and that without these latter the country's agricultural output can never increase significantly enough to help make the nation economically and militarily strong. Thus, insofar as agriculture was concerned, Mao's aim in staging the GPCR was not to seek more collectivization as many outsiders have believed, but rather to prevent further dilution of collectivization or, to be more accurate, its subtle abandonment. The struggle over whether agricultural collectivization should be preserved at all was far more acute than one over whether there should be more or less of it.

Industrial and commercial policies. In the industrial and commercial fields, one of the major factors contributing to the split between Mao and Liu Shao-ch'i centered around Mao's emphasis on the people's consciousness as a key to economic development and the Liuist attempt to make greater use of material incentives in stimulating productivity.[2] Mao made the following major assumptions: First, given the scarcity of exploited resources and the pressing need for rapidly accumulating development capital, the nation simply could not afford to rely upon extensive use of material rewards. Second, extensive use of material incentives would have revived socio-economic stratification, and thus enable a relatively small number of privileged individuals such as administrators, managers, scientists, and the like to enjoy affluence at the expense of the broad masses. Third, since people are the only productive force in abundant supply in today's China, it would have been wasteful and foolish not to have given full play to their energy, talents, and zeal in

[2] Mao Tse-tung, "On the Ten Major Relations," *CB*, No. 892 (October 21, 1969), pp. 21–24; The Writing Groups of the Ministry of Metallurgical Industry and of the Anshan Municipal Revolutionary Committee, "Long Live the Victory of the Constitution of the Anshan Iron and Steel Company," *Peking Review*, No. 14 (April 3, 1970), pp. 11–15, 38; The Writing Group of the Kirin Provincial Revolutionary Committee, "Socialist Construction and Class Struggle in the Field of Economics: A Critique of Sun Yeh-feng's Revisionist Economic Theory," *ibid.*, No. 16 (April 17, 1970), pp. 6–12; Ching Hung, "The Plot of the Top Ambitionist to Operate Trusts on a Large Scale Must Be Thoroughly Exposed," *SCMP*, No. 3049 (May 29, 1967), pp. 1–9; and Proletarian Revolutionaries in the Office in Charge of Finance and Trade of the State Council, "Struggle Between the Two Lines on Transforming Capitalist Industry and Commerce," *Peking Review*, No. 29 (July 19, 1968), pp. 22–23, 28.

various nation-building endeavors. Fourth, Mao believed, partly from personal experience, that once the masses have become conscious of the significance of the tasks and have been given an opportunity to help fulfill them, they can accomplish miracles in any undertaking. In this way, China will be better able not only to overcome its material, financial, and technical handicaps but she can also insulate her socio-political institutions from bureaucratism and other exploitative and repressive practices of self-seeking elites.

Specifically, Mao's emphasis on popular consciousness called for the inculcation of certain values such as hard work, frugality, inventiveness, self-reliance, defiance of difficulties, and selfless service for the collective. These tenets smack of the Puritan ethics in the early stages of American history. The only glaring difference between the two sets of values is the absence in the Chinese scheme of acquisitiveness. Mao's other major emphases included: (1) workers' participation in industrial management and technical experimentation; (2) the development of indigenous industries on a large scale in the midst of developing modern industries to make full use of the vast labor force and scattered raw materials at a time when there are severe constraints on the country's ability to develop modern industries; (3) proper attention to the basic needs and welfare of the broad masses as a whole while formulating economic plans, organizing production, and providing supplies and services; and (4) the development of close relations between cadres, technicians, and workers by requiring them all to work side by side in productive labor.

In the meantime, the Liu Shao-ch'i faction had lost faith in the efficacy of relying on people's consciousness to overcome the objective problems of economic development. They accused the Maoists of "using ultra-economic methods to guide the country's economic construction," and advocated "using economic methods to run the economy." Liu Shao-ch'i is said to have raised the question: "Why must we run the economy by administrative methods instead of by economic methods?" Convinced that material incentives would be more effective in spurring productivity, Liu allegedly said: "Give him a good reward if he works honestly"; "If you don't give him more money, there will be no incentive and he will not do a good job for you."

Consistently refraining from airing his views publicly, Liu also tried to de-emphasize the large-scale mass movement in production on the ground that it was wasteful and inefficient. Giving top priority to professionalism and the division of labor, Liu and his adherents in the early 1960's and even earlier worked hard to boost the one-man leadership system in business enterprises and to enhance the role of experts, while opposing the policy of requiring managers and technicians to participate in productive labor. The Liuists also belittled the development of indigenous industries and even small and medium-sized modern industries, all of which they thought to be inefficient and detrimental to the development of large-scale enterprises to which they wanted to give maximum autonomy.[3]

Another major dispute between the Maoists and the Liuists over industrial and commercial development stemmed from the Maoist policy of "putting politics in command" and the Liuist advocacy of "putting profit in command." These opposing approaches were most directly related to the formulation of economic plans, the management of business enterprises, and the evaluation of business efficiency. In summary, the Liuist policy of placing profit in command, which clearly had its genesis in "Khrushchev revisionism," meant that economic plans should be grounded on profits. Sun Yeh-feng (Director of the Research Institute of Political Economy at the Chinese Academy of Sciences, and a protege of Liu Shao-ch'i) said: "I doubt the statement that 'capitalist society produces for profits, but socialist society produces for use value, not for profits'; we raise labor productivity and technical standards for the purpose of obtaining profits." He also said: "Profits are the motive force and they can push business management forward"; "once you get hold of [emphasize] profits, you are leading an ox by its nose and its legs naturally follow; otherwise, you will be carrying the legs." Sun proposed: "Let profits be the main quotas in planning and in compiling statistics, and in its relations with enterprises the state only has to get a grip on profit quotas; it should not bother with anything else but leave it to the enterprises." He further stated that profits were the sole index for judging whether an enterprise was being run well or poorly. "The amount of profit," he declared, "should be the most sensitive index for an enterprise's technical progress and the effectiveness of its management."

The Maoists, on the other hand, held that "politics is the concentrated expression of economics" and that "planning is subject to politics." Thus they insisted that China's national economic planning must serve her comprehensive goals and should proceed from all her domestic and international needs and the

[3] The Writing Group of the State Capital Construction Commission, "Simultaneous Development of Large-Size, Medium, and Small-Size Enterprises," *SCMP*, No. 4731 (September 2, 1970), pp. 67–75.

demands of socialist construction. If planning were based on considerations of profit, the state could not develop the unprofitable national defense industry; heavy industry in the interior could not be built; a given area, province, or city could not protect itself from war by a diversified industrial system; industries that support agriculture but yield a low output and temporarily bring low returns could not be developed, and therefore the state could not increase the people's daily necessities, which must be subsidized for a time. It would also be impossible to produce the goods necessary to support the international proletarian struggle.

As concern about industry's adverse impact on ecology grew in the West, the Maoists found another serious pitfall in the Liuist policy of placing profit in command. They argued that the ecological damages caused by Western industries and other private enterprises were an excellent example of what society could expect if its business enterprises were concerned with profit only. However, the Maoists did not want to do away with profit completely; they only insisted on using it as a tool in planning and business accounting rather than as the controlling factor. Refuting the Liuist charge of using ultra-economic methods to run the economy, the Maoists pointed out that "giving prominence to politics should never be taken as not doing economic work, adopting business accounting, lowering production costs, and increasing accumulation." They often quoted Mao as having said: "Corruption and waste are very great crimes. A Socialist economic enterprise must do its utmost to make full use of manpower and equipment, improve the organization of labor, improve management, raise labor productivity, use manpower and materials economically, and launch emulation drives and practice economic accounting to reduce production costs and increase personal income and public accumulation year by year."

To give substance to their policy of placing politics in command, the Maoists called for strengthening party leadership in national economic planning and in production at the factory level. They therefore were strongly opposed to the Liuist attempt to give greater autonomy to individual enterprises and to have a single professional manager, instead of a party committee, to run each factory.

Party building. In the early 1960's, Mao and Liu also began to disagree on how to run the CCP itself, which by then had been in power for more than a decade and whose specific functions and responsibilities had been constantly changing along with the profound and rapid social, economic, and political changes in the whole country.[4] The Liuists seemed to feel that with the seizure of power in 1949 and with the implementation of various socialist transformation programs in the ensuing decade, the CCP had basically carried out the revolutionary phase of its mission and that it now must address itself primarily to the task of modernizing the nation. They apparently also believed that whereas the revolutionary phase of the party's mission owed much of its success to mass mobilization, ideological remolding, and periodical rectifications of the party and its auxiliary organizations, the nation-building phase of its mission called for professionalism, rationalism, and stability in both organization and procedure. To promote organizational stability, the Liuists allegedly advanced "the theory of the dying out of class struggle," "the theory of intraparty peace," and "the theory of the party of the whole people." Believing in professionalism, the Liuists curtailed the admission of "culturally backward" elements such as peasants and workers and endeavored to recruit intellectuals and other "culturally advanced" elements, regardless of their ideological impurities. Emphasis on professionalism also led the Liuists to restrict the role of the rank-and-file members in party affairs, which, in their opinion, only the cadres could handle with competence. This, coupled with the practice of allowing the First Secretary of each party committee to make too many single-handed decisions, bred authoritarianism and dampened the enthusiasm of the masses inside and outside the party. Preaching rationalism, the Liuists grew increasingly more skeptical about the efficacy of ideological studies as a means of motivating people even within the party. Consequently, they "slandered" the movement to study Mao's Thought as "oversimplification, vulgarization, and formalism," and, as noted before, took steps to "smother" it. Meanwhile, they tried to motivate party members by appealing to their self-interest. They thus encouraged the practice of "entering the party in order to be an official" and talked about "merging private and public interests."

Mao, on the other hand, believed that, if the CCP was to fulfill the herculean task of transforming a "poor and blank" country into a nation with modern industry, agriculture, national defense, culture (but without new socio-economic cleavages, which, in his opinion, had been the root cause of human misery and injustice in the past), it must retain its revolutionary élan. In other words, Mao wanted the party to concern itself not only with how to lead economic production but also with how to continue revolutionizing

[4] "Thoroughly Repudiate Liu Shao-ch'i's Counterrevolutionary Revisionist Line on Party Building," *Peking Review*, No. 51 (December 20, 1968), pp. 10–15.

society and man, especially completely eradicating the ideological influences of the exploiting classes. Mao therefore would not cherish party unity if it had lost its "revolutionary orientation and political foundation." On the contrary, he put a premium on "true proletarian unity" through ideological struggle and periodical rectification. While Mao would not bar the culturally advanced from joining the CCP, he was for active recruitment of qualified workers, peasants, and "revolutionary soldiers" to prevent the party from becoming an instrument for the privileged. Naturally, Mao was adamantly opposed to the policy of attracting individuals to the party by subtly appealing to their instinct for self-aggrandizement. Rather, he preferred to appeal to the candidates' idealism and patriotism. To enable party members to come to grips with the fundamental questions of "what road to take" and "whom to serve," and to rid them of the "pernicious influence" of the norms and values of the old society, Mao insisted that ideological studies be continued and that cadres and rank-and-file members alike spend some time in workshops or on farms. As already noted, Mao also favored giving rank-and-file members a greater voice in party affairs and sought to place the party apparatus under popular supervision so that it would be less likely to degenerate into a self-seeking institution. As for the relationship between the First Secretary of a party committee and his colleagues, Mao was disturbed by the undue concentration of authority in the former's hand. He therefore proposed that party committees at all levels operate in accordance with the principle of "combining unified leadership with collective responsibility."

Foreign policy. Disagreement over whether to reactivate the Sino-Soviet alliance was another important cause of the Mao-Liu split. Until the steady escalation of American attacks on Vietnam from 1964 on, which threatened China with war, Liu had actively supported Mao in continuing the "ideological struggle" against Moscow. However, Yang Hsien-chen, one of Liu's proteges on the CCP Central Committee and head of the Higher Party School, did put forward in the early 1960's the theory of "two combined into one" to provide a philosophical base for "such reactionary political lines as the 'Three Peaces and One Less' [peace with imperialism, peace with reaction, and peace with modern revisionism; less support for the revolutionary struggles in other countries]." [5] In the face of the mounting American threat, Liu deemed it necessary

[5] *Red Flag** editorial, "Long Live the Great Proletarian Cultural Revolution," *SCMM*, No. 530 (June 27, 1966), p. 5.

to seek a rapprochement with Moscow.[6] He therefore wanted to send a Chinese delegation to the twenty-third Soviet party congress in 1966 to arrange a compromise solution to the repeated Soviet offers of "united action" on Vietnam, which the Japanese Communist Party, with the concurrence of Pyongyang and Hanoi, had been urging both Peking and Moscow to do. Mao, on the other hand, considered the Soviet offers a ruse to make China halt its ideological struggle with Moscow, which had been undermining Moscow's influence in the world Communist movement. He questioned the Soviet leaders' sincerity in supporting Hanoi, and thus believed that Moscow was trying to put itself in a position to later sponsor a peaceful settlement of the Vietnam question in the interest of Soviet-U. S. collaboration, but at the expense of the Vietnamese people's struggle. He also probably suspected that, in the name of taking "united action," Moscow could reestablish its military presence in China. If so, this could easily lead to further Soviet encroachment on Chinese sovereignty and interests, which, of course, Mao would not tolerate. Last but not least, Mao apparently thought that, instead of deterring Washington from attacking China, China's taking "united action" with Russia might very well tempt Washington to justify an attack only on China and not the Soviet Union. After all, since the onset of the Sino-Soviet dispute, many American strategists and policy-makers had been advocating a stricter policy toward China on the assumption that she was more intransigent than the Soviet Union. Instead, Mao sought to deter both Washington and Moscow by retaining an independent initiative in diplomacy and by preparing the whole country to fight a people's war. This foreign policy dispute made it all the more necessary for Mao to remove Liu from power.

Educational policies. In the educational field, the Mao-Liu rift had much to do with the vexing problem of how to achieve an optimum balance between "redness" (political and ideological orthodoxy) and "expertness" (professional proficiency).[7] By 1961, the Liuists were advocating "expertness" in education while ostensibly repeating Mao's precept on the equal importance of both qualities. They therefore greatly reduced extracurricular activities

[6] Edgar Snow, "Aftermath of the Cultural Revolution," *New Republic,* Vol. 164, No. 15 (April 10, 1971), p. 19.

[7] Shih Yen-hung, "Down with the Chief Backer of the Revisionist Educational Line," *CB,* No. 836 (September 25, 1967), pp. 11–19; and The Shanghai Revolutionary Mass Criticism Writing Group, "Who Transforms Whom? A Comment on Kairov's 'Pedagogy,'" *Peking Review,* No. 10 (December 6, 1970), pp. 7–13.

at all levels, de-emphasized ideological training, cut back the amount of physical labor required of students, and gave more weight to scholastic achievements when matriculating students and assigning them jobs. Mao was appalled by these changes, as well as others, which he thought were making the schools and colleges spawning grounds of bourgeois elitism rather than training grounds for future builders of socialism. As already noted in Chapter XI, as soon as the GPCR got under way, Mao's ardent supporters launched a frontal attack on the Liuist educational policy and unfolded a comprehensive experimental reform program to harmonize the entire educational system with Mao's image of a new society.

Literature and art. There were also sharp differences between the two factions on literature and art. Since his famous lectures at the Yenan Forum on Arts and Literature in 1942, Mao had consistently rejected the idea that literature and art are generally apolitical and should be created and appreciated for their intrinsic value. Adhering to the Marxist-Leninist tradition, Mao insisted that literature and art have always had a class or political content and have always been used to serve a definite political or class interest. In the case of contemporary China, he wanted to place literature and art exclusively in the service of "workers, peasants, and soldiers." In other words, all literary and artistic works must be geared to the colossal task of mobilizing, reeducating, and sustaining the Chinese masses in the interest of the socialist revolution and socialist construction. Mao therefore adamantly opposed any attempt to relax control over intellectual expressions lest the impact of socialist art be diluted by works that either challenged or undermined the two "sacred" undertakings. In Mao's opinion, literary works depicting romance "between gifted scholars and great beauties," would encourage hedonism among youths instead of teaching them the importance of rendering dedicated service to the people.

The Liuists, on the other hand, were more concerned about the paucity of really substantial artistic works since the mid-1950's and the growing tendency of writers and artists to play it safe by not engaging in any creative activity at all. They naturally sought to relax these controls in order to stimulate literary and artistic activity. They advanced the theories of "portraying realities," "the diversification of subject matters in literature," and "the convergence of the spirits of the age." They deplored "the smell of gunpowder" in movies and novels portraying the exploits of the People's Liberation Army, and wanted the movie industry to make more films with "light and cheerful themes." They lamented "the excessive party control of literature," and called defiant writers "resolute Leftists" or "democratic fighters." They stressed the importance of "expert leadership" in the arts and preached "individualism, humanitarianism, and class reconciliation." In addition, they claimed the right to "speak for the people" and to expose "the dark side" of society.

The Liuists attack Mao. Not only did the Liuist writers and artists clamor for the right to criticize, but many of them, as has been noted before, actually wrote articles, novels, and plays surreptitiously attacking Mao Tse-tung and his various policies. If Liu Shao-ch'i and his top political associates, such as P'eng Chen, Lu Ting-i (Director of the CCP Propaganda Department), and Chou Yang (a Deputy Director of the CCP Propaganda Department), did not personally inspire all these attacks, they clearly condoned them. Indeed, Liu's repeated circumvention of Mao's unpublicized efforts to stamp out "antiparty and antisocialist" criticism and uphold "the class line" finally impelled Mao to have his faithful supporters launch an open counterattack against the various "ghosts and monsters who have sneaked into the party and the cultural organizations."

According to official indictments, "the most reactionary and outrageous" elements at the time were Teng T'o, Wu Han, and Liao Mo-sha, three of P'eng Chen's top aides in the CCP Peking Municipal Committee and the Peking Municipal People's Government; they were labeled as the "Three-Family Village Black Gang." Wu Han, a famous historian and a Vice-Mayor of Peking, first published an article on June 9, 1959, entitled "Hai Jui Scolds the Emperor." In February 1961, a play called "Hai Jui's Dismissal" appeared. Ostensibly depicting the political turmoil of the late Ming Dynasty (1368–1643) and the uprightness of Hai Jui, an official who was dismissed from office by the emperor after he had defended the peasants against powerful oppressors, the play was actually an allegorical attack on Mao Tse-tung's dismissal of P'eng Teh-huai as Minister of National Defense in 1959 and Mao's policies on collectivization and other matters. In March 1961, Teng T'o and Liao Mo-sha joined forces with Wu Han in making continual attacks on the Great Leap Forward and on Mao Tse-tung personally. They began to publish articles in the "Evening Chats at Yenshan" and "Notes from the Three-Family Village" series in the fortnightly *Ch'ien-hsien,* the *Peking Daily,* and the *Peking Evening News,* official organs of the CCP Peking Municipal Committee.

Using the same allegorical method of attack and ridicule, the trio mocked Mao Tse-tung for his famous slogan "The East Wind Prevails Over the West Wind." They insinuated that Mao, believing himself omniscient, was often inclined to reject good advice from below while trusting "flatterers." They wrote symbolically of good officials who were arbitrarily dismissed, and praised "the rebellious spirit" of those who continued their opposition despite dismissal. They hinted that the Great Leap Forward was no more than "big talk," that the CCP did not take good care of the labor force during that campaign, and that the cause of building socialism had collapsed. By using allusions, they described Mao as a victim of amnesia and suggested that he should "quickly retire to take a rest."

Regarding these surreptitious critics as spokesmen for capitalism, and determined to uphold socialism and revolutionary discipline, Mao first responded to the covert opposition in September 1962 at the tenth plenum of the CCP Eighth Central Committee when he admonished the whole party and all the people in the country "not to forget class struggle." Although this admonition immediately precipitated the socialist education movement in the countryside, Liu Shao-ch'i, P'eng Chen, and others primarily responsible for overseeing culture and education apparently failed to take any effective step to implement Mao's policies. In December 1963, Mao told the Chinese Writers' Union that "problems abound in all forms of art" and that "very little has been achieved so far in socialist transformation," complaining that "'the dead' still dominate many departments." He then asked: "Is [n't] it absurd that many Communists are enthusiastic about promoting feudal and capitalist art, but not socialist art?" In June 1964, on the occasion of the rectification campaign carried out by the All-China Federation of Literary and Art Circles (which since has been denounced as a sham rectification), Mao warned: "In the past 15 years these associations and most of their publications by and large have not carried out the policies of the party. . . . In recent years, they have even slid to the verge of revisionism. Unless they make serious efforts to remold themselves, they are bound at some future date to become groups like the Hungarian Petofi Club." * At the same time, the party press unleashed a campaign against some of the "revisionist" writers, including Yang Hsien-chen. But the

* The Petofi Club was an organization of Hungarian intellectuals and university students formed in the wake of the Twentieth Congress of the Soviet Communist Party. It arranged public discussion on topics relating to "Stalinist oppression" in Hungary, and its activities helped lay the groundwork for the anti-Communist uprisings which broke out in October of that year.

most outspoken dissidents were not directly attacked during this phase of Mao's counteroffensive.

The purge of P'eng Chen. According to official revelations, Mao did not call for a thorough exposure and repudiation of Wu Han and his "gang" until September 1965, when a "working conference" of the CCP Central Committee was in session.[8] At this conference Mao suggested that a proletarian cultural revolution be launched to "combat revisionism in general." A "Group of Five" with P'eng Chen as its chairman was put in charge of the proposed revolution—a move designed to force P'eng's hand. If he did not fulfill the responsibilities of the post, Mao would then be justified in taking stern measures against him. Since P'eng had been Liu Shao-ch'i's most important protege, any political chastisement of P'eng under such circumstances would also undercut Liu's own position in the party.

P'eng, reportedly with the support of Liu Shao-ch'i, only "feigned compliance with" Mao's instructions; instead, he worked assiduously to soften the political significance of the GPCR. He tried to subvert the campaign to expose and repudiate Wu Han by spreading the notion that "the question of Wu Han should be treated as an academic question" and that the party must not behave like "scholar-tyrants who always act arbitrarily and try to overwhelm people with their power." Aware of P'eng's devious actions and those of the regular party apparatus (manned largely by Liu Shao-ch'i's proteges), Mao decided to employ outside means to carry out his cultural revolution and regain effective control of the party. The first step was the appearance in the Shanghai *Wen-jui Daily* on November 10, 1965, of an article entitled "On the New Historical Drama 'Hai Jui's Dismissal,'" by a journalist named Yao Wen-yuan. Written under the direct guidance of Mao's wife, Chiang Ch'ing, who—hitherto politically obscure—was shortly to play a leading role in the GPCR, Yao's article attacked Wu Han's play "Hai Jui's Dismissal" as a "big poisonous weed" serving the ends of the class enemies who had been attacking the party since the Great Leap Forward. Instead of taking the initiative and disciplining Wu Han for his anti-Mao writings, P'eng Chen instructed Teng T'o and others in the Peking Municipal Committee to make reports and write articles in support and defense of Wu Han while purporting to criticize him. Early in February 1966, P'eng even concocted a document known as the "Outline Report on the Cur-

[8] *Red Flag** editorial, "Two Diametrically Opposed Documents," *ibid.*, No. 23 (June 2, 1967), p. 22.

rent Academic Discussion Made by the Group of Five in Charge of the Cultural Revolution." In this document P'eng allegedly continued his effort to "oppose Mao's line on the cultural revolution and to divert the great struggle to criticize and repudiate Wu Han and the considerable number of other antiparty and antisocialist representatives of the bourgeoisie into a nonpolitical discussion of academic errors." He also placed restrictions on the "proletarian Left" while "shielding and giving free rein to various ghosts and monsters who have sneaked into the party and the cultural organizations." [9]

This attempt to circumvent Mao's policy quickly led to P'eng's downfall, and he appeared in public for the last time in late March 1966. In the meantime, Mao proceeded to broaden his campaign against "those in the party taking the capitalist road." On April 14, Shih Hsi-min, Vice-Minister of Cultural Affairs, made a report to the Standing Committee of the National People's Congress, "Holding High the Great Red Banner of the Thought of Mao Tse-tung and Resolutely Carrying the Socialist Cultural Revolution Through to the End." On May 16 under Mao's personal guidance, the CCP Politburo drew up and issued to all the organs of the party a document known as "The Circular of the Politburo" revoking P'eng Chen's "Outline Report," dissolving the "Group of Five in Charge of the Cultural Revolution" and its offices, and announcing the establishment of a new Cultural Revolution Group directly under the Standing Committee of the Politburo with Ch'en Po-ta as head and Chiang Ch'ing as Chen's First Deputy. Putting forward the basic principles of the GPCR, this document stated that the whole party must follow Mao's instructions, completely expose the reactionary bourgeois stand of so-called "academic authorities," thoroughly criticize and repudiate reactionary bourgeois ideas in academic work, education, journalism, literature, art, and publishing, and seize the cultural leadership. "To achieve this," the document continued, "it is necessary at the same time to criticize and repudiate those representatives of the bourgeoisie who have sneaked into the party, the government, the army, and all spheres of culture, to clear them out or transfer some of them to other positions."

As noted earlier, P'eng Chen's dismissal as the First Secretary of the CCP Peking Municipal Committee was made known on June 3. It seems that the CCP Propaganda Department also was purged at about the same time, although Lu Ting-i's replacement by T'ao

[9] "Circular of the Central Committee of the Chinese Communist Party (May 16, 1966)," *ibid.*, No. 21 (May 19, 1967), pp. 6–9.

Chu as director was not revealed until early July. This preliminary purge of wayward veteran Communists was accompanied by a reorganization of the editorial staff of the *People's Daily,* which, under the control of Liu Shao-ch'i's proteges, had lagged conspicuously behind the *Liberation Army Daily* and some of the party organs in Shanghai in pressing the campaign to expose alleged anti-Mao "revisionists" in the party. On June 4, by contrast, the *People's Daily,* while commenting on the reorganization of the Peking Municipal Committee, gave the ominous warning: "No one who opposes Chairman Mao, Mao Tse-tung's Thought, the party's Central Committee, the dictatorship of the proletariat, or the socialist system can escape the censure and condemnation by the whole party and the whole nation, whoever he may be, whatever high position he may hold, and however much of a veteran he may be. The only possible result is his total ruination."

The big-character wall posters. The main medium used to expose and repudiate those in authority opposing Mao and "taking the capitalist road" was the big-character wall poster; and the main forces utilized were the "Red Guards," the "revolutionary rebels," and the Peoples' Liberation Army. Big-character wall posters had been used previously in Communist China. For example, during the Anti-Waste and Anti-Conservatism Campaign in the spring of 1958, the staff of the Central People's Government in Peking pasted up more than a quarter of a million such posters. But never before had wall posters played as significant a role in an intraparty struggle and thus attracted such worldwide attention as had those that appeared during the GPCR. Instead of concentrating, as in the past, on the shortcomings and inadequacies of ordinary party members, lower and middle-echelon cadres, and nonparty personnel, the GPCR posters attacked high-ranking officials, including those at the very top, in order to totally discredit them and remove them from power.

The first poster to espouse the cause of the GPCR appeared on May 25, 1966, at Peking University. Produced by a woman philosopher-lecturer, Nieh Yuan-tzu, and six others of the university, it attacked the president and some officials of the CCP Peking Municipal Committee for their efforts to "suppress" the incipient cultural revolution at the university. On June 1, Mao Tse-tung decided to publicize "the first Marxist-Leninist big-character poster" throughout the party and the country. Soon posters were plastered on walls nationwide and had become one of the most potent vehicles of the so-called "extensive democracy," by which Mao set "the revolutionary masses" on a campaign to attack "those overt and covert cliques opposing him and his Thought." The posters proved so effective that they were officially compared with "swords and daggers that hit the vital part of the enemy and make his sore spot hurt." [10]

The significance of the posters lies in the fact that during the GPCR they often went beyond the bounds of the official press: they attacked high-ranking officials by name; they frequently gave the first news that an important person was in trouble; they provided detailed stories on how certain "revisionists" were rounded up and tried by "the revolutionary masses"; and they reported speeches never released through the official press—including some by Mao Tse-tung. More important, they provided virtually unlimited opportunities for the masses to take part in a movement like the cultural revolution and thus help arouse and maintain interest in the campaign. The wall posters were cheap, and anyone who could write could make one. Although often officially inspired, their method of exposure and attack lent the appearance of spontaneity and therefore created popular support for whatever action the party leadership eventually took against the culprits. Moreover, given their unofficial character, wall posters allowed the leadership to chastise certain recalcitrant officials without committing itself to any specific action on their ultimate fate; if a chastised person had to be "rehabilitated" for one reason or another, it could be done without undue embarrassment to the leadership itself.

When wall posters first appeared on the university campuses in Peking, Liu Shao-ch'i and Teng Hsiao-p'ing had not yet been directly attacked and were still in charge of the party apparatus. In June and July, Liu and Teng took advantage of Mao Tse-tung's absence from the capital to "smother the raging flames" Mao had lit. They personally directed many units in "attacking the revolutionaries from all sides, suppressing the revolutionary masses, practicing a white terror, and branding large numbers of the revolutionary masses counterrevolutionaries or 'Rightists.'" [11] This they did largely through so-called "work teams" sent out to the various educational institutions. In particular, the work teams "forbade the cadres to read big-character posters, take part in the movement, or attend any meetings." At this crucial moment, Mao Tse-

[10] "Saluting the Revolutionary Youths and Teenagers," *Red Flag,** No. 11 (August 21, 1966), p. 33.

[11] Hsieh Fu-chih's Speech at a Mass Rally to Found and Celebrate the Peking Municipal Revolutionary Committee," *Peking Review,* No. 18 (April 28, 1967), p. 18.

tung returned to Peking and began to deal with the situation. From August 1 to 12, he presided over the eleventh plenum of the Eighth Central Committee. This plenum, the first in four years, adopted a "Decision Concerning the Great Proletarian Cultural Revolution" that, in effect, restated Mao's basic policies on the GPCR as contained in the above-mentioned May 16, 1966, Circular; it rebuked—albeit obliquely—Liu Shao-ch'i's attempt to "strangle the revolutionary masses and to stamp out the cultural revolution itself." The resolution further provided for the establishment of "cultural revolution groups, committees, and congresses" to supplant the former work teams and serve as "organs of power." It instructed the new agencies to "put daring above everything else," "boldly arouse the masses to join the cultural revolution," and "make the fullest use of big-character posters and great debates, so that the masses can clarify the correct views, criticize the wrong views, and expose all the ghosts and monsters."

The forming of the Red Guards. One of the major groups set in motion immediately after the plenum was the "Red Guards," mostly high school and college students, who appeared for the first time on August 18, 1966, at a mammoth rally in Peking, in the presence of Mao Tse-tung, Lin Piao, and other leaders of the country. During seven additional rallies in the next three months or more, Mao and Lin reviewed a total of 11 million "revolutionary students and teachers." As a shock force of the GPCR, the Red Guards were exhorted at the rallies to guarantee that the "fatherland will never change color"; to raise the "iron broom" and make a clean sweep of the "old ideas, culture, customs, and habits of the exploiting classes"; "to foster the new ideas, culture, customs, and habits of the proletariat"; and to "smash all kinds of monsters and freaks who were attempting to subvert the proletarian dictatorship." The main targets of the movement, the Red Guards were told, were "those in authority within the party who are taking the capitalist road."

The Red Guards responded to this call with a pledge to study, disseminate, apply, and defend Mao Tse-tung's Thought, which was proclaimed to be the highest directive for all kinds of work. They vowed to display "the spirit of daring thought, speech, and action, and to break through, rise up in revolution, and clean up the muck left over by the old society." After each rally the Red Guards went on trips to "exchange revolutionary experiences." The "iron broom" was soon felt across the country: Stores were ordered by the Red Guards not to sell perfumes, cosmetics, and other luxury goods.

Streets and shops bearing names inconsistent with the spirit of the GPCR were changed. Officials and scholars believed to be harboring bourgeois or revisionist ideas were criticized by posters or other means of exposure like mass rallies, where "guilty" persons were forced to sit on stools and wear dunce caps while "the revolutionary masses" taunted and accused them.

The Red Guards were soon reinforced by "the revolutionary rebels"—pro-Maoist workers, peasants, and cadres in the party, government, and business enterprises. They were backed by units of the PLA stationed in the localities concerned. This coalition of "revolutionary masses, cadres," and the PLA was officially described as the "three-in-one combination," whose main task was to "bombard the headquarters of the bourgeoisie" and launch "a struggle from below to seize power from the handful of party people in authority taking the capitalist road." To overcome any reluctance to revolt against the established authorities "who were antiparty and antisocialism," the Maoist leadership advanced such slogans as "Down with Slavishness," "To Rebel Is Justified," and "All Erroneous Leadership that Endangers the Revolution Should Not Be Accepted Unconditionally but Should Be Resisted Resolutely." Knowing that the proteges of Liu Shao-ch'i still constituted the majority in many party committees, the pro-Mao elements contended that one cannot talk about the question of "majority" or "minority" independently of class viewpoints and that "it is necessary to see who has grasped the truth of Marxism-Leninism and the Thought of Mao Tse-tung." They also quoted Stalin as having said, "Lenin never became a captive of the majority, especially when that majority had no principles."

The campaign to seize power from "the revisionists" began in the mass media and the educational institutions. After this phase of the struggle was completed in December 1966, the attack was quickly directed toward those party, government, and business organizations where "seizure of power was necessary." The arrest of P'eng Chen and Lu Ting-i and the de facto dismissal of Liu Shao-ch'i and Teng Hsiao-p'ing occurred at this time. During "the January Revolution" in 1967, pro-Maoists seized power from Liu Shao-ch'i's followers in the CCP Shanghai Municipal Committee and People's Government, marking the beginning of the first series of "power seizures" in the country—including the provinces of Shansi, Heilungkiang, Shantung, and Kweichow, and the cities of Peking and Tsingtao. In many places the pro-Maoists met subtle but active resistance from the followers of local "revisionist" leaders, and in some cases there were armed clashes. But in all cases active resistance was short-lived, for the Maoists generally had the support of the local units of the PLA, despite the fact that until the fall of 1967 the armed forces in some areas "committed the mistake of supporting one particular group of the rebels, while restraining or even suppressing other groups." Upon seizing power in their respective localities, the "revolutionaries" invariably scrapped the existing party and government machinery in favor of a provisional organ known as the "revolutionary committee," composed of representatives of the "revolutionary masses," the "revolutionary cadres" of the abolished organs, and local units of the PLA, thus preserving the "three-in-one combination." Pending the establishment of a local revolutionary committee, a "preparatory committee" for its formation and a local military control commission usually took charge.

To minimize resistance and maximize the educational impact of the GPCR, the Maoist leadership constantly reminded its followers that the struggle against the "revisionists" and bourgeois ideology had to be conducted mainly by reason and not by coercion or by force, because "struggle by coercion or by force can only touch the skin and flesh while struggle by reasoning can touch the soul." [12] To salvage from the abyss of "revisionism" the largest possible number of experienced cadres and experts whose practical talents and skills the country sorely needed, Mao's associates repeatedly called attention to the necessity and desirability of making it possible for people who had been "hoodwinked" by the "bourgeois reactionary line" to correct their mistakes and devote themselves to the revolution—"if they make a clean break with the handful of top party persons in authority taking the capitalist road." To overcome various shortcomings and errors of "the revolutionary masses" during the power struggle, the Maoist leadership launched a campaign early in 1967 to combat "the tendencies of departmentalism, small-group mentality, ultra-democracy, individualism, anarchism, and the inclination to seek the limelight." The "revolutionary masses" and all the people of the country were exhorted to "eliminate self-interest and put public interest in the van." In fact, the *Liberation Army Daily* (November 30, 1966) stated: ". . . fundamentally speaking, the present Great Proletarian Cultural Revolution is a great revolution to destroy all the exploiting classes' concept of self-interest of the last several hundred years and to foster the socialist concept of devotion to the public interest, a great revolution to remold people to the depths of their

[12] "Speech of Comrade Chiang Ch'ing," *ibid.*, No. 50 (December 9, 1966), p. 7.

souls." In view of Mao's heavy reliance on "voluntarism" for constructing a new China, this description, if stripped of the Communist jargon, certainly cannot be dismissed as mere propaganda.

The factions struggle for power. Despite these exhortations, factionism and violent struggles for influential positions resulted from the massive destruction of the established power structure in the winter of 1966–1967 and from the lack of adequate central control of the myriad of hastily formed "revolutionary mass organizations," which had attracted opportunists as well as idealists. The first factional units were organized by function and occupation at the early stages of the GPCR. With the reins of power hanging free after the capitalist roaders had been "dragged out," the uncoordinated and often fortuitously formed tiny organizations of Red Guards and "revolutionary rebels" began to fight among themselves. Many of them would augment their strength by absorbing entire factions from other groups; others effected loose federations with other factions that maintained their separate identities while acting in rough concert. Ultimately, most of the factions in any given locality coalesced into "two large contending factional organizations," with hundreds of thousands of members on their rolls. Although their organizational jurisdiction did not extend beyond provincial borders, some factions did maintain contact with their counterparts in other provinces and in Peking, principally through a network of "liaison stations." Opposing factions fought "civil wars" not only on wall posters and tabloid newspapers but also in the streets, schools, factories, government offices, railroad stations, and other places. Some combatants fought hand to hand, others used poles and daggers; still others resorted to small arms, automatic weapons, and, in some rare instances, even tanks and armored cars, that they had stolen or seized from local army units which were strictly forbidden to "hamstring the revolutionary Left."

The violent factional strife, declared the *Wen-hui Daily,* "creates splits, prevents unity, undermines fighting will, damages the revolution and production, covers up bad elements, and lets loose all kinds of evil-doers." The influential newspaper then characterized factionalism as "the most dangerous enemy hidden in our revolutionary ranks." The contending factions harmed the GPCR mostly by their persistent quarrels over the eligibility of various mass organizations and revolutionary cadres for membership on the revolutionary committees in their respective localities. Their obstructionism delayed the formation of revolutionary committees, upset the pace of the GPCR, and prolonged the disruption of industry and transportation, although the seriousness and magnitude never approached that caused by the civil disorders in certain American cities in the 1960's.

Mao pulls the reins on the GPCR. Determined to curb the disruptive activities of the contending factions, but careful not to alienate the "revolutionary youth" and Red Guards who, in Chiang Ch'ing's words, "have made tremendous contributions to the GPCR at its initial and middle stages," the Maoist leadership took additional corrective measures in 1967 and 1968. On February 3, 1967, it issued the first of a series of notices forbidding long journeys by foot to revolutionary teachers, students, and Red Guards, who wanted to "exchange revolutionary experience and establish ties all over the country." About two weeks later, the mass media featured an open letter from the CCP Central Committee to the peasants and rural cadres; it emphasized the importance of doing a good job of spring cultivation. To shield most of the rural administrative personnel from the fire of the GPCR, the letter stated that the absolute majority of the rural cadres were good, or comparatively good, and that former poor and lower-middle peasants should "show understanding and support" for even those cadres who had made mistakes but were making amends by good deeds. This letter was shortly followed by another announcing a parallel policy toward "workers and staff and revolutionary cadres" in industrial and mining enterprises throughout the country. On March 7, 1967, Mao directed the army to "give political and military training in the universities, middle schools, and the higher classes of primary schools stage by stage and group by group." But before the army could undertake the gigantic task of remolding the contentious young students, two serious incidents occurred in the summer of 1967, which momentarily added more confusion to the GPCR.

Counterrevolutionary conspiracies: the May 16 Corps. The first was the abduction in Wuhan on July 20 of Hsieh Fu-chih and Wang Li, two important emissaries from Peking, by a conservative local mass organization known as the "One Million Heroic Troops."[13] The abductors had acted on the orders of some senior officers of the Wuhan Military District, including Commander Ch'en Tsai-tao. The kidnapped officials were rescued two days later; the "One Million Heroic Troops" were disbanded; and Com-

[13] *SCMP*, no. 4089 (December 29, 1967), pp. 3–13; *ibid.*, No. 4095 (January 9, 1968), pp. 18–19; and Thomas W. Robinson, "The Wuhan Incident: Local Strife and Provincial Rebellion During the Cultural Revolution," *China Quarterly*, No. 47 (July–September, 1971), pp. 413–438.

mander Ch'en Tsai-tao and his principal accomplices were swiftly dismissed from their posts and placed under military custody in Peking. This episode greatly shocked the nation, since Commander Ch'en's action in the case had been tantamount to open defiance of Peking's authority, although subsequent developments suggested that the abduction was not meant to challenge Mao, but was precipitated by Wang Li's petulance and "ultra-leftist" insinuations against Ch'en and some other military officers.

The other serious incident involved the "May 16 Red Guard Corps" of Peking.[14] They were organized by a group of ostensibly ultra-leftist intellectuals in the Academy of Sciences, and were secretly supported by Wang Li, Kuan Feng, and Ch'i Pen-yü, members of the CCP Central Committee's Group in Charge of the Cultural Revolution. The May 16 Corps began to emerge in the fall of 1966, but was not formally inaugurated until August 3, 1967. According to initial indictments in some Red Guard wall posters, the May 16 Corps plotted to "split the proletarian headquarters" headed by Mao, "provoke discord" in the army, and undermine Peking's international image. Camouflaging its real identity behind an extremely leftist stance, the group was really extremely rightist. To set Chou En-lai and the Cultural Revolution Group against each other, the May 16 Corps clamored: "Chou En-lai is the general root of capitalist restoration." "The current struggle," they asserted, "is one between the new Cultural Revolution Group and the old government." "Premier Chou," they added, "is a member of the old government and we should not listen to him." In addition, they issued a call to overthrow all the remaining vice-premiers, including Li Fu-ch'un, Li Hsien-nien, Ch'en I, Nieh Jung-chen, and Hsieh Fu-chih. They also compiled "blacklist information" against Chiang Ch'ing; some even attacked Mao Tse-tung.

Discord in the army was spread when, shortly after his return to Peking from Wuhan, Wang Li "made use of the mistakes some military districts committed by supporting the Left in spreading the slander that 'the military districts do not heed what the Central Committee says.'" On July 30, Wang, in his capacity as Acting Director of the CCP's Propaganda Department, ordered the Central People's Broadcasting Station to air the editorial, "Fiercely Fire at the Chief Enemies of the People," which he and another "backstage boss of the May 16 Corps had cooked up." In this editorial they vigorously advocated "dragging out the handful in the army."

[14] "The May 16 Red Guard Corps of Peking," *CB*, No. 844 (January 10, 1968), pp. 1–30; and "May 16 Corps Condemned by Central Leaders," *SCMP*, No. 4068 (November 28, 1967), pp. 14–15.

Meanwhile, Kuan Feng released an editorial, "The Proletariat Must Tightly Grasp the Gun," in the *Red Flag* (No. 198; August 1, 1967). This editorial quickly "whipped up a counterrevolutionary adverse current of attacking the People's Liberation Army." On the diplomatic front, Ch'i Pen-yü inspired the attack on the Soviet and Burmese embassies and had the office of the British Charge d'Affaires in Peking burned in August—events that shocked even many open-minded foreign observers. By late August, however, the "counterrevolutionary conspiracies" of the May 16 Corps had been brought to a halt; and soon most of its leaders, as well as many of the "sinister hands" manipulating the group, were said to have met the same fate that had befallen their alleged masters including Liu Shao-ch'i, Teng Hsiao-p'ing, and T'ao Chu. However, as certain unidentified Chinese leaders subsequently revealed in 1971 during private conversations with foreign visitors, it was Ch'en Po-ta, rather than Liu Shao-ch'i and the other early victims of the GPCR, who had actually inspired the May 16 Corps. The earlier reports in some Red Guard publications naming Liu Shao-ch'i as the principal conspirator behind the May 16 Corps could have been planted by Ch'en Po-ta to conceal his role in it after the group had been labeled as counterrevolutionary. The group's call to "drag out" some senior officers of the army might have been made in anticipation of Lin Piao's desire to put his own proteges in command of all the important units of the PLA. As noted in Chapter VI, since Lin's demise there have been thinly veiled charges that he had once worked very closely with the former high official in charge of the GPCR "in carrying out splittist and factional activities."

The suppression of the May 16 Corps and the purge of some of its "backstage bosses" marked a major turning point in the GPCR. In the ensuing months more steps were taken to curb factionalism and extreme leftism and steer the GPCR back to the right course. On September 5 an order was issued forbidding the seizure of arms, equipment, and other military supplies from the army and authorizing it to take forceful action against those who would violate the injunction. In early and mid-September Mao toured the central and eastern parts of the country, including Shanghai, Honan, Hupeh, Hunan, Kiangsi, and Chekiang. This relatively extensive inspection tour served to demonstrate his effective control over the outlying regions, and thus deter ambitious and unruly elements. During the journey he issued the ideologically significant "instruction": "There is no conflict of fundamental interests within the working class. Under the dictatorship of the proletariat, there is no reason whatsoever for the working class to split into two big irreconcilable groupings."[15] The media throughout the country immediately publicized this new directive from the leader and called for a speedy formation of "grand alliances of rebel groups." On October 17, the central authorities of the party and the government specifically decreed that "all factories, schools, departments, and business units must form revolutionary grand alliances according to different systems, trades, and lines of business and classes in schools" and that "in accordance with the voluntary principle all organizations that embrace several trades or lines of business should make the necessary adjustments."[16]

The training classes. Coinciding with this latest call was the disappearance of the wall posters, many of which had degenerated by now into convenient vehicles for factional strife among the "rebel groups" themselves.[17] Meanwhile, there emerged all over the country "classes for the study of Mao Tse-tung's Thought."[18] Making their first appearance on October 1, the first round of classes in Peking alone had a total enrollment of over 70,000 leading members of "revolutionary mass organizations, young Red Guards, and revolutionary cadres." All classes were short-term, lasting from several days to a few weeks. Some were full-time residential courses, others were full-time or part-time training centers within various agencies. The objectives of these classes were to "help the people carry out Chairman Mao's instructions, grasp Chairman Mao's Thought and policies, and carry the cultural revolution forward along the correct course." Self-criticism played an important role, and helped to forge unity. Mao's Thought was taken as the guide to distinguish "what is correct thinking and what is erroneous thinking." In all these activities, representatives of the army actively "helped" the Left, assisted industry and agriculture, exercised control, and gave military and political training.

Purifying the revolutionary ranks. Although the training classes and other rectifying measures from the spring of 1967 on apparently reduced factionalism and self-interest and thus facilitated the formation in late 1967 and early 1968 of more revolutionary committees in many municipalities and provinces, "mountain-stronghold mentality, sectarianism, and ambitious bourgeois individualists and double-dealers" continued to "instigate the masses to struggle against one another and to carry on other sinister activities

[15] *Ibid.*, No. 4026 (September 22, 1967), pp. 1–2.
[16] *NCNA*, October 17, 1967.
[17] *Tokyo Asahi*, September 25, 1967.
[18] *NCNA*, October 27, 1967.

undermining the cultural revolution." Even where great revolutionary alliances had been established, factional strife and conspiracy often caused much reneging on pledges to abide by agreements. In consequence, many revolutionary committees were seriously paralyzed. Faced with this situation, the Maoist leadership, in February 1968, urged the revolutionary mass organizations to vigorously purify their ranks by ridding themselves of "bad people and black hands who had infiltrated their units and usurped their power." Many organizations responded by weeding out "those who appeared to be 'leftists' but actually were rightists and capitalist roaders." The purification campaign soon culminated in the dismissal, on March 22, 1968, of Yang Ch'eng-wu, Acting Chief of the General Staff; Yü Li-chin, Political Commissar of the Air Force; and Fu Chung-pi, Commander of the Peking Garrison.[19] Denounced in Red Guard publications as "refined schemers, who had instructed the pseudo-leftist clique of Wang Li, Kuang Feng, and Ch'i Pen-yü to put forward the reactionary slogan 'Drag Out a Small Handful in the Army,'" the three senior military officers were accused of "using malignant and tricky tactics in a vain attempt to destroy the proletarian headquarters headed by Chairman Mao with Vice-Chairman Lin Piao as his deputy, to demolish our great wall—the People's Liberation Army—and to shake the new-born revolutionary committees in order to achieve their criminal purpose of usurping the party, the army, and the state and restoring capitalism." Specifically, they were indicted for: (1) attempting to reverse the verdict on the "February Adverse Current" in 1967 (see Appendix I); (2) collecting "black materials" against Chou En-lai, Ch'en Po-ta, K'ang Sheng, and Chiang Ch'ing; (3) suppressing information from Mao Tse-tung and Lin Piao; (4) conspiring to depose Hsieh Fu-chih as chairman of the Peking Municipal Revolutionary Committee; (5) plotting to eliminate several regional commanders of the army and the commander of the air force; (6) attempting to arrest certain members of the Cultural Revolution Group; (7) instigating the masses to struggle against one another; and (8) ostensibly denouncing but actually supporting the political and military line of P'eng Teh-huai, Lo Jui-ch'ing, and other high-ranking capitalist sympathizers in the party. Without identifying the three erring officers by name, the official press at the time characterized their activities as "right opportunism, right splittism, and right capitu-

[19] *SCMP*, No. 4169 (May 2, 1968), pp. 4–6; *ibid.*, No. 4172 (May 7, 1968), pp. 1–10; *ibid.*, No. 4186 (May 27, 1968), pp. 1–5; *ibid.*, No. 4188 (May 29, 1968), pp. 1–4; *ibid.*, No. 4222 (July 22, 1968), pp. 1–3; *ibid.*, No. 4234 (August 8, 1968), pp. 15–16; and *CB*, No. 857 (July 9, 1968), pp. 1–28.

lationism." In view of Lin Piao's collusion with Ch'en Po-ta during the GPCR, and the fact that Yang Ch'eng-wu, Yü Li-chin, and Fu Chung-pi had long been Lin's proteges, this account of the three senior officers' disgrace (particularly their alleged scheming with Wang Li, Kuan Feng, and Ch'i Pen-yü, who were Ch'en Po-ta's top aides) seems to have been contrived by Lin Piao and Ch'en Po-ta for the same purpose they used in forming the May 16 Corps. If so, in due course Peking may set the record straight by identifying the three officers as executors of Lin Piao's "splittist and factional schemes." Lin Piao and Ch'en Po-ta had conveniently made them sacrificial lambs in 1968 by accusing them of following the political and military line of P'eng Teh-huai and other top capitalist sympathizers in the party and army, and of slandering Ch'en Po-ta, as well as Chou En-lai and Chiang Ch'ing. The Maoist leadership's acquiescence in the false accusations against the May 16 Corps and the three senior military officers could be due to the fact that it was not yet ready to call Lin and Ch'en to account for their activities.

Taming the youngsters. In any event, the dismissal of the three military officers in Peking and the "dragging out of chameleons and small reptiles" in various parts of the country went a long way toward restoring order and discipline. This was evidenced by the formation in the spring of 1968 of additional revolutionary committees at the provincial level and below and by reports of rising industrial and mining outputs in the following summer months. In many educational institutions, however, "civil wars" between contending groups of students showed little sign of abatement. On the contrary, some of these groups reportedly even advanced the theory of "many centers" to justify their "sectarianism and other reactionary bourgeois trends undermining the leading role of Chairman Mao's proletarian headquarters." To more effectively tame the contentious youths, Mao launched another spectacular drive at persuasion that also displayed some force. A "workers' Mao Tse-tung's Thought propaganda team" was sent to the Tsing-hua University campus in Peking to straighten out ideological kinks among Red Guard factions there. Conveying his approbation to the new vanguard shock force of the GPCR, which was backed by unarmed soldiers, Mao made his much-publicized presentation of mangoes to the worker's propaganda contingent on August 5. The mangoes were a "treasured gift" that the Chinese leader had just received from foreign friends. Soon it was announced that throughout the country worker-peasant-soldier propaganda teams were entering colleges, schools, and all other units "where the tasks of struggle-criticism-transformation had not been carried out well." The teams reportedly "expressed their determination to do their propaganda work in a deep-going, thorough, patient, and sustained way and ensure that Mao Tse-tung's Thought is truly transformed into practical action on the part of the revolutionary masses." In the meantime, Mao issued his latest instruction, stating that "the leading role of the working class in the cultural revolution and in all fields of work should be brought into full play." [20] He also called upon youths to integrate themselves with the broad masses and accept the leadership of the working class. The Red Guards' response, he added, would determine whether or not they were true revolutionaries.

While the propaganda teams were reeducating young people in colleges and schools and helping them correct their mistakes, the arduous and time-consuming task of creating new ruling bodies in mainland China was completed at long last on September 5; autonomous regional revolutionary committees were established in Sinkiang and Tibet. This development, coupled with favorable trends on other fronts, enabled Lin Piao to make the following statement on October 1 at the rally celebrating the nineteenth anniversary of the founding of the Peking regime: "Our great Proletarian Cultural Revolution has now scored great victories. Revolutionary committees have been established in twenty-nine provinces, municipalities and autonomous regions—that is, in the whole country except Taiwan Province. Industry, agriculture, science, and technology and revolutionary literature and art are all thriving. The counterrevolutionary plot of China's Khrushchev and the handful of his agents in various places to restore capitalism has been completely aborted. . . . The dictatorship of the proletariat in the country has become more consolidated and powerful than ever. . . ." [21]

The purge of Liu Shao-ch'i. The final, definitive action against the principal target of the GPCR was taken at the unheralded, "enlarged" twelfth plenary session of the Eighth Central Committee of the CCP, held in Peking from October 13 to October 31.[22] Attended not only by those full and alternate members of the Committee who had survived the GPCR but also by members of the Cultural Revolution Group, "principal responsible comrades of the revolutionary committees of the provinces, municipalities, au-

[20] *People's Daily,** August 13, 1968.

[21] *Peking Review,* No. 40 (October 4, 1968), p. 13.

[22] For an English text of the communique of the plenum, see *ibid.,* Supplement to No. 44 (November 1, 1968), pp. v–viii.

tonomous regions, and . . . the Chinese People's Liberation Army," the plenum was the first since August 1966. According to a communique released on November 1, the Central Committee formally decided to expel Liu Shao-ch'i. This was the first time that Liu was named in an official party declaration in connection with revisionism in China. Up till then he was identified simply as "China's Khrushchev" or some other insulting description. Calling Liu a "traitor, renegade, and scab" and a "lackey of imperialism, modern revisionism, and the Kuomintang reactionaries," the statement reported that the plenary session "expressed its deep revolutionary indignation" at Liu's "counterrevolutionary crimes" and unanimously adopted a resolution, based on an investigation by a special party group, to expel him from the party "once and for all" and "to dismiss him from all posts both inside and outside the party," presumably including the Chairmanship of the People's Republic, and "to continue to settle accounts with him and his accomplices for their crimes in betraying the party and the country." As might be expected, the meeting hailed the GPCR as a sweeping success and declared that all the policies and actions of Mao Tse-tung and Lin Piao had been correct. Indicating that a new national party congress, the first since 1958, would be held "at an appropriate time," the plenary session announced that "through the storms of the Great Proletarian Cultural Revolution ample ideological, political, and organizational conditions have been prepared for convening the Ninth National Congress of the Party." Pending that, the Maoist leadership insisted on carrying out the tasks of "struggle-criticism-transformation" conscientiously. "That," in Lin Piao's words, "means to consolidate and develop the revolutionary committees, to do a good job of mass criticism and repudiation, purifying the class ranks, consolidating and building the party, revolutionizing education, simplifying the administrative structure, changing irrational rules and regulations, grasping revolution, promoting production, and carrying the Great Proletarian Cultural Revolution through to the end."

Rebuilding the CCP. The CCP Ninth National Congress opened in Peking on April 1, 1969. Officially described as "a congress of unity, a congress of victory, and a congress that resolves to seize still greater victories throughout the country," it laid the foundation to rebuild the shattered party in accordance with Mao's "revolutionary line"; the convention was attended by a total of 1512 delegates. Among them were veteran party leaders who had survived the recent purge as well as many "advanced elements" in the party who had emerged in the course of that tumultuous event.

These included a great number of industrial workers, poor and lower-middle peasants in rural communes, officers and soldiers of the PLA, and Red Guards. Mao Tse-tung presided over the opening session of the Congress and made "a most important speech," which, however, was not made public. Upon the election of a presidium with Mao as its chairman, Lin Piao as its vice-chairman, and Chou En-lai as its secretary-general, the Congress adopted an agenda consisting of: (1) a political report by Lin Piao on behalf of the Eighth Central Committee; (2) revision of the Constitution of the party; and (3) election of a new Central Committee. Delivered on the same day that the agenda was adopted, Lin Piao's 24,000-word report reviewed the course and policies of the GPCR, set forth certain guidelines for rebuilding the CCP, and discussed China's relations with foreign countries.[23] A remarkably shorter document in comparison with the party Constitution of 1956, the new charter, as noted in Chapter VI, reaffirmed the Thought of Mao Tse-tung and Marxism-Leninism as the theoretical basis for the party's thinking and explicitly stipulated that Lin Piao would be Mao's eventual successor. The reference to Lin has, of course, become obsolete as a result of Lin's subsequent demise. As a result of the prominence given to Mao's Thought, the new Constitution called for uninterrupted revolution to ward off the danger of capitalist restoration and the threat of subversion and aggression by imperialism and modern revisionism. It stressed the need to strengthen the dictatorship of the proletariat and enjoined the party to remain a vigorous vanguard organization leading the proletariat and the 700 million Chinese people in building socialism independently, through hard work and dauntless determination. As noted in Chapters VI and VII, the new party charter also prescribed certain new principles of party organization and function to combat bureaucratism and preserve revolutionary élan. On April 24, the Congress formally elected the Ninth Central Committee at its last plenary session and then adjourned. The process of restructuring the central leadership organs of the party was completed five days later on April 29 when the newly elected Ninth Central Committee, at its first plenum, elected a new Politburo and Standing Committee. The new party Constitution and central leadership within the party were decisive achievements in the Maoists' pro-

[23] For an English text of Lin's report, see *ibid.*, No. 18 (April 30, 1969), pp. 16–35. On October 9, 1972, Premier Chou En-lai told a delegation of the American Society of Newspaper Editors that Lin's report was actually prepared by the Central Committee after the Committee had rejected an earlier draft prepared for Lin by Ch'en Po-ta on the grounds that it did not conform to Mao's policies. *Wall Street Journal,* October 11 and 12, 1972.

tracted campaign to rid the CCP of "revisionists" and to uphold Mao's "revolutionary line" on party and state affairs. This alone, they believe, will enable the Chinese people to liberate themselves from hunger, greed, exploitation, ignorance, war, and humiliation from foreign encroachments.

XIV

Conclusion

Having traced the Chinese Communist movement from its inception to the present, one cannot help wondering how its real significance to China should be assessed, how the movement is likely to develop in the foreseeable future, and what are its international implications if any. These are complex and controversial questions, and no definitive and comprehensive answers can be supplied here. Nevertheless, some brief observations are appropriate and are offered for the reader's reference.

Insofar as the movement's significance to the Chinese nation is concerned, the most striking fact is that, despite the material and human costs involved and regardless of how repugnant its approaches to problems may be to Western observers and disaffected elements in China itself, the CCP—of all the revolutionary and reformist parties of modern China that have sought to save and rejuvenate their country—alone has achieved any significant successes, even if only initially in some respects. Domestically, one of the party's greatest accomplishments has been the political unification of the nation. For the first time since the middle of the nineteenth century, when the Manchu regime in Peking began to lose its grip not only on outlying regions such as Tibet and Sinkiang but also on many provinces in "China Proper," China now has a central government exercising effective control from the Yalu and Amur Rivers in the northeast to the Himalayan mountains in the southwest and from the seacoast in the southeast to Sinkiang in the northwest. The significance of this fact cannot be overestimated. First, unification has freed the more than 700 million Chinese from the scourges of banditry, lawless-

中國共產運動簡史

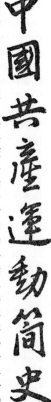

ness, and warlordism, which had afflicted them for more than a century. Second, except for the effects of officially inspired "revolutionary" struggles, political reunification has made it possible for the nation to achieve greater integration in the economic, social, and cultural spheres, thus enabling it to better utilize its human and material resources for the good of all the people in its various territorial-administrative subdivisions. Third, political reunification has strengthened the country's ability to resist foreign intrigues to fan separatist movements in the outlying regions. The persistent and unbridled nature of such intrigues can be seen from Japan's sponsorship of "Manchukuo" and the "Inner Mongolia Autonomous Government" in the 1930's, Russia's promotion of an "independent" Outer Mongolia both prior to and after the Bolshevik Revolution in 1917, Soviet Russia's collaboration with General Sheng Shih-ts'ai in Sinkiang from 1932 to 1942, Moscow's support of the revolt in the Ili district of the same province in 1944, and British activities in Tibet in the decades preceding the CCP's "peaceful liberation" of that region in 1951.

Another significant accomplishment of the CCP is the fact that it has set the nation on the road to industrialization, without which she cannot solve many of her other problems. This achievement can be best appreciated if one recalls that the CCP began its drive in the field in the early 1950's with a far inferior scientific and technological base than the Soviets in the 1920's, although for a number of years the CCP was able to overcome part of this disadvantage with Soviet technical assistance and Soviet industrial equipment. Closely related to the initial success in industrialization has been the tremendous expansion of educational opportunities at all levels and the fight against illiteracy among the huge adult population. Inasmuch as industrialization is not attainable unless the citizenry of a nation has achieved a certain level of literacy and technical skill, this development is of great significance. Equally important have been the achievements in the agricultural field. Since the initial setbacks more than a decade ago, collective farming and a host of other Maoist rural policies, including the undertaking of massive public works, have been bearing increasingly more fruit, as evidenced, among other things, by the rising farm outputs, the improving quality of rural life, and the diminishing vulnerability of farm production to the vagaries of weather conditions, which in the past had made famine a specter constantly stalking China. What is more, by reordering the priorities in capital investment, by "walking on two legs" in agriculture and industry, by aiming at local self-sufficiency, by appealing to man's sense of involvement and public-mindedness rather than to his acquisitiveness, and by earnestly bringing the role of the masses into full play while relentlessly combating elitism and bureaucratism, the Maoist leadership seems to have found a genuinely unique way of economic development and nation-building which had previously been condemned in various quarters as "utopian" or "anachronistic" but whose efficacy has now impressed more and more foreign observers with vastly different political views.[1]

In the social field, the CCP has derived and is likely to continue to derive considerable strength and popularity from the development of extensive medical and hospital facilities, the promotion of a mass program of health and hygiene, the reform of the family system, the mobilization of women for nation-building tasks outside the household, the improvement of the cultural and material life of the various national minorities, and the fight against ethnic prejudices and discrimination, including Han Chauvinism. In due time the CCP's effort to curb population growth also may yield beneficial results.

Externally, the CCP must be credited with having made China "stand up" once again after more than a century of foreign invasions and humiliation. Saving China from further foreign encroachments and restoring her to a respectable position among nations has been the common goal of all the revolutionary and reformist movements in the nation's modern history; that the CCP has accomplished this goal has won it immense esteem and support from the Chinese, including many of those who strongly abhor its other policies.

How has the CCP been able to do what it has done? There is no question that much of it is due to the vision and resourcefulness of its leaders, the dedication of its cadres, and the comprehensive nature of its control of the population. Equally important factors contributing to the CCP's effectiveness are its emphasis on thoroughgoing changes, the skillful use of Chinese nationalism, and the bold mobilization of the masses for attaining the goals it has set for the nation. It may not be an exaggeration to say that, in the final analysis, the most important achievement of the CCP has been the revival of dynamism, self-reliance, and a sense of national purposefulness on the part of the Chinese people.

Needless to say, the CCP's record as a ruling party has not been

[1] See, for example, John Kenneth Galbraith, "Galbraith Has Seen China's Future—And It Works," *The New York Times Magazine*, November 26, 1972, pp. 38–40; and Joseph Alsop's reports on his China tour in his syndicated column carried by various American newspapers in December 1972 and January 1973.

an unmixed one. In the preceding chapters we have noted many of its shortcomings, inadequacies, mistakes, and "excesses." It should be pointed out, however, that except for those shortcomings and excesses which it does not regard as real, but rather as legitimate concomitants of and measures necessitated by the revolution, the Maoist leadership itself has made timely exposure and rectification of errors a cardinal principle of building the party and the nation. This can be seen from the party's many shifts in policy and tactics; the launching of rectification campaigns; the unfolding of the GPCR; and the undertaking of a series of corrective measures to check deviations and excesses both during and after the GPCR, including the "purge" of Lin Piao. This trait of the Maoist leadership must be borne in mind if the CCP's shortcomings and mistakes are to be viewed in a proper perspective. Some of the most serious problems facing the Maoist leadership at present are how to preserve dedication, discipline, and solidarity of the party after 20-odd years of rule and many intraparty struggles and how to foster a younger generation of people who will be willing and able to carry on the unfinished tasks of the revolution in the same austere and dauntless manner that Mao deems absolutely necessary. While it is always risky to predict the shape of things to come, it is this writer's belief that, with all the major "revisionists" and "political swindlers" stripped of power and publicly discredited and given the imperatives of China's economic and demographical peculiarities, Mao's determined efforts to perpetuate revolutionary zeal and to stamp out revisionism will continue to enable him and his immediate successor or successors to enforce his austere programs, with the help of a thoroughly reconstructed party, even though necessary changes and adaptations within the general framework of Maoism will have to be made from time to time as has been the case in the past. As for the speculation that Mao's eventual death might precipitate violent struggles for power and even national disintegration, one must be reminded of the integrating effect of contemporary Chinese nationalism and the much expanded nationwide networks of mass transportation and communications.

As for the international implications of the Chinese Communist movement, the most encouraging development since the appearance of the first edition of this book has been the repudiation by a growing number of people of their earlier belief that the leaders in Peking were fanatically belligerent and irrational and that the theory of "people's war" was liable to inflame the continents of Asia, Africa, and Latin America. The bulk of the world now seems to have accepted the view that while Peking is determined to safeguard China's territorial integrity and political independence, to elevate further her international position, and to provide inspiration and aid to peoples fighting against "imperialism," "colonialism," "neo-colonialism," and Soviet "social-imperialism," there is little reason to believe that in the years to come China will forsake the patience and prudence in action that have characterized her external conduct since 1949.[2] Nor are many people in the world still apprehensive that the prescription for a people's war will soon gain wide acceptance in the developing world. There has been a belated understanding of the Chinese position that a people's war cannot succeed in a country unless there exist the necessary objective conditions as well as subjective qualifications on the part of those people who wage it. The Chinese Communist revolution itself has amply demonstrated that a protracted people's war entails enormous sacrifices and countless risks. It is difficult to see that as of now there are many places where forces seeking to change the status quo must perforce have recourse to a people's war. Rather, the source of Peking's influence on peoples struggling for modernization and "a place in the sun" has been and may continue to be the dynamic image projected to those peoples by its deeds and propaganda. For them, China represents a revolutionary force rapidly transforming a huge illiterate population into a literate one, eliminating disease and pestilence, and developing scientific, technical, and industrial capabilities, mainly through self-reliance. More significantly, such an image promises quick acquisition and mobilization of power as well as influence and dignity for a people who have languished under "imperialism," "colonialism," and domestic misrule. However, this image is no guarantee that those peoples whom it has impressed will uncritically follow the "Chinese model" in its entirety, let alone accept Chinese domination. Rather the model's greatest impact may very well lie in the self-confidence that it engenders in the people of emerging countries—people that are likely to say to themselves: "If a once backward and oppressed China can do it, why can't we?"

[2] Franklin W. Houn, "The Principles and Operational Code of Communist China's International Conduct," *The Journal of Asian Studies*, Vol. 27 (November 1967), pp. 21–40.

Appendix

The Evolution of the CCP Politburo Membership Since 1949

Since 1949, the Politburo has been expanded in size. When the party seized power, the Bureau consisted of only eleven members: Mao Tse-tung, Liu Shao-ch'i, Chu Teh, Chou En-lai, Kao Kang, Ch'en Yun, Jen Pi-shih, Chang Wen-t'ien, K'ang Sheng, Lin Po-ch'ü, and Tung Pi-wu. Liu Shao-ch'i's rise to the summit of the CCP hierarchy occurred in the later 1930's because of his support of Mao in consolidating the latter's power in the party after the Long March. Chu Teh, as already noted in Chapters III and IV, had been Mao's principal military collaborator in the CCP since 1928. Chou En-lai, who had been a member of the Politburo since the 1920's, assumed the premiership of the new regime at its very inception in 1949. Kao Kang, together with Liu Tzu-tan, had been in charge of the Communist stronghold in northern Shensi before Mao and other central leaders arrived there in 1935. By 1949 Kao had become the party's top man in the Northeast. Ch'en Yun had been prominently involved in labor union movement, party organization and economic affairs prior to the CCP's final victory in 1949. Jen Pi-shih supported Mao in 1935 when Chang Kuo-t'ao challenged the latter's newly acquired leadership. After reaching Yenan in 1936, he served at a number of important posts, including the directorship of the General Political Department of the Eighteenth Group Army. Chang Wen-t'ien had been a leader of the Returned Student Clique who chose to support Mao after the Tsung-i Conference in January 1935. K'ang Sheng once represented the CCP at the Comintern in the 1930's and subsequently cast his lot with Mao upon his return to Yenan. Both Lin Po-ch'ü and Tung Pi-wu had been "elder statesmen" of the CCP.

In June 1950, P'eng Chen was elected to fill the seat vacated by Jen Pi-shih, who died in that year. Toward the end of 1953, P'eng Teh-huai, who had just returned from Korea where he commanded the Chinese People's Volunteers, joined the executive club for the first time; and in March 1955, Lin Piao and Teng Hsiao-p'ing became the newest members after the purge of Kao Kang. Like the disgraced Kao Kang, Lin and Teng had headed separate regional apparatuses of the party, government, and army. In October 1956, the newly elected Eighth Central Committee enlarged the Politburo to include seventeen full and six alternate members. The seventeen full members were Mao Tse-tung, Liu Shao-ch'i, Chou En-lai,

Chu Teh, Ch'en Yun, Teng Hsiao-p'ing, Lin Piao, Lin Po-ch'ü Tung Pi-wu, P'eng Chen, Lo Jung-huan, Ch'en I, Li Fu-ch'un, P'eng Teh-huai, Liu Po-ch'eng, Ho Lung, and Li Hsien-nien. All the newcomers to the Politburo on this occasion had long been top generals of the People's Liberation Army but had recently been summoned to Peking to assume important positions in the Central People's Government. The six alternate members then elected to the Bureau were Ulanfu, Chang Wen-t'ien, Lu Ting-i, Ch'en Po-ta, K'ang Sheng, and Po I-po. Except for Chang Wen-t'ien and K'ang Sheng, who were actually demoted, the election of such a sizeable number of alternate members for the first time and the simultaneous increase in the number of full members of the Politburo enabled the party to duly recognize those who had contributed the most to the party's seizure of power in 1949 and its consolidation in the following years.

In May 1958, at its fifth plenum, the Eighth Central Committee further enlarged the Politburo by including K'o Ch'ing-shih (Mayor of Shanghai), Li Ching-ch'üan (party boss in the populous Szechwan Province), and T'an Chen-lin (soon to take charge of the party's rural work) among its full members. From August 1959 to June 1966, however, the membership of the Politburo was depleted continuously. First P'eng Teh-huai, Ch'en Yun, and Chang Wen-t'ien were suspended as active members in the fall of 1959 because of their reported misgivings about a number of the party's policies. P'eng Teh-huai was said to have criticized Mao's policies concerning the Great Leap Forward and the communes, questioned the continuing validity of certain Maoist ideas on building the armed forces, and was not willing to attack Soviet revisionism because of the risk of losing Russian economic and military aid, which he considered essential to China's fledgling modern defense programs. Instead, P'eng carried on "illicit traffic" with Khrushchev to strengthen his hand in challenging Mao and in "usurping power in the army and the party." [1] On July 14, 1959, he wrote Mao "a letter of opinion," attacking the latter for "petty bourgeois fanaticism," "hot-head mentality," and "exaggeration" in connection with the ill-fated Great Leap Forward and the Commune Movement, and clamoring that in the aftermath of these disastrous campaigns "a Hungarian Incident would have occurred and the Soviet Red Army would have to be called in if our people had not been good." A few days later, P'eng repeated his criticism at the Lushan Conference of the CCP Central Committee. Although P'eng had allegedly been "disloyal" to Mao on several previous occasions, including his advocacy of the deletion from the party Constitution of 1956 all direct references to Mao's Thought and his "collusion with the antiparty clique of Kao Kang and Jao Shu-shih" in 1954, his latest challenge to Mao was the most uninhibited and most serious one and, therefore, caused his de facto separation from the Politburo.[2] The suspension of Chang Wen-t'ien as an active

[1] "Excerpts of 'The Resolution of the 11th Plenary Session of the Communist Party of China Concerning the Anti-Party Clique Headed by P'eng Teh-huai,' " *Peking Review*, No. 34 (August 18, 1967), pp. 8–10.

[2] David A. Charles, "The Dismissal of Marshal P'eng Teh-huai," *China Quarterly*, No. 8 (October–December 1961), pp. 63–76.

alternate member of the Politburo was accompanied by his outright dismissal as a deputy minister of foreign affairs. His fall was linked with that of P'eng Teh-huai, whose criticism of Mao's policies he echoed at the Lushan Conference. Regarded in non-Communist circles in China as a pro-Soviet leader in the CCP, Chang might have been particularly unhappy about the "ideological controversy" with Moscow that had been developing. As for Ch'en Yun, it is believed that his absence from party meetings and other public functions from late 1959 on was due to his opposition to the Great Leap Forward and the Commune Movement. Until his partial oblivion, Ch'en had been the CCP's top expert on economic affairs, and had a strong disinclination to take bold action. Next, in the early 1960's the Politburo lost the services of three additional members as a result of the deaths of Lin Po-chü (May 29, 1960), Lo Jung-huan (December 16, 1963), and K'o Ch'ing-shih (April 9, 1965). Then late in the spring of 1966, P'eng Chen and Lu Ting-i suddenly dropped out of sight. Early in the summer, it became known that they had lost some of the important posts that they held concurrently, and it was generally assumed that by then they had also been denied the right to actively serve on the Politburo.

The Politburo was restored to full strength after its reorganization at the eleventh plenum of the Eighth Central Committee in August 1966, in the midst of the GPCR. Although the party did not release a complete list of names, fragmented information suggested that the reorganized Politburo consisted of twenty-one full members and five alternates. The full members were Mao Tse-tung, Lin Piao, Chou En-lai, T'ao Chu, Ch'en Po-ta, Teng Hsiao-p'ing, K'ang Sheng, Liu Shao-ch'i, Chu Teh, Li Fu-ch'un, Ch'en Yun, Tung Pi-wu, Ch'en I, Liu Po-ch'eng, Ho Lung, Li Hsien-nien, Li Ching-ch'üan, T'an Chen-lin, Hsu Hsiang-ch'ien, Nieh Jung-chen, and Yeh Chien-ying. T'ao Chu, Ch'en Po-ta, Hsu Hsiang-ch'ien, Nieh Jung-chen, and Yeh Chien-ying were newcomers. T'ao's elevation to the Politburo followed his appointment as the party's new director of propaganda. Formerly First Secretary of the CCP Central-South China Bureau and concurrently Vice-Premier of the State Council, his emergence as the fourth ranking member of the party's policy-making board attracted worldwide attention at the time. Ch'en Po-ta's promotion to full membership coincided with his appointment as the leader of the Central Committee's group in charge of the GPCR. Ch'en had been an alternate member of the Politburo and long-time ghost writer for Mao. The reinstatement of K'ang Sheng to full membership was preceded by his appointment as advisor to the group in charge of the GPCR. For many years K'ang had been active in liaison work with foreign Communist parties and in cultural and educational affairs at home. The election of Hsu Hsiang-ch'ien, Nieh Jung-chen, and Yeh Chien-ying to the Politburo brought in all the surviving former marshals of the People's Liberation Army, in which military ranks had been abolished. Former marshals who were holdovers in the Politburo included Lin Piao, Chu Teh, Ch'en I, Liu Po-ch'eng, and Ho Lung. Li Hsien-nien, concurrently Vice-Premier and Minister of Finance, was also a high-ranking general, although he never was a marshal. The presence in the Politburo of as many as eight men with military backgrounds indicated a conscious effort on the part of Mao Tse-tung and his heir-apparent, Lin Piao, to cement the bond between the party and the army while the party apparatus was being overhauled during the GPCR.

The reorganization restored Ch'en Yun to active membership in the Bureau, a move probably designed to emphasize Mao's unflagging effort to preserve unity and solidarity at a time when he had to formally remove P'eng Chen, P'eng Teh-huai, Lu Ting-i, and Chang Wen-t'ien—all of whom had committed more serious errors than Ch'en. Of the alternate members, two were holdovers and three were newcomers. Ulanfu and Po I-po, the two holdovers, had been vice-premiers in charge of minority nationality affairs and economic construction, respectively. The three new alternate members were Li Hsueh-feng. Hsieh Fu-chih, and Sung Jen-ch'iung. Among the high posts concurrently held by Li were the First Secretaryship of the CCP North China Bureau and of the CCP Peking Municipal Committee. Li's appointment to the latter post in June 1966, which until then had been occupied by P'eng Chen, obliquely but nevertheless officially disclosed P'eng's downfall from the CCP power structure. Hsieh Fu-chih, the second new alternate member, had been Minister of Public Security since August 1959 and Vice-Premier since January 1965. Sung Jen-ch'iung, the third new alternate member, had been the First Secretary of the CCP's Northeast Bureau since 1961.

No sooner had the membership of the Politburo been replenished than it began to shrink again, when the spearhead of the GPCR was directed toward "those in authority taking the road of capitalism." Toward the end of 1966, Liu Shao-ch'i, who had already been demoted at the eleventh plenum of the Eighth Central Committee from second to eighth place on the roster of party leaders, was identified in wall posters in Peking as the chief exponent of "the bourgeois black line" and the number-one opponent of "the proletarian revolutionary line represented by Chairman Mao." The earlier decision not to exclude him from the Politburo outright apparently was based on tactical considerations. Other members of the Bureau vehemently attacked in wall posters included T'ao Chu, Teng Hsiao-p'ing, Chu Teh, Ch'en Yun, Ho Lung, Li Ching-ch'üan, Ulanfu, Po I-po, and Li Hsueh-feng. Chu Teh, Ch'en Yun, and Li Hsueh-feng, having been withdrawn from the political limelight for about five months, joined Mao Tse-tung on the Heavenly Peace Gate during the May Day Parade in 1967. This indicated that they were still in good grace, although their influence seemed to have declined. However, by this time, Liu Shao-ch'i, T'ao Chu, Teng Hsiao-p'ing, Ho Lung, Li Ching-ch'üan, Ulanfu, and Po I-po had all lost their official positions even though formal announcements of dismissal had not yet been made in some cases. Shortly after the May Day Parade, T'an Chen-lin, too, vanished from the scene. Later he was accused of being the arch-villain behind "the February adverse current" against the Red Guard movement. It was said that during the period from mid-February to early March 1967, he and "his ilk" jumped forth to stir up a countercurrent for capitalist restoration. They allegedly attempted to sway the headquarters of the GPCR from the right by discrediting and dissolving the "revolutionary rebel organizations" in the agricultural and forestry system, by staging "a sham seizure of power" there, and by seeking a reversal of verdicts on "innocent veteran revolutionaries including Liu Shao-ch'i." T'an was quoted as having said: "I would speak on behalf of all veteran revolutionaries . . . and I am not afraid of being beheaded, or being thrown into prison, or being expelled from the party." In the summer of the same year, Ch'en I also found himself under attack by "rebels" in his own Ministry of Foreign Affairs for having executed certain aspects of Liu Shao-ch'i's "revisionist" foreign policy. For several weeks Ch'en even was prevented from functioning as the head of that Ministry. But shortly he reemerged in good standing after having examined his errors reportedly with the help of Premier Chou En-lai. Toward the end of the year, Sung Jen-ch'iung became a new target of the "rebels," especially those in Northeast China. Although at first he enjoyed the protection of Mao and Premier Chou, the party eventually adjudged him as "a turncoat and unrepentant capitalist roader" who must be repudiated. On the eve of its reorganization in April 1969, the Politburo actually consisted of fifteen full members and two alternates. The full members were Mao Tse-tung, Lin Piao, Chou En-lai, Ch'en Po-ta, K'ang Sheng, Chu Teh, Li Fu-ch'un, Ch'en Yun, Tung Pi-wu, Ch'en I, Liu Po-ch'eng, Li Hsien-nien, Hsu Hsiang-ch'ien, Nieh Jung-chen, and Yeh Chien-ying. The alternates were Li Hsueh-feng and Hsieh Fu-chih.

The election of a new Politburo in April 1969, along with the adoption of a new party Constitution and the election of the Ninth Central Committee, put Mao Tse-tung, Lin Piao, and their loyal supporters in more effective control of the CCP apparatus. The new Politburo consisted of twenty-one full members and four alternates. Dropped from the revamped body were such figures as Vice-Premier and Foreign Minister Ch'en I, Vice-Premier and Chairman of the State Planning Commission Li Fu-ch'un, Vice-Premier Ch'en Yun, former Marshal Hsu Hsiang-ch'ien, and former Marshal Nieh Jung-chen. Their exclusion probably stemmed from their reported reservations about certain aspects of the GPCR and their refusal to confess some "errors in work." However, all four were seated at a place of honor during the plenary sessions of the Ninth National Party Congress and were reelected to the Ninth Central Committee. In addition, the press continued to identify them by their other impressive titles. All these facts suggested that despite their failure to retain their seats on the Politburo, they still enjoyed considerable stature in the CCP after the GPCR. Aside from Mao and Lin, holdovers among the full members of the new Bureau were Chou En-lai, Ch'en Po-ta, K'ang Sheng, Yeh Chien-ying, Liu Po-ch'eng, Chu Teh, Li Hsien-nien, Tung Pi-wu, and Hsieh Fu-chih. Hsieh's promotion to full membership had been expected because of his important role during the GPCR. He had been Chairman of the Peking Municipal Revolutionary Committee since its inception in April 1967, while continuing to serve as Vice-Premier and Minister of

Public Security. Newcomers to the Politburo were Chiang Ch'ing, wife of Mao Tse-tung and First Deputy Director of the Group in Charge of the Cultural Revolution; Yeh Ch'un, wife of Lin Piao and director of Lin's office in the CCP Military Affairs Commission; Chang Ch'un-ch'iao, Deputy Director of the Group in Charge of the Cultural Revolution, Political Commissar of the Nanking Military Region, and Chairman of the Shanghai Municipal Revolutionary Committee; Yao Wen-yuan, leading theoretician of the Cultural Revolution and Vice-Chairman of the Shanghai Municipal Revolutionary Committee; Hsu Shih-yu, Commander of the Nanking Military Region and Chairman of the Kiangsu Provincial Revolutionary Committee; Ch'en Hsi-lien, Commander of the Shenyang (Mukden) Military Region and Chairman of the Liaoning Provincial Revolutionary Committee; Huang Yung-sheng, Chief of the General Staff; Wu Fa-hsien, Commander of the Air Force and Deputy Chief of the General Staff; Li Tso-p'eng, First Political Commissar of the Navy and Deputy Chief of the General Staff; and Chiu Hui-tso, Director of the army's General Rear Service Department and Deputy Chief of the General Staff. Listed as alternate members of the new Politburo were Ch'i Teng-k'uei, Vice-Chairman of the Honan Provincial Revolutionary Committee; Li Hsueh-feng, Chairman of the Hopei Provincial Revolutionary Committee; Li Teh-sheng, Chairman of the Anhwei Provincial Revolutionary Committee, who also was to become Director of the General Political Department of the People's Liberation Army; and Wang Tung-hsing, Director of the General Office of the CCP Central Committee and Deputy Minister of Public Security.

Partly because of Mao's continuing efforts to rid his "proletarian headquarters" of both "right and 'left' opportunists" and partly because of death, by April 1972 the reconstructed Politburo had already lost more than one-third of its members. The process of attrition began in the spring of 1970 with Hsieh Fu-chih's illness. After long medical treatment, he eventually died of cancer on March 26, 1972, at the age of sixty-three. A few months after Hsieh was taken ill, political misfortune hit Ch'en Po-ta when he unexpectedly disappeared from public view just before the second plenum of the Ninth Central Committee. As of the summer of 1973, there had been no formal announcement of Ch'en's fall into disfavor, but implicit attacks on him in a number of newspaper articles and radio broadcasts, including the joint *People's Daily–Red Flag–Liberation Army Daily* editorial on July 1, 1971, commemorating the fiftieth anniversary of the CCP, had made his ouster almost beyond doubt. Briefly, Ch'en's downfall seemed to have been caused mainly by the "ultra-leftist" excesses of the GPCR, which he, as the principal man in charge of that campaign, not only failed to prevent in advance but actually abated. By dismissing him, the Maoist leadership obviously hoped to make clear that those excesses were intolerable deviations at the operational level and had never met its approval. However, the immediate cause of Ch'en's removal from the Politburo might have been his opposition to Mao's seeking a detente with the United States in response to President Nixon's overtures; Ch'en's public disappearance coincided with the intensified indirect contacts between Peking and Washington. In resisting the new foreign policy, Ch'en reportedly allied himself with Lin Piao.

Li Hsueh-feng was the next man to be dropped from the Politburo. He made his reported public appearance on October 1, 1970, at the provincial capital of Hopei. Like Ch'en Po-ta, Li's fall from favor had not been formally disclosed as of the summer of 1973. But an alleged secret Chinese Communist document which the Chinese Nationalist authorities in Taipei claimed to have obtained through their intelligence sources named Li as one of those who supported Lin Piao's "devious" but unsuccessful attempt at the second plenum of the CCP Ninth Central Committee (August 23–September 6, 1970) to provide in a new draft national constitution a chairmanship for the state, which Lin Piao himself aspired to occupy if and when the draft charter became the supreme law of the land. Mao, according to the same document, was against the reestablishment of that office, and his view prevailed at the plenum. Thus Li Hsueh-feng was one of the earliest casualties of the gradually widening split between Mao and his then heir-designate.

The most far-reaching and the most surprising shake-up of the Politburo occurred in September 1971 as a result of the political demise of Lin Piao, Yeh Ch'un, Huang Yung-sheng, Wu Fa-hsien, Li Tso-p'eng, and Ch'iu Hui-tso, who had long been Lin's proteges even before their elevation to the Politburo. Lin's dramatic rise and fall in the CCP political vortex has been discussed in Chapter VI. After all these attritions, the Politburo, by the summer of 1972, actually consisted of only thirteen full members and three alternates. The full members were Mao Tse-tung, Chou En-lai, K'ang Sheng, Chiang Ch'ing, Yeh Chien-ying, Tung Pi-wu, Chu Teh, Liu Po-ch'eng, Chang Ch'un-ch'iao, Yao Wen-yuan, Li Hsien-nien, Hsu Shih-yu, and Ch'en Hsi-lien. The alternates were Chi Teng-k'uei, Li Teh-sheng, and Wang Tung-hsing. Of these remaining members, poor health had kept K'ang Sheng inactive since November 1970, though he was present when Mao Tse-tung received President Nicolae Ceausescu of Romania on June 3, 1971. Meanwhile, advanced age and their reportedly lukewarm support of the GPCR had also made the continuing presence of the venerable Chu Teh (b. 1886) and Liu Po-ch'eng (b. 1892) more of an honor than a symbol of their power.[3]

[3] For more information on most of the personalities mentioned in this appendix, see Donald W. Klein and Anne B. Clark, *Biographic Dictionary of Chinese Communism, 1921–1965* (Cambridge, Mass.: Harvard University Press, 1971), 2 vols. It should be pointed out that Teng Hsiao-p'ing, one of the most powerful members of the Politburo from 1955 to 1966 and the second most important target of Red Guard wall posters during the GPCR, reappeared in public on April 13, 1973, as a Vice Premier of the State Council—apparently after having atoned for his errors, although he was not reinstated as a member of the Politburo. Teng's rehabilitation was in line with the policy of "liberating" repentent cadres in the post-GPCR era, especially after the demise of Lin Piao.

Index